Risk and EU Law

Risk and EU Law

Edited by

Hans-W. Micklitz

European University Institute, Italy

Takis Tridimas

Chair of European Law, Director, Centre of European Law, The Dickson Poon School of Law, King's College London, UK and Professor and Nancy A. Patterson Distinguished Scholar, School of Law, Pennsylvania State University, USA

Edward Elgar PUBLISHING

Cheltenham, UK • Northampton, MA, USA

Published by
Edward Elgar Publishing Limited
The Lypiatts
15 Lansdown Road
Cheltenham
Glos GL50 2JA
UK

Edward Elgar Publishing, Inc.
William Pratt House
9 Dewey Court
Northampton
Massachusetts 01060
USA

A catalogue record for this book
is available from the British Library

Library of Congress Control Number: 2015938374

This book is available electronically in the Elgaronline
Law subject collection
DOI 10.4337/9781783470945

MIX
Paper from
responsible sources
FSC® C013056

ISBN 978 1 78347 093 8 (cased)
ISBN 978 1 78347 094 5 (eBook)

Typeset by Columns Design XML Ltd, Reading
Printed and bound in Great Britain by TJ International Ltd, Padstow

Contents

Contributors

Alemanno, Alberto is Jean Monnet Professor of EU Law and Risk Regulation at Ecole des Etudes Commerciales (HEC), Paris and Global Clinical Professor at NYU School of Law, where he runs the EU Public Interest Clinic. Alberto's research focuses on the role of evidence and public input in policymaking and adjudication. Due to his commitment to bridge the gap between academic research and policy action, he regularly provides advice to a variety of organizations, such as the European Commission, the European Parliament, the Organisation for Economic Co-operation and Development, World Health Organization, and numerous NGOs and governments across the world. Originally from Italy, he holds LLM degrees from the College of Europe and Harvard Law School and a PhD in International Law and Economics from Bocconi University. He is the Editor-in-Chief of the *European Journal of Risk Regulation*, a member of the Editorial Board of the *Revue du Droit de l'Union Européenne* and is the founder of the Summer Academy in Global Food Law and Policy. He is a qualified lawyer attorney at law in New York.

Allen, Franklin is the Executive Director of the Brevan Howard Centre and Professor of Finance and Economics at Imperial College London. He is on leave from the Wharton School of the University of Pennsylvania where he is the Nippon Life Professor of Finance and Professor of Economics. He has been on the faculty there since 1980. He is Co-Director of the Wharton Financial Institutions Center. He was formerly Vice-Dean and Director of Wharton Doctoral Programs, Executive Editor of the *Review of Financial Studies* and is currently Managing Editor of the *Review of Finance*. He is a past President of the American Finance Association, Western Finance Association, Society for Financial Studies, Financial Intermediation Research Society and Financial Management Association, and a Fellow of the Econometric Society. He received his doctorate from Oxford University. Dr Allen's main areas of interest are corporate finance, asset pricing, financial innovation, comparative financial systems and financial crises. He is a co-author with Richard Brealey and Stewart Myers of the eighth through eleventh editions of the textbook *Principles of Corporate Finance*.

Brean, Donald is a Professor of Finance and Business Economics at Rotman School of Management, University of Toronto. Donald teaches courses in International Finance and International Economics. His research interests centre on international investment, public finance and economic policy, specifically in economies in transition. He was the former Director of Centre d'Etudes de la France et du Monde Francophone.

Cafaggi, Fabrizio is Professor of Comparative Law at the School of National Administration (SNA) and Director of the Centre for Judicial Cooperation at the European University Institute (EUI) in Florence. He is the Director of a Master's programme in Behavioural Sciences and Administration at SNA/Libera università studi sociali. He is a former Professor of Comparative Law at the EUI, founding member and member of the Council of the European Law Institute and member of the American Law Institute. He has been a Visiting Professor at Columbia Law School, New York University School of Law, University of Pennsylvania Law School and at the San Andres Law School in Argentina. He is currently collaborating with Unidroit for a Guide on contract farming and with the Food and Agriculture Organization and International Fund for Agricultural Development on public–private partnerships in agriculture. The current subjects of his research include transnational private regulation, global supply chains and contractual governance, network contracts, European private law, judicial dialogue and remedies in EU law.

Carletti, Elena is Professor of Finance at Bocconi University. Prior to this she was Professor of Economics at the European University Institute, where she held a joint chair in the Economics Department and the Robert Schuman Centre for Advanced Studies. She is also Research Fellow at the Centre for Economic Policy Research, Extramural Fellow at the Tilburg Law and Economics Centre, Fellow at the Centre for Financial Studies, at the Centre for Economic Studies and Ifo Institute, at the Innocenzo Gasparini Institute for Economic Research, and at the Wharton Financial Institutions Center. Her main research areas are financial intermediation, financial crises and regulation, competition policy and corporate governance. She has published numerous articles in leading academic journals, and has co-edited various books. She has worked as consultant for the OECD and the World Bank, and she has served in the review panel of the Irish Central Bank and of the Riskbank. She has also been a board member of the Financial Intermediation Research Society and a review panel member for the creation of Financial Market Centres in Stockholm. She has been a member of the Scientific Committee of Confindustria since 2014. She participates regularly in policy debates and roundtables at central banks and international organizations and has also organized numerous academic and policy-oriented events.

Cremona, Marise is Professor of European Law at the European University Institute (EUI) in Florence. Between 2009 and June 2012 she was Head of the Law Department and between June 2012 and August 2013 she was President ad interim of the EUI. She is a Co-Director of the Academy of European Law and General Editor (together with Professors Loic Azoulai and Nehal Bhuta) of *The Collected Courses of the Academy of European Law*. Until 2006 she was Professor of European Commercial Law, Centre for Commercial Law Studies at Queen Mary, University of London. She is also a member of the International Advisory Board of the Centre for European Research, University of Göteborg; member of the Advisory Board of the *European Foreign Affairs Review*; and a member of the Editorial Board of the *European Law Review*.

Duquet, Sanderijn (Master of Laws, Ghent U. and LL.M. International Legal Studies, American U. Washington College of Law) is PhD Fellow at the Research Foundation – Flanders (FWO), the Leuven Centre for Global Governance Studies and the Institute for International Law, University of Leuven. Sanderijn is preparing a PhD on the contribution of the European Union to international diplomatic and consular law. She has published on topics such as diplomatic and consular law, EU external relations, foreign direct investment and informal international law-making.

Garde, Amandine is Professor of Law at the University of Liverpool. She previously lectured at King's College London, where she obtained her PhD; at the Faculty of Law in Cambridge, where she was also a Fellow of Selwyn College; at the University of Exeter and at the University of Durham. Her research interests lie in the fields of EU internal market, consumer, advertising, food and public health law. In particular, she has developed an expertise on the legal aspects of obesity prevention and other risk factors for non-communicable diseases such as tobacco and excessive alcohol consumption. Her book *EU Law and Obesity Prevention* was the first to offer a critical analysis of the EU's Obesity Prevention Strategy. She is Co-Editor (with Alberto Alemanno) of *Regulating Lifestyle Risks: The EU, Alcohol, Tobacco and Unhealthy Diets*. As one of the few legal experts on the prevention of non-communicable diseases, she has been invited to take part in a broad range of policy initiatives for – among others – the World Health Organization, the Directorate General of the European Commission for Health and Consumers, the UK Government, the Scottish Government, the Swedish

Institute for European Policy Studies, and the National Institute for Health Education and Promotion and the National Institute for Health and Medical Research in France. Amandine Garde spent a year as a postdoctoral Jean Monnet Fellow at the European University Institute in Florence in 2005–2006 and is a qualified solicitor, having trained at Simmons & Simmons in their London and Paris offices.

Herberger, Tim is a research and teaching assistant at the Department of Finance, Bamberg University. He received his PhD from Bamberg University and his MSc degree in finance from the Friedrich-Alexander-University Erlangen-Nuremberg. His fields of interest include risk management, behavioural finance, valuation of intangible assets, financing in higher education, mergers and acquisitions, and initial public offerings and sport finance and management.

Höfer, Andreas, MSc, Bamberg.

Kobrak, Christopher is Professor Emeritus of Finance at the ESCP Europe and currently teaches financial and business history at the Rotman School of Management, University of Toronto. An International Fellow at the Centre for Corporate Reputation, Oxford University, he serves on the Editorial Boards of several business history journals. He holds the following degrees: a BA in Philosophy from Rutgers University; an MBA in Finance and Accounting and a PhD in Business History, both from Columbia University; and the French Habilitation in Management from the University of Toulouse. A CPA and former business practitioner, his publications include *History and Financial Crisis: Lessons from the 20th Century* (ed. with Mira Wilkins), *Banking on Global Markets: Deutsche Bank and the United States, 1870 to the Present* and *European Business, Dictatorship and Political Risk, 1920–1945* (edited with Per Hansen), as well as journal articles on a wide range of business and financial topics.

Ladeur, Karl-Heinz is Professor Emeritus of Public Law at the University of Hamburg; he was also Distinguished Bremen Professor at the Bremen International Graduate School of Social Sciences and Professor at the European University Institute Florence. He is Doctor Honoris Causa of Fribourg University and has also worked as legal advisor of German public broadcasting stations (ARD, ZDF).

Micklitz, Hans-W. is Professor for Economic Law at the European University Institute in Florence. He is also Jean Monnet Chair of Private Law and European Economic Law at the University of Bamberg (on leave) and Head of the Institute of European and Consumer Law in

Bamberg. He took Studies of Law and Sociology in Mainz, Lausanne, Geneva, Giessen and Hamburg. He has acted as a Consultant for many public and private organizations, including the OECD in Paris, UNEP Geneva/Nairobi and Consumers International Den Haag/Penang (Malaysia). He has also acted as an advisor for ministries in Austria, Germany, the UK, the European Commission, OECD, UNEP, the Gesellschaft für Internationale Zusammenarbeit and other non-governmental organizations. He was Visiting Scholar at the University of Michigan, Ann Arbor; Jean Monnet Fellow at the European University Institute Florence; Visiting Professor at the Somerville College at the University of Oxford; and co-founder of the Centre of Excellence at the University of Helsinki. He is holder of an ERC Grant 2011–2016 on European Regulatory Private Law.

Oehler, Andreas is Full Professor at Bamberg University and has held the Chair of Finance there since 1994. He received his PhD at the University of Mannheim and his Habilitation degree at the University of Hagen. He has published widely, in particular in the area of credit risk management, banking, behavioural and empirical finance, and investor protection. His fields of interest also include financial markets, retirement provisions/funded pension plans, pension systems, consumer protection, personal finance and household finance. Since 2012 he has been Director of the Research Centre 'Household Finance and Financial Literacy'. He is a member of various expert committees, including Chairman of the Board of the Stiftung Warentest, Germany's leading product-testing institute, and the German Council of Consumer Policy Experts.

Tridimas, Takis is Professor of European Law at the Dickson Poon School of Law of King's College London and Director of the Centre of European Law. He is also the Nancy A. Patterson Distinguished Faculty Scholar and Professor at Pennsylvania State University and a Visiting Professor at the College of Europe, Bruges. He has acted as advisor to many public and private organizations, including the European Central Bank, the European Parliament, the European Commission and the EU Court of Auditors. He was senior legal advisor to the EU Presidency (2003) and Chairman of the Committee set up by the EU Council of Ministers to draft the Treaty of Accession of 2003 by which ten new States joined the EU. He is a barrister of England and Wales and a qualified advocate in Greece.

van Asselt, Marjolein B.A. holds the Risk Governance chair at Maastricht University. From January 2008 until July 2014 she was also a member of the Scientific Council for Government Policy (Wetenschappelijke Raad voor het Regeringsbeleid). In July 2014 she was appointed a member of the Dutch Safety Board. She studied Computer Science and Philosophy of Science, Technology and Society at the University of Twente and obtained her PhD at the Faculty of General Sciences, Maastricht University (2000). She was Visiting Scholar at King's Centre for Risk Management, London, and at Saïd Business School, Oxford University. From 2005–2010, she was a member of the Young Academy (De Jonge Akademie) of the Dutch Royal Academy of Sciences, being a member of the first board.

Vieweg, Klaus is Director of the Institute of Law and Technology (Institut für Recht und Technik), Chair for Civil Law, Law of Information Technology, Law of Technology and Business at the Law School of Friedrich-Alexander University Erlangen-Nuremberg. He is also a member of the Acatech German Academy of Sciences of Technology. His selected publications can be found at: http://www.irut.jura.uni-erlangen.de/Forschung/Veroeffentlichungen/Veroeffentlichungen.html.

Vos, Ellen is Professor of European Union Law at the Law Faculty of Maastricht University. She is Co-Director of the Maastricht Centre for European Law of Maastricht University. She is also research coordinator of the research programme 'Integration, Differentiation and Flexibility: New Perspectives on EU Law and Policy' under the umbrella of the Ius Commune Research school. She studied Law at the Universities of Utrecht and Bologna. She was a trainee at the European Commission, the European Consumer Organization and the European Court of Justice. She wrote and obtained her PhD in Law at the European University Institute in Florence. She was a Jean Monnet Fellow at the Robert Schuman Centre of the European University Institute. From 2001–2005 she served as the Director of the advanced master programme in Comparative, European and International Law, Magister Iuris Communis programme of the Law Faculty of Maastricht University.

Wendt, Stefan is Assistant Professor of Finance at the School of Business of Reykjavik University. From March 2005 until March 2015 he was Research and Teaching Assistant at the Department of Finance at Bamberg University, where he received his PhD in 2010. His fields of interest include financial markets and asset pricing, risk management, corporate finance and governance, small and medium-sized enterprises, behavioural finance and financial intermediation.

Wouters, Jan is Jean Monnet Chair *ad personam* EU and Global Governance, Full Professor of International Law and International Organizations, and founding Director of the Institute for International Law and of the Leuven Centre for Global Governance Studies, an interdisciplinary centre of excellence, at the University of Leuven (KU Leuven). As Visiting Professor at Sciences Po (Paris), Luiss University (Rome) and the College of Europe (Bruges) he teaches EU External Relations Law. He is a member of the Royal Academy of Belgium for Sciences and Arts, and President of the United Nations Association, Flanders Belgium. He also practises Law as Of Counsel at Linklaters, Brussels. He is Editor of the International Encyclopedia of Intergovernmental Organizations, Deputy Director of the *Revue belge de droit international*, and an Editorial Board member of ten international journals. He has published widely on international, EU, corporate and financial law (including 50 books, 100 international journal articles and 150 chapters in international books). He is coordinator of a large-scale FP7 Programme FRAME, 'Fostering Human Rights Among European (External and Internal) Policies' and of the InBev-Baillet Latour EU China Chair at KU Leuven.

Introduction

Hans-W. Micklitz and Takis Tridimas

RISK AND RISK CONTROL MECHANISMS

Although the assessment and management of risk has always been an integral part of government and private decision-making, it has acquired particular importance in contemporary polities. Multiple factors, such as the openness of liberal societies, market competition, the constant endeavour to innovate, globalisation and new technologies, have increased the types and diversity of risks as well as the potential magnitude of their undesirable effects. Furthermore, risk awareness and with it the struggle to prepare, pre-empt and confront have also increased.

A series of recent events have brought to the fore the importance of risk management. In 2008, the world experienced the deepest financial crisis since the 1930s. Its effects, which are still unfolding, have been compounded by the on-going Eurozone crisis. Events such as terrorist attacks, international health scares and natural disasters poignantly illustrate that sudden and unpredictable events may have far-reaching consequences in economic, social and political life at a global level. The financial crisis, in particular, is set to have a long-lasting impact on the regulatory regime in Europe and the US. Although risk is an innate element of economic and political life, a worldwide discussion is taking place with a view to facilitating better prevention and suppression mechanisms in modern complex societies.

Risk regulation is well established in various sectors, such as health and safety, food and medical law, but is also gaining pace in other areas, such as financial services and contract governance, where it has been less prominent. The possible transfer of models from established areas of regulation to new sectors invites us to revisit our understanding of risks, how they should be managed, the respective roles of preventive control mechanisms and post-market remedial models, and, last but not least, the shape and structure of institutional design. In parallel, since the terrorist attacks of 9/11, there has been a heated debate among scholars, and a lively constitutional conversation between judges and politicians, on how to manage security risks. Citizen expectations, public security, economic prosperity and human rights are some of the parameters within which institutional actors form their decisions.

The interaction of EU law with risk control has inevitably increased. The transnational character of many economic, social, security and political threats leads Member States to entrust more risk control responsibilities to the EU. The Union's intervention is further enhanced by its own institutions' appetite for power and empire building. EU law now has presence in all areas of risk regulation, broadly understood, including food and health law, consumer protection, product liability, environmental protection, counter-terrorism and financial markets supervision. EU law, being an important source of norm creation and peremptory regulation for the Member States, poses itself a legal risk for Member States and private actors. From that perspective, the normative function of EU law may become as much the problem as it is the solution.

A comparative analysis of risk regulation in various sectors is beneficial in enhancing our understanding of risk, facilitating cross-fertilisation of ideas and, ultimately, contributing to better solutions. Such an analysis should take into account a number of key concepts and questions. These include the following:

- *The concept of risk.* Whilst risk may generally be defined as the possibility of occurrence of a harmful event, a number of classifications may be made. Risk can be seen as incomplete information, complexity or indeterminacy. In a historical perspective, distinctions may be drawn between danger, stemming from experience, risk, as systematised knowledge generated by societal networks, and advanced control mechanisms provided by private or public law normative frameworks.
- *The objectives of risk regulation.* Prevention and suppression are the twin goals of risk regulation but any legal intervention would need to identify specific goals and mechanisms and enter into a balancing exercise weighing different risks and taking into account other competing interests. A correlation may be drawn between the mode of risk regulation (self-regulation, shared regulation and mandatory regulation) and the types of risk posed or the sector where they arise. The gradual disappearance of the public/private divide seems to be a common denominator.
- *The parameters of decision-making.* Effective risk control can only take place within a set system of governance and rational decision-making. Whilst the distinction between risk assessment and risk

management appears clear cut from a theoretical perspective, the two are closely intertwined and in practice they may be fused. A number of questions arise here as to who should take decisions (authority boundaries), the institutional and procedural safeguards available (process and accountability), the balancing between risk prevention and economic freedoms (politics), and the justiciability of outcomes (the role of the judiciary).

- *The trigger mechanism of risk regulation.* Key events, such as crises or scandals, political activism, state paternalism and even media attention, push the regulatory impulse one step further. But do they do so in the right direction? Are they, perhaps, too focused on regulating past events rather than coping with future mutating risks? What is the optimum time of intervention? Regulatory responses triggered by specific events may be a more efficient way of legislating but do they make for good law?

PERSPECTIVES ON RISK REGULATION

This volume brings together contributions from different disciplines and with various perspectives dealing with selected aspects of EU risk regulation. They seek to address the questions listed above. The first group of chapters (1 to 3) looks at risk regulation in context. It deals with broad, horizontal issues focusing on epistemological, economic and sociological aspects of risk. The second group (Chapters 4 to 10) provides legal and economic perspectives in specific areas of risk regulation.

The identification and management of risk is not an easy process. *Vieweg* sets the scene by raising a number of key questions that should guide the risk prevention and management inquiry. What is the object of protection? What risks should we safeguard against? Which authority should take decisions and by what process? How is the probability of occurrence of an undesired event to be determined? How can risk be quantified? To what extent and at what stage should cost-related aspects be included? There is a need for consistency and coherence between EU and national action, and also between legislative and executive responses. Uniformity in the methodology for the identification, assessment and suppression of risk should be encouraged.

Vieweg offers a grid which identifies sources of risk and regulatory models for their prevention and management. Whilst such systematisation does not do away with the need to calibrate responses to the specificities of uncertainty, it provides a framework for transversal action. Sources of risk include human error, technical error, natural occurrence and interference by an unauthorised third party. In relation to regulatory models, Vieweg distinguishes self-regulation, where a private actor seeks protection by contract against a perceived risk; cooperative regulation, where private networks develop common responses or power is shared between public and private actors; and classic imperative regulation through orders and prohibition. He provides a systematic list of factors to be taken into account in drawing risk regulation and argues that risk-determination and prevention processes should be transparent.

Based on economic analysis, *Oehler, Herberger, Höfer and Wendt* point to the dangers arising from simplified or incomplete assumptions made in risk modelling. Risk management is a cybernetic process which includes its identification, measurement, evaluation and control. The use of risk models, whilst necessary to mitigate the lack of information, gives rise to enormous challenges. Economic literature identifies three economic paradigms for the management of risk. The neoclassical paradigm starts from the premise that the idealised *homo economicus* takes rational decisions to maximise utility. In perfect market conditions, individuals are fully able to make assessments and can adjust their risk levels to reflect their preferences with little need for the introduction of externally imposed risk management protocols. The new institutional economics paradigm accepts that market participants possess incomplete information and that information is unevenly distributed. Such asymmetries lead to agency conflicts which in turn require institutional intervention. Under this model, risks include informational risks, delegation risks and risks with respect to asymmetric distribution of economic consequences which vary depending on the circumstances and conduct of individuals. The behavioural economics paradigm asserts that the cognitive limitations of individuals result in their decisions falling short of full rationality. Focusing on individual conduct, this paradigm asserts that individuals will not be able to assess all threats and their risk perception will differ even in identical situations.

Oehler, Herberger, Höfer and Wendt point out the limitations of the neoclassical paradigm and the institutional paradigm in risk modelling. By relying on the efficiency of market mechanisms under idealised conditions, the first model gives results which deviate from reality. The second model assumes that the reduction of information asymmetries will lead to risk reduction. Given, however, that the perception of risk among individuals differs even in identical situations, models should take into account variations arising from factors such as information overload, choice overload and overconfidence.

Model risks may also arise from poor data quality or data processing where mathematical calculation and quantification leads to erroneous estimates. The authors identify three types of model risk: the use of a model that does not fit the situation (over-optimism); the use of a model in a different way from or another purpose than intended (ignorance); and the failure to use a suitable model (agnosticism). The failure to identify the risk of modelling gives rise to an illusion of control. The mitigation of model risk requires the implementation of governance and control procedures and techniques such as model validation and back testing.

Ladeur seeks to analyse epistemological aspects of risk management focusing on the interrelationship between the legal system and the societal knowledge base. Risk regulation can be seen as a process of homogenisation of the social knowledge infrastructure. Norm creation crystallises risk control experience developed in a fragmented way at the local level, thus universalising knowledge. But in modern democracies, the internalisation of uncertainty is much more complex. In a liberal society where innovation is a virtue, uncertainty is the inevitable result of progress. Risk is a bridging concept establishing links between experience and normativity. The bridging takes place through complex and sophisticated mechanisms. The shift from *ex post facto* private law remedies to public law *ex ante* preventive mechanisms and the corresponding increase in institutions and specialised agencies is well documented. Science has replaced experience as a more advanced form of knowledge. This in turn requires intermediation through the establishment of institutions to translate scientific information to normative outcomes.

Ladeur identifies the emergence of new models of governance where risk assessment and management no longer take place within the unitary and largely homogeneous hierarchical channels of the nation state but at supranational level through networks which disperse power and bring down the public–private law divide. He places particular emphasis on the establishment of networks and the growth of new objectives-oriented epistemic communities necessitated by the need to process and articulate the normative implications of specialist knowledge. Such developments make the process of standardisation more complex and call for a redefinition of the role of public authorities.

Cremona's chapter brings to the fore the interdependence between internal and external EU action, and the different types of risk involved in decision-making in the external relations sphere. Tracing the travails of the EU–US Agreement on the Processing and Transfer of Financial Messaging Data, Cremona identifies risks at three different levels: legal risk, namely legal uncertainty arising from different regulatory approaches to data protection; constitutional or political risk arising from the vicissitudes of the political process which is exacerbated by the EU's complex institutional architecture; and factual risk, which arises from the need to balance conflicting policy objectives, *in casu* the need to have in place a meaningful anti-terrorism regime and maintain the EU's relevance on the international stage with the need to protect personal data.

Two aspects, perhaps, stand out in Cremona's analysis. As she points out, although it is commonly considered that transferring more powers to the EU would increase its voice as an international political actor, it may in fact lead to the opposite result. The complex EU institutional set-up and the posturing of different political actors may inhibit decisive action and executive discretion which are necessary for the swift conduct of international negotiations. Secondly, her analysis highlights the difficulty in striking a balance between security and data protection in the sphere of international negotiations, especially in the light of competing security models that prevail at the national level. The multiplicity of the actors involved, the dispersal of power and the need to pursue various and diverse objectives increase the possibilities of sub-optimum results. Yet, somehow, the EU's complex decision-making procedures appear to be working and may overall be said to be a success.

Wouters and Duquet examine whether and, if so, how the EU advances risk-oriented approaches in its management of counter-terrorism. Although counter-terrorism action has been integrated into both the Area of Freedom, Security and Justice and the Common Foreign and Security Policy, it retains prominent inter-governmental features. Since 2005, strategic thinking grounded in risk analysis has slowly found its way into EU policy making. Its implementation, however, has often occurred in an uncoordinated way. The authors propose a dual approach based on threat reduction and vulnerability mitigation measures. The first relate to the reduction of terrorist threats (focus on the 'other') whilst the second relate to measures and policies necessary to make the EU less vulnerable in the event of a terrorist attack (focus on the 'self').

When it comes to the assessment and prevention of terrorism, primary responsibility lies with the Member States but the EU has gradually built a supportive and coordinating role. Prevention has become a constitutive part of the EU's counter-terrorism strategy. The EU plays a role, for example, in coordinating national intelligence services and facilitating the collection, analysis and exchange of data. The authors argue that the EU must also enhance its vulnerability reduction measures. Taking a risk-based approach to counter-terrorism goes beyond analysing and diminishing potential threats. Prospective targets also have to be made less vulnerable to terrorism. The development of defence mechanisms requires the adoption of policies and instruments which include measures not specific to terrorism such as cooperation in the field of criminal law and the European Arrest Warrant. The EU's efforts are here hampered by competence limitations in the field of criminal law, the principle of minimum harmonisation under Article 83 TFEU and the patchwork of available opt-outs. The European Public Prosecutor's Office and the solidarity clause of Article 222 TFEU may offer promising possibilities but they are not unproblematic. The prosecutor does not directly cover terrorism and it has proved very difficult to adopt measures under the solidarity clause. In a nutshell, despite a great effort to embed risk regulation in the EU's counter-terrorism strategy, the EU's policy remains fragmented.

Van Asselt and Vos examine the role of science in decision-making and explore the 'uncertainty paradox' in the field of food regulation. In an effort to cope with risk and uncertainty and strengthen the objective basis of regulation, decision-makers turn to science, thus leading to the scientification of law. This in turn leads to an expert dependency syndrome. Specialised agencies tend to be entrusted with extensive powers sometimes going beyond risk assessment. The Commission, as the EU executive, tends to over-rely on advice provided by such agencies, leading to a blurring of the boundaries between risk assessment and risk management. The authors demonstrate the central position of the European Food Standards Agency in decision-making and the technocratic dominance in taking GMO decisions despite the societal and political controversies surrounding them.

Whilst risk assessment is a *sine qua non* for sound management of risk, and has to be carried out in a transparent, objective and competent manner, it is not a substitute for risk management, which is perforce a political act. The force of science as a neutral arbiter may distort the decision-making process, especially in cases of scientific uncertainty. Science cannot provide answers where scientific evidence is uncertain. Yet, decision-makers may rubber-stamp risk assessment based on inconclusive evidence even where political support for the chosen solution may be lacking. Two further points arise from Van Asselt and Vos's analysis. Whilst the European Court of Justice (ECJ) increasingly pays attention to the scientific base of market regulation, it continues to be deferential to EU choices. Van Asselt and Vos caution against judicial bodies becoming 'super experts' on scientific matters. Ultimately, risk assessment is itself a political exercise. It does not occur in a policy vacuum but is determined by answering a number of specific questions regarding the appointment of experts, the scope of their mandate, the process of collecting evidence and their role in executive decision making.

Alemanno and Garde explore the EU's increasing presence in the field of lifestyle risk regulation. EU intervention is interesting from many points of view. Recent EU measures suggest a policy shift. Whilst in earlier years EU law was preoccupied with facilitating free movement, the emphasis increasingly appears to be on regulating undesirable products. Just as in a previous era the expansive interpretation of Article 34 TFEU sought to challenge entrenched consumer habits by liberalising inter-state trade, a new policy generation is emerging where regulation rather than liberalisation seeks to change consumer behaviour. This in turn raises important points about personal freedom, the role of government and the outreach of the EU.

EU measures in the field of lifestyle regulation share some features but also present important and marked differences. They seek to promote an environment conducive to public health and are based on coordination and concerted action at multiple levels seeking to engage stakeholders from a wide spectrum. But they vary in terms of instruments, intensity and scope. The EU has adopted a hard approach in relation to tobacco consumption, a soft strategy to combat alcohol abuse, and a somewhat intermediate approach in relation to nutrition.

The central pillar of EU intervention remains the 'information paradigm'. Consumers must be adequately informed to be able to take responsibility for their health choices. This achieves a golden balance. By placing the onus on consumers to take decisions, it limits interference with personal freedom. At the same time, the EU's approach to information is a qualitative one placing emphasis on the requirement that the information supplied must not be misleading. Given the limitations on the information paradigm, it is supplemented by other techniques provided at EU and national level. Those include marketing bans, measures affecting product availability, product reformulation through ingredients regulation, and fiscal measures. The need to take action in several sectors along with the fragile and fluid division of powers between the EU and the Member States point to the need for coordination and coherence.

The authors focus on an aspect which lies at the core of risk regulation, namely the evidence required to justify a restriction and the burden of proof. Providing evidence, however, raises important challenges. Given that undesirable outcomes are the result of multiple factors, it is often impossible to establish with any certainty a cause and effect relationship between a specific risk and a specific outcome. How much obesity is caused by advertising of foods containing sugar? How much health harm is caused by allowing the sale of tobacco by automatic vending machines? Also, given that lifestyle regulation tends to include many interconnected initiatives, it becomes very difficult to isolate the specific effects of a measure which forms part of a comprehensive regulatory network. Such difficulties make the application of the principle of proportionality difficult. How can a judicial body determine the suitability of a measure? How is it possible to establish if there are less restrictive alternatives? Balancing becomes more difficult when one adds the precautionary principle to the factors to be taken into account. A distinct aspect of recent case law is the enhancement of process aspects in proportionality analysis. The need for impact assessments and the articulation of criteria which they must fulfil inevitably will increase their value as objective yardsticks which the courts will take into account in determining the proportionality of a measure. The authors argue in favour of evidence-based judicial review. Such an approach will promote a 'broader culture of proof, evidence and rationality' and may open the judiciary to evidence based on other disciplines such as statistics, economic analysis and psychology.

Cafaggi analyses a relatively new phenomenon, namely transnational risk regulation in global supply chains. Supply chains are interlinked via up-stream and down-stream contracts. Contracts, however, are not only a means of building supply chains vertically but also a means of interconnecting them horizontally. Transnational private regulation has a long history, reaching back to the Middle Ages and, maybe, even further. What is really new is the combination of risk regulation and contracting. Building on previous research, Cafaggi provides a deep insight into how various public and private actors in global supply chains are interconnected, interact and develop techniques to manage product risks via contract governance. His analysis focuses on food safety and the management of food risks in supply chains. There are other domains of product regulation where similar phenomena could be observed, such as supply chains in chemical products, pesticides, pharmaceuticals and technical products where risks to health and safety are inherent. It seems, however, that the debate around risk regulation and contract governance is most advanced in the area of food supply chains.

Cafaggi argues that the integration of risk regulation into contracts leads to mutual transformation from transnational private regulation to contract governance and also from risk assessment and risk management via public authorities to risk assessment and risk management through a whole variety of public and private actors who are interconnected horizontally and vertically. This does not mean privatisation of risk assessment and risk management, as cooperation between the public and the private sector is crucial in transnational risk regulation. The public/private divide, however, is vanishing away. There is another argument, which stands out from the analysis of global supply chains in the food sector. This is the key role that standard and certification bodies have gained in transnational risk regulation. They are gradually turning from mere compliance managers into risk managers, monitoring and surveying not only the production process but also distribution and marketing. This brings the third-party impact of risk regulation through contract governance to the fore. One cannot agree more with Cafaggi's plea for more research in order to get a deeper understanding of contractual practice.

Allen and Carletti provide an economist's perspective focusing on the concept of systemic risk in the context of the global financial crisis of 2008. They identify six types of such risk, namely exposure to asset price bubbles, particularly property bubbles; inefficient liquidity provision and mispricing of assets; multiple equilibria and panics; contagion; sovereign default; and currency mismatches in the banking system. They argue that microprudential regulation focusing on the risks of individual credit institutions is not sufficient to prevent crises because it ignores systemic risk. Its inadequacy was spectacularly exposed in the 2008 crisis. They outline a number of policies to advance macroprudential supervision.

Three elements, perhaps, stand out from Allen and Carletti's analysis. The first pertains to contagion. Although there can be no doubt that contagion was an important contributing factor to the 2008 crisis, our understanding of the effects of contagion risk remains limited. Whilst empirical literature suggests that close connection between credit institutions via network structures reduces the likelihood of widespread default, the authors caution against the claim that contagion is unlikely to occur where financial institutions are closely linked. Secondly, the authors highlight the close relationship between sovereign default risk and banking crises as evidenced by the Eurozone crisis, especially in Greece, Ireland and Portugal. As Alexandre Lamfalussy famously pointed out, the EMU is characterised by a strong 'M' and a weak 'E'. Whilst the EU Treaties framework provides the structures and disciplines for centralised Monetary policy, competence on Economic policy and fiscal matters remains a national competence. The tension proved impossible to manage as markets misread the potency of the EMU construct to guarantee discipline. The Eurozone crisis also illustrated the difficulties caused by the lack of a common resolution procedure and agreed arrangements on burden sharing.

Finally, although the authors outline specific initiatives that could be taken with a view to putting in place an effective system of macroprudential supervision dealing with each type of systemic risk, the challenges of such an exercise should not be underestimated. Measures which may be appropriate for a region with a homogeneous economy may be more difficult to implement in heterogeneous environments such as the Eurozone. Thus reliance on increasing interest rates to counter a property bubble may come at the price of slower growth or recession in another part of the Eurozone. Effective management requires the employment of a combination of measures including targeted use of taxes, tightening monetary policy, and putting in place a more coherent and representative system of international supervision. As a practical solution to the global imbalance problem, the authors recommend elevating the Chinese Rmb to a reserve currency. The authors are critical of the ability of deposit guarantee schemes to increase stability and suggest that the problem of bank runs could be dealt with through lender of last resort policies. Furthermore, they point out that financial institutions hold little capital relative to other industries and suggest measures to reduce their reliance on debt, such as counter cyclical capital regulation and the use of contingent convertible debt.

Kobrak and Brean discuss attempts to introduce a system of financial regulation at the supranational level focusing on the role of the G20 and the EU's efforts to establish a banking union. Although many changes were introduced in the aftermath of the 2008 crisis, they doubt that the reform has been robust enough and prefer to view the glass as half empty. Many G20 initiatives have in fact not been followed up and a number of reforms remain unimplemented. The gap between rhetoric and reality suggests that the G20 forum is an ineffective mechanism to push forward the solutions needed. Whilst recognising the inevitability of national political priorities as a dominant force, they argue that closer international cooperation is the only course capable of addressing the needs of citizens and the markets. In that respect, the global financial crisis and the ensuing Eurozone crisis may be seen as a lost opportunity. They did not precipitate the effective and decisive action for which one might have hoped.

Kobrak and Brean identify two problems: the cumbersome decision-making process at G20 level which requires unanimity, and the subordination of sound international reform and coordination to divergent national objectives. In relation to Europe, the authors applaud banking union as an effective and efficiencies-generating risk mitigation strategy. They consider that banking union is a welcome development, with centralisation in bank oversight fulfilling the subsidiarity criteria. The establishment of banking union can be seen as a new stage in the management of risk in financial markets. It is not only retrospective, seeking to avoid the Eurozone crisis that beset Europe, but also prospective: by subjecting banks to common supervision and earmarking funds for rescue it seeks to limit the vice of contagion and break the vicious circle between weak banks and weak sovereigns. However, whilst a technocratic efficiency-driven analysis of the virtues and vices of banking union would suggest that the case is clearly made in its favour, its political dimensions and repercussions for the nation state pose enormous challenges and may change the reading of the scales.

In conclusion, Kobrak and Brean consider that, despite the recent dramatic challenges to global finance on both sides of the Atlantic, regulation remains largely the privilege of state action. National priorities, especially in countries in which the financial sector plays a very large economic role, have curtailed cross-border coordination. A formal or informal consensus among major economies about the appropriate rules of the game for national and international financial organisations is still elusive.

GENERAL TRENDS

Looking at the evolution of EU risk regulation across sectors, one could identify a number of salient features and trends. These include the growth of agency power at EU level, the prevalence of reactive, 'events driven' legislative intervention, the fusion between management crisis and law reform, the decline of the public/private divide, the tension between EU and national competence, and the evolution of proportionality review. Another feature, which transcends specific areas, is the integration risk paradigm built by the case law.

Growth of EU Agencies

The enhanced presence of the EU in the field of risk regulation has led to the proliferation of EU agencies. The growth of agency power has been remarkable. Whilst there were just two Community agencies in the 1970s[1] and only four in 1993, there are currently more than 40 agencies.[2] This has made for a qualitative change in EU governance. The growth of independent agencies and the substantial increase in their powers lead to profound issues pertaining to accountability and democracy, and raise the

---

[1] These were the European Centre for the Development of Vocational Training and the Foundation for the Improvement of Living and Working Conditions.

[2] See http://europa.eu/about-eu/agencies/index_en.htm; last accessed on 1 June 2015.

spectrum of the emergence of a 'headless fourth branch of government'.[3] Traditionally, the *Meroni* doctrine[4] imposed severe limitations on the power of EU institutions to establish agencies by prohibiting them from being vested with discretionary powers. More recent case law appears to have relaxed the *Meroni* criteria, recognising that agencies have an important role to play in the internal market and can be delegated some discretion provided that their powers are well circumscribed and subject to process and substantive requirements.[5] In some cases, to preserve the limits on delegation, agencies operate under a reverse accountability rule: an agency proposes draft standards to the Commission but the latter can only depart from or amend them if it provides reasons.[6] The net effect of this is to bring agency powers close to regulatory competence.[7]

Events- or Scandal-Driven Legislation

A prominent feature of many regulatory initiatives is that they are scandal or events driven. The legislature reacts after a specific scandal or crisis with a view to closing a regulatory gap and avoiding a similar event in the future. This has been a perennial feature of financial and capital markets regulation. The initiatives which followed the financial crisis and the Eurozone crisis are no exception. As various contributions in this book show, it is also a feature of other areas such as counter-terrorism and health regulation. Whilst it is appropriate for policy makers to respond to specific problems, too much preoccupation with specific events might lead to backward- rather than forward-looking law reform. Crises tend to mutate and there is a danger of policy making suffering from the 'mazinot line syndrome'. Government and society will be ready to fight a past war but not the next one.

---

[3] The expression was coined by President Franklin Roosevelt's Committee on Administrative Management; see Breyer, Stewart, Sunstein and Spitzer, *Administrative Law and Regulatory Policy*, at 146.

[4] Case 9/56 *Meroni v High Authority* [1958] ECR 133.

[5] C-270/12 *UK v Council (ESMA case)*, judgment of 22 January 2014.

[6] See for example Regulation No. 1095/2010 establishing a European Securities and Markets Authority [2010] OJ L 331/84, Art. 10(1), sub-para. 6.

[7] See, for a recent discussion, among others, M. Scholten and M. van Rijsbergen, The Limits of Agencification in the European Union, 2014 (15) *German Law Journal*, 1223.

Law Reform versus Crisis Management

It would appear that the European Union is better equipped to contribute to law reform than to crisis management. The latter requires clear and specific competence and wide executive discretion,[8] elements which the Treaties did not traditionally grant to the EU institutions. Law reform, on the other hand, is a reflective exercise which the EU appears well placed to conduct. It has the advantage of pan-European expertise and can master the knowledge of several national legal systems. It acts in the EU interest as a whole and can be presumed to be less susceptible to capture by national interests. Also, being one step further away from the national electorates, it should be under less political pressure to act immediately in the aftermath of a crisis and can instead engage in thoughtful long-term law reform. Notably, the Commission's reaction in the aftermath of the 2008 financial crisis gave a different picture. The Commission felt under pressure to react immediately and initiated long-term reform leading to the adoption of a bewildering plethora of institutional and substantive measures within a short period. Such fusion of crisis management and law reform may not make for optimum policy choices. Still, the resulting picture following the global financial crisis and the ensuing Eurozone crisis shows the European Union as a winner. There is more centralisation of powers, more norm creation at EU level, extension of EU presence beyond rule making to the field of monitoring and enforcement, and recognition of a crisis management role for the EU.

The Blurring of the Line between the Public and the Private

Risk regulation in whatever form was long based on regulatory attempts to earmark bright lines; namely, to draw clear distinctions between private and public responsibilities, between the scientific-technical definition of risk and the political decision on risk assessment, between private parties who had to follow the risk assessment which was publicly decided and the public entities which accepted responsibility for value judgements. It seems that those lines of separation are disappearing. This holds true for the distinction between an objective, scientific definition on risk, and subjective, political value judgements. It holds equally true in the

[8] See E.A. Posner and A. Vermeule, Crisis Governance in the Administrative State: 9/11 and the Financial Meltdown of 2008 (13 November 2008). U of Chicago Law & Economics, Olin Working Paper No. 442; available at SSRN: http://ssrn.com/abstract=1301164 or http://dx.doi.org/10.2139/ssrn.1301164; last accessed on 1 June 2015.

interplay between science and politics and between private and public responsibilities. The interaction between the various actors is much stronger and crosses the boundaries of objective science vs. political assessment. What can be observed from the cross-subject and cross-sector analysis is the growing idea of cooperation, mutual dependence and joint rather than shared responsibilities. The implications for the legal system are just about to come to the fore. Who can hold responsibility for what? The vanishing divides make matters more difficult for the legislature, the executive and the courts which have to attribute responsibilities.

The Tension between EU and National Competence

Perhaps two areas of risk regulation stand out in contemporary EU law: counter-terrorism initiatives and measures seeking to cope with the double financial crises that hit Europe in the late 2000s. Both areas exposed the tensions and equivocations surrounding the division of powers between the EU and the Member States. On the one hand, national governments long for bright lines delineating the boundaries of EU competence. On the other hand, where expedient, they favour collective action at EU level with as few constraints as possible. The adoption of economic sanctions against non-state actors to combat terrorism is a case in point. Following the terrorist attacks of 9 September 2001, the Council adopted sanction measures giving effect to UN Security Council Resolutions despite the feeble legal basis in the Treaties for the imposition of economic sanctions against individuals. Whilst in *Kadi*[9] the ECJ recognised competence to the EU, it also found that the Union has its own enclosed constitutional space which cannot be penetrated by international law obligations and which requires compliance with the Union's fundamental rights.

Competence issues have also played a prevalent role in financial governance. The need for urgent and effective action to cope with the Eurozone crisis, whilst respecting national red lines, gave rise to parallel international treaties sitting alongside the EU system. Those arrangements pose strong challenges not only to the integrity of EU law but also to democracy, the rule of law and the rights of the individual.

The tension between EU and national competence is also evident in other areas. The ECJ has encouraged the use of Article 114 TFEU by

---

[9] Joined Cases C-402/05 P and C-415/05 P *Kadi & Al Barakaat International Foundation v Council and Commission* [2008] ECR I-6351.

exercising a light standard of review. Still, EU and national action are closely intertwined. In the absence of common rules, Member States can regulate areas of shared competence where the EU has not yet legislated or occupied the field. Similarly, if the EU approximates the laws of the Member States through minimum harmonisation, Member States can exceed the minimum standards laid down at EU level. The fact remains that drawing the boundaries between legitimate and illegitimate EU intervention under Article 114 TFEU is far from straightforward.

Proportionality as Process and Substance Review

Proportionality permeates the EU legal order. Its appeal to the judiciary is such that in recent years it has evolved into a global standard of justice. Whilst it hides varying degrees of judicial scrutiny, one may identify some general features in the application of the principle. First, following the entry into force of the Charter, the analysis of the ECJ tends to be more structured, examining separately each of the conditions of Article 52(1) for determining whether a restriction on a right is acceptable, namely whether it is provided by law, whether it affects the essence of the right and whether it is proportionate. Secondly, although the Court continues to apply a more generous standard of review to EU measures than to national ones, the gap has perhaps become narrower. This is not only a sign that the internal market has reached a stage of maturity but also indicates that many of the national interests which are invoked to justify restrictions on free trade are now fully embraced by EU law and receive express recognition in the Treaty. The juxtaposition in the balancing exercise becomes less one between an EU and a national interest and more between two EU interests. Finally, the procedural aspects of proportionality have been enhanced. Proportionality is less a subjective merits analysis and more an exercise in consistency, cost–benefit analysis and due process.

Integration Risk and the Case Law

A final point may be made in relation to judicial construction. A risk analysis may also be applied to the case law of the ECJ. The expansive conception of EU competence, the doctrines of primacy and direct effect, the employment of effectiveness as a strong enforcement mechanism, and the preference for a uniform interpretation of EU law, may be seen as risk control mechanisms employed by the judiciary to contain threats to the integration paradigm. There are two areas where the Court's understanding of risk appears particularly wide. In the context of internal market harmonisation, the ECJ has opted for a broad interpretation of Article 114 relying on potential obstacles to trade.[10] According to the established case law, recourse to Article 114 TFEU is possible in order to prevent the emergence of future obstacles to trade resulting from multifarious development of national laws, provided that the emergence of such obstacles is likely and the measure in question is designed to prevent them.[11] It suffices that there is a reasonable probability that Member States will adopt divergent measures in the foreseeable future. The ECJ is averse to integration risks, even potential ones, but the case law lacks an economic analysis and the burden of proof for the EU institutions appears relatively light.

There is another area where the Court has adopted a broad conception of risk. Perceived threats to the integrity of the EU legal order, even indirect, are examined with a heightened degree of scrutiny as are, especially, threats to the exclusivity of the ECJ's own jurisdiction. Thus in the pre-Lisbon era the ECJ adopted a broad interpretation of the first pillar going even beyond an obstacle pre-emption criterion to hold that any measure which could potentially be adopted under the Community pillar could not be adopted under the second or the third pillar.[12] Similarly, the case law reveals some distrust towards international arbitration tribunals. This is evident in the Court's approach towards international treaties which provide for the establishment of courts,[13] and also in its Opinion on the EU's accession to the ECHR.[14] In short, the case law suggests a heightened degree of vigilance towards any risk to integration.

---

[10] See for example Case C-359/92 *Federal Republic of Germany v Council* [1994] ECR I-3681.

[11] See *Swedish Match*, para. 30; *Second Tobacco Advertising case*, para. 38.

[12] See Case C-176/03 *Commission v Council* [2005] ECR I-7879, Case C-440/05 *Commission v Council* [2007] ECR I-9097; Case C-91/05 *Commission v Council (ECOWAS case)* [2008] ECR I-3651.

[13] Opinion 1/91 *on the EEA Agreement* [1991] ECR I-6079; Case C-205/06 *Commission v Austria* [2009] ECR I-1301; Case C-249/06 *Commission v Sweden* [2009] ECR I-1335.

[14] Opinion 2/13 *on the compatibility of the draft agreement on the Accession of the European Union to the European Convention for the Protection of Human Rights and Fundamental Freedoms*, Opinion delivered on 18 December 2014.

1. Risk and the regulatory State – various aspects regarding safety and security in the fields of technology and health*

Klaus Vieweg

I. INTRODUCTION

The topic of safety and security is a classic problem which, following the process of industrialization, continues to appear in a variety of new forms. Examples of current problems include risks arising from various sources, starting with toys and children's jewellery and extending to the risk of infection in hospitals and while flying, as well as risks attached to nuclear power plants and international terrorism. Reactions to technical developments can be observed in the areas of business, law and in society in general. A good historical example is the founding of boiler monitoring organizations in Germany in the late 1800s, which was a direct result of frequent cases of boilers exploding. These organizations later became the Technische-Überwachungsvereine (TÜV), which are non-commercial organizations for the monitoring of technical installations. Industrial mass-production and globalization are two further relevant developments in the business world. These developments were accompanied by political decisions, for example to create a European single market.

The matter of safety and security is a multidisciplinary topic the world over. In this chapter, however, as a German lawyer, I wish to concentrate mainly on the legal systems and practical experience in Germany and Europe. The most important decisions in the field of safety and security are made in the areas of politics, technology, economics and law. A

* Original wording of lecture without citations. With thanks to Mairéad Boland for the translation.

considerable amount of background information is provided by persons and bodies in the areas of science, psychology, sociology, philosophy, ethics and history. The starting point for most of those decisions is usually a set of undesired circumstances and occurrences which may be described by terms such as 'endangerment', 'risk', 'danger' and 'damage'. These decisions are not generally made in accordance with a unified method or approach. Rather, these tend to diverge depending, on the one hand, on the function and subject-specific alignment of the person making the decision, and, on the other, on the type and level of the undesired circumstances or occurrences. The debate as regards safety and security must also be mentioned. Too rigid a focus on one's own area of competence and, more importantly, the ignoring of decisions reached in the areas of politics and law, can mean that the diagnostic value of scientific experiments must be relativized considerably. On the other hand, the establishment of bridges between the various disciplines can improve the quality of decision-making and avoid time-wasting and additional costs.

In this chapter, I will first address the issue of consistency between terms and scenarios. I will then talk about tasks and responsibilities, and, finally, I will discuss decision-making processes.

II. CONSISTENCY REGARDING TERMS AND SCENARIOS

1. The terms used in the area of technical security and safety reflect the different roles and responsibilities of the various disciplines involved in this field (for example, technical measures in order to avoid or reduce undesired circumstances and occurrences, or legal provisions relating to the quality and composition of objects, responsibility, competence, and liability of persons and organizations). The terms used in different areas diverge substantially from one another for the most part. Even within individual areas, the meanings of particular terms and definitions diverge and so the assessment and weighting of particular areas are concealed (for example, the anthropocentric containment of the subjects requiring protection, the acceptance of risks, the fading-out of so-called development risks).

2. The coining of working definitions leading to an interdisciplinary – as the case may be, an intradisciplinary – and, where possible, international agreement is recommended. This is vital for the solution of difficult factual problems. Definitions used within a legal system and in technical standardization (DIN, VDE, DKE, DVGW, CEN, CENELEC,

ETSI, ISO, IEC[1]) are of particular importance. These should almost be viewed as non-negotiable terms of reference. They should be framed so as to match each other.

3. The starting point for the clarification of definitions is that an absolute outright state of security or safety cannot exist. In particular, the following questions should be posed: 'How safe is safe enough?' and 'Who decides, and according to which principles and criteria?'

4. The working definitions must facilitate agreement in relation to the following questions:

- Who and/or what is the object of protection? Is it man and his (material) goods, or can assets which are not attributable to him – that is, goods which are 'unattached' to a particular person – also be taken into account (here, the problem of so-called ecological risk, or rather, damage, must be addressed)?
- Against what is the object of protection to be safeguarded? Against targeted attacks and interferences (security) and/or other negative effects of undesired conditions and occurrences (safety – technical error, human and organizational error, natural occurrences)? Should undesired situations and occurrences (so-called development risks, that is, risks which are not yet known, but the occurrence of which cannot be excluded should new technology be developed) be included?
- In each individual case, one must ask whether the problem relates to undesired situations and occurrences which can be ascertained statistically, or at least estimated, or whether it relates to tactically adjusted behaviour, or a dynamic process (for example, a terrorist attack; but also – as a natural occurrence – the mutation of viruses which can then lead to their resistance to treatment)?

---

[1] The acronyms stand for the following: DIN – Deutsches Institut für Normung (German Institute for Standardization); VDE – Verband der Elektrotechnik Elektronik Informationstechnik (German Association for Electrical, Electronic and Information Technologies); DKE – Deutsche Kommission Elektrotechnik Elektronik Informationstechnik im DIN und VDE (German Commission for Electrical, Electronic and Information Technologies of DIN and VDE); DVGW – Deutscher Verein des Gas- und Wasserfaches (German Technical and Scientific Association for Gas and Water); CEN – Comité Européen de Normalisation (European Committee for Standardization); CENELEC – Comité Européen de Normalisation Électrotechnique (European Committee for Electrotechnical Standardization); ETSI – European Telecommunications Standards Institute; ISO – International Organization for Standardization; IEC – International Electrotechnical Commission.

- Should measures be put in place even at the starting point? In other words, should measures be put in place where a factual situation exists which may be defined as an unwanted situation or occurrence; that is, should this state of affairs result in repercussions (for example, the implementation of technical-organizational measures, the intervention of an authority, the refusal to grant permission for the operation of a factory, liability, penalization)?
- Should advantages and chances also be included in the definition even if they extend beyond the level of the undesired situation or occurrence (the potential extent of damage) and the probability of the occurrence of this undesired situation (taken together, these two aspects form the classic risk definition)? If yes, how? Should, for example, quantifications of risk be decisive? Should the principle of proportionality hold good in the weighing up of the risk and its accompanying advantages and chances?
- Should cost-related aspects be included? If yes, how (quantification problems, weighting problems)?

5. Consistency – both between the various disciplines and, in particular, consistency between the legislature, administrative decisions and case law – requires transparency in the methodical approach.

The steps which occur in the various disciplines between the identification of problems (risks) and the solution of problems (reduction of the risks) should be made clear. In relation to the multitude of risks and the measures taken in order to reduce them, simplifications are unavoidable in order to create a basis for understanding. As a basis for orientation, it is suggested that all scenarios are systematically included in a 'risk grid' which is made up of sources of risk – human error (including organizational error), technical error, natural occurrences, the unauthorized interference of third parties – and three ideal types of regulatory models to be found within legislation (self-regulation, cooperative regulation and imperative regulation). These regulatory models reflect the affected interests (individual and general) and correspond (ideally) to the principle of proportionality. The measures included in the grid as examples of risk reduction are the results of weighing-up exercises in the areas of utility and proportionality (see Table 1A.1). Of course, various combinations of the sources of risk and gradations in the three regulatory models are common in practice.

Further differentiations and variations of the – very rough – 'risk grid' are possible. In each individual case, it must be examined whether or not the taking into account of additional aspects is helpful. In this way, the differentiation by the 'regulatory (legal) instruments' between criminal responsibility, civil liability and public law obligations can be targeted at regulation of behaviour. It is of no help in cases of intentional interferences by third parties (in particular, in the case of terrorist attacks). Differentiation based on the intention of the person causing damage – whether the damage is desired or not – does not get us any further because the most important cases of the intentional causing of damage are already to be found in the 'risk grid' classified as interferences by third parties.

The 'risk grid' serves not only as a source of information but also as a touchstone for the integrity of a transverse systems theory. By making reference to the 'New Approach' and the 'New Legislative Framework', the 'risk grid' also makes clear the function of technical standardization which, in practice, has achieved an importance which should not be underestimated, and which the EU legislators have carried over into their specification of general security requirements in the standardizing organizations CEN, CENELEC and ETSI.

III. TASKS AND RESPONSIBILITIES

1. The general goal of security and safety is generally pursued in an aim-oriented manner by the assignment of tasks and obligations according to technical qualifications and interests. This assignment takes place in various different ways. It is important to the extent that the regulations set out in statute allow self-regulation or contain concrete guidelines. It must be taken into account that, in this area, lobby groups are hugely influential.

Cases of self-regulation are characterized by the facts that the individual interest of the endangered party takes priority over the interests of society in general, and that the legislator chooses not to take action, but rather deems the general legal framework to be sufficient. The assignment of tasks and obligations ensues bilaterally on a contractual basis between those who wish to allay an undesired risk and those who claim to be able to prevent the risk, or at least to reduce it to an acceptable level (for example, the testing of electrical terminal equipment by an expert, the installation of a lightning conductor to protect against lightning or an alarm system to protect a ('single family') detached house against burglary). Should the risk be wholly dependent upon a human error made by the endangered person, then safeguarding against financial damage ensuing from the risk could take the form of insurance.

If the risk extends beyond the individual person and, above all, if third parties are in need of protection because their (material) assets could be affected (for example, fire protection), the assignment of tasks and responsibilities takes place on a tri- or multilateral basis. As a rule, there are provisions set out in statute intended to regulate the types of cases which relate to concrete risk. In particular, standards relating to the jurisdiction of authorities and courts, criminal responsibility and civil liability must be taken into account.

2. Insofar as the assignment of tasks and obligations takes place in accordance with legislative standards (tri- or multilaterally), two legislative regulatory approaches should, ideally, be differentiated from one another. First, 'classic' imperative regulation by concrete orders and prohibitions plays as important a role today as it did in the past, both on a national as well as on a European level. This becomes particularly important when substantial interests of the general public are affected. Secondly, the meaning of cooperative regulation between the EU and the State, on the one hand, and between the affected company and private individual on the other, is clearly gaining in importance. The 'New Approach' (1985) and the 'New Legislative Framework' (2008) are particularly practice-oriented. Usually, cooperative regulation is rooted in the interest of the general public, as well as in the interests of the individual.

The differentiation made in some sections of theory and practice between so-called 'safety problems' and 'security problems' has not yet fully manifested itself in legal regulations (for example, there are still no special regulations for terrorist attacks on nuclear power plants). There are two probable reasons for this: first, a time-lag within the legal system which can be denoted as a 'legal lag' (ever since 11 September 2001, it has been clear that terrorist attacks cannot be prevented by the threat of punishment) and, secondly, an overreaching legislative protection concept which – in relation to the risk – does not differentiate between 'safety' and 'security' but has regard to the protection of legally protected interests.

IV. DECISION-MAKING PROCESSES

1. Regarding the regulatory model of self-regulation (where individual interests are affected above all) and the risk source of unauthorized third-party interference (see Table 1A.1), the decision process (individual decision of the endangered party) may be characterized as laid out in Figure 1A.1.

The knowledge, experience, feelings and interests of the endangered party shape the individual assessment of risk, for which the extent of the damage, the probability of occurrence, individual measures (such as insurance) and the degree of fear that damage will occur are also of importance. In addition, all relevant information provided by those technical experts who have been consulted for advice will be taken into account. The solutions suggested by technical experts will also be individually assessed by the endangered party under the headings of the expected increase in safety, costs, time input, alternatives and consequences. The internal weighing-up process of the endangered party is of central importance. His negotiations with technical experts result – in contract form – in the selection of a technical solution, the level of safety of which he regards as being optimal in view of all relevant costs and time-input. In the case of a negative decision, the situation will remain a hazardous one.

2. As to the regulatory model of cooperative regulation and European or national imperative regulation on the one hand and the sources of risk emanating from technical error, natural occurrences and the interference of unauthorized third parties on the other, the decision process relating to the solution of security and safety problems (simplified) can be characterized as demonstrated by Figure 1A.2.

The decision process is, on the one hand, influenced to a large extent by statutory regulations which exist in relation to the prevention or the reduction of risks. Standards relating to competence, responsibility, the process of arriving at a decision, all relevant technical, organizational and administrative procedures, and insurance solutions, as well as – above all – security and safety standards, must be included under this heading. On the other hand, information regarding the risk plays a substantial role – in other words, information about the starting point, as well as the technical possibilities available to solve the problem. Legal standards, as well as information regarding the risk, influence communication and cooperation between those responsible for the source of risk, technical experts and the State, in particular, the authorities with competence for these matters. The decision regarding the solution of the safety problem is therefore dependent upon concrete legal regulatory approaches which are specific to the risk.

3. In the point of view of an individual drawing up regulations – in particular in the European or national context – a systematic approach in relation to a concrete risk (for example, a terrorist attack on a nuclear power plant or another plant requiring authorization) could be laid out as follows:

- identification of the risk (or, possibly, risks) and decision regarding whether regulations are necessary;

- formulation of the security or safety aim for the concrete scenario within the scope of the legislative aim;
- determination of the regulatory approach regarding the affected interests and the principle of proportionality;
- investigation of any relevant preventative, compensatory or repressive measures which could prevent or reduce the risks (for example, technical or administrative measures, user information);
- determination of the tasks and obligations of the decision-makers (authorities, industry in general, producers and delivery companies, standardization organizations, technical experts, operators/users/consumers);
- regulation of the decision-makers' behaviour (civil liability, costs relating to administrative measures such as recall, penalization, loss of reputation);
- determination of regulations for the prevention or reduction of the risks (for example, technical or administrative measures, user information) for the purpose of assessment of risk.

The question of whether the regulations which have been in place until this point are based upon a similar systematic approach and, in particular, whether the constitutional principle of proportionality is taken into account must be clarified. Independently of this, a transparent procedure should lead to a mutual understanding between all parties concerned. The difficulties faced by those drawing up regulations become clear when the various contexts are viewed in a regulatory circuit model (see Figure 1A.3).

V. CONCLUSION AND RECOMMENDATIONS

As an interdisciplinary and international topic, there must exist within the area of security a common understanding regarding definitions and methodical approaches. Problems of comprehension lead to time-wasting, cause additional costs and, frequently, lead to a reduction in the quality of decision-making.

The working definition of 'risk' is taken as a starting point. The term can then be further defined by characteristics such as 'potential level of damage' and 'probability of occurrence'. Proceeding from this point, an efficient harmonization of definitions can be facilitated by considering differences between definitions and by restructuring the relationships between definitions. The differentiation between definitions relates in particular to the obligation to take certain measures on the one hand, and, on the other, to the assertion that no measures must be taken because the risk is acceptable. Furthermore, it can be clarified conceptually whether advantages and chances may be taken into account in weighing up the decision.

A glossary of all definitions used in the context of security and safety problems – including details of how they relate to one another – would be useful. Keeping in mind the process of decision-making in practice, these glossaries should be compiled within the three key areas of technology, law and business – on a national as well as an international level. In doing so, the area of technology could be represented by technical standardization; the area of law by all relevant legislation, administration and case law; and the area of business by the insurance industry and various groups of companies. The foundations have already been laid by DIN technical report 144[2] and the results of the working group 'Taxonomie'.

Using these glossaries as a basis, it would be advisable to clarify in a second step whether or not the definitions can be used and understood consistently within each individual area, between disciplines and internationally, or if the terms require harmonization.

As regards the methodical approach which characterizes safety and security decisions, it is suggested that a 'risk grid' based on the four sources of risk – human error (including organizational error), technical error, natural occurrences and the unauthorized interference of third parties – as well as on the three ideal-typical legal regulatory models – self-regulation, cooperative regulation and imperative regulation – should be used as a means of clarifying the process. To this end, the framing of methodical approaches within a grid of 12 fields arranged as described above would be a step in the right direction. Leading safety experts also play an important role in the areas of technology, technical standardization and in those areas of risk which have not yet been covered by technical standardization. Considerable advances have been made by the preliminary work of standardization organizations on the one hand, and by the acatech[3] working group 'Creation of System Capability' on the other. In addition, legislation, administration and case law, as well as the insurance industry and company groups, are of importance. Taking the aforementioned risk grids as a basis, it should be clarified if, and to what extent, the methodical approaches correspond to each other, or

---

[2] DIN Deutsches Institut für Normung (ed.), DIN-Fachbericht 144: Sicherheit, Vorsorge und Meidung in der Technik, Berlin 2005.

[3] acatech (Deutsche Akademie der Technikwissenschaften) is the German Academy of Science and Engineering.

if they require harmonization or clarification. In this case, solutions specific to particular branches and products should also be taken into account.

APPENDIX

Table 1A.1 Risk grid

Regulation (affected interests) / Source of risk	Human error (including organizational error)	Technical error	Natural occurrence	Interference by unauthorized third party, in particular an attack from external sources
Self-regulation **(personal interest of the endangered party and, possibly, of his contractual partner)**	Domestic accident, e.g. fall from a stool which was being used incorrectly as a substitute for a ladder	Fire caused by incorrect wiring, wear and tear (after the item has been placed on the market and its guarantee has expired)	Flooding of basements by heavy rain; strike by lightning of a detached 'single family' house (lightning conductor not compulsory)	Burglary of a detached 'single family' house (State intervention occurs after the act only)
Cooperative regulation EU/State – company/private individual **(general public interest and personal interest)**	Operational error which runs contrary to the behavioural requirements set out in the 'New Approach' and the 'New Legislative Framework'	Errors in the construction or fabrication of an object which run contrary to the requirements relating to condition as set out in the 'New Approach' and the 'New Legislative Framework'	Lightning/flooding in industrial plant which requires planning permission – section 3 sub-section 2 No. 2 in connection with section 9 sub-section 1 No. 2 Accident Regulation (Störfall-VO). (See Enforcement Aid (9.2.6.1.2 in connection with appendix 1.2.1.1 and 1.2.2))	Intentional causing of an interference in an industrial plant which requires planning permission – section 3, sub-section 2, No. 3 in connection with section 9, sub-section 1, No. 2, Accident Regulation (Störfall-VO). SFK Guidelines, GS 38. (See Enforcement Aid, 13.3)
European/State imperative regulation **(considerable general public interest)**	Infringement of, e.g., - ban on alcohol for learner drivers – section 24 c, Road Traffic Regulations (StVO) - certificates of proof of technical qualifications - obligation to wear protective equipment; section 21 a, Road Traffic Regulations – safety belt, protective helmet (StVO)	Sources of risk are contained within the security report (directed specifically at industrial plants) – section 9, Accidents Regulation (Störfall-VO). 7,800 industrial plants (within the meaning of section 3, sub-section 5, Federal Emission Control Act – BIMSchG) within Germany are affected	- earthquakes: interpretation of industrial plants which require planning permission – section 5 sub-section 1 No. 1 Accidents Regulation (Störfall-VO) - lightning: lightning conductor required for all places of assembly – Art. 38 para. 3 No. 4 Federal Criminal Code and Regulations of Bavaria (LStVG); Art. 44 of the Bavarian Building Regulations (BayBO) - protection against fire for all buildings - protection against floods (building prohibition, dam height)	Targeted causing of a disturbance in an industrial plant which requires planning permission – section 3, sub-section 2, No. 3 in connection with section 9, sub-section 1, No. 2, Accidents Regulations (Störfall-VO). (See Enforcement Aid 13.3)

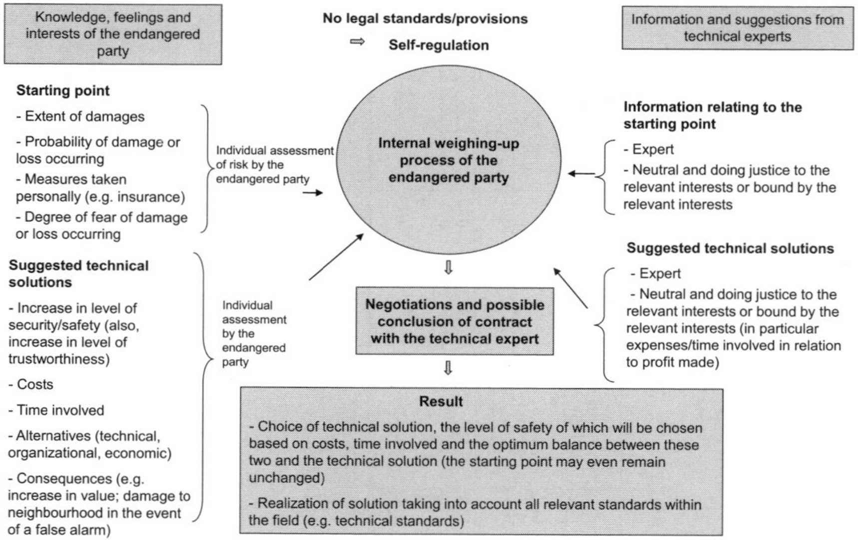

Figure 1A.1 Bilateral security/safety solution in the event of individual endangerment (for example, alarm system for a detached, one-family house)

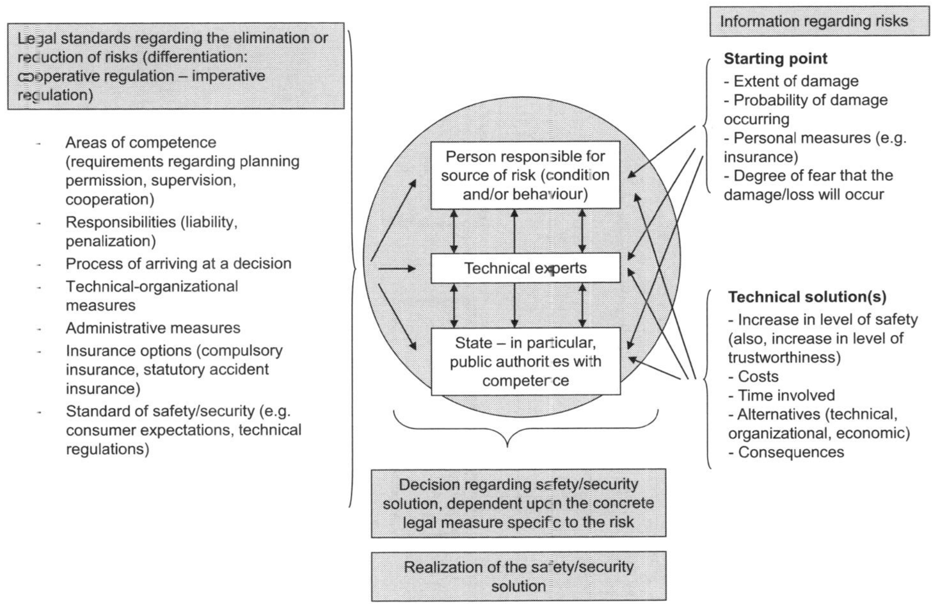

Figure 1A.2 Tri-/multilateral safety/security solution in the event of general endangerment (in particular, endangerment of third parties and the assets of third parties, as well as assets of the general public)

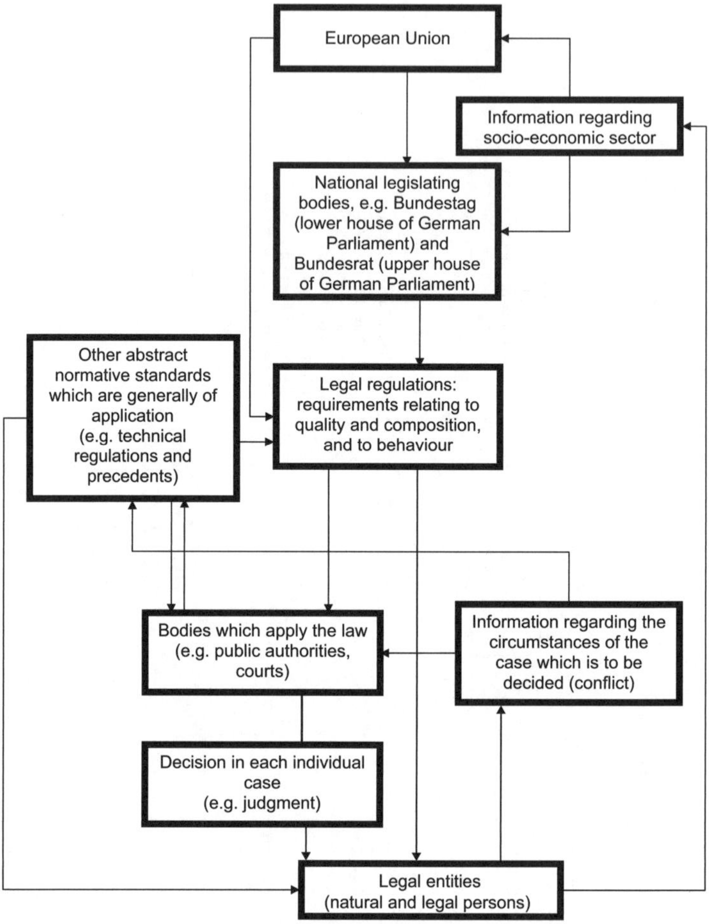

Figure 1A.3 Legislating and applying the law

2. Risk assessment and risk management in economics

Andreas Oehler, Tim Herberger, Stefan Wendt and Andreas Höfer

It is probable that improbable things will happen.
(Aristotle, *Rhetoric*, Book II, Chapter 24)

I. INTRODUCTION

Risk is a core aspect of decision-making in economic situations. This covers decision-making on both the corporate and the individual level, and also economic policy making including regulatory issues. However, risk is not limited to economic situations. Instead, risks may arise in every area of life which leads to the necessity of differentiated approaches to risk management and policy making depending on individual characteristics and risk exposures but also on respective situations in specific areas of life.[1]

The economic idea of risk management is based on the assumption that all possible states of the nature and the probability of their occurrence are known. Real-life economic situations, however, are characterized by

[1] Andreas Oehler, 'Behavioral Economics and Consumer Policy: Basic Reflections and Practical Examples from Consumer Finance' ['Behavioral Economics und Verbraucherpolitik: Grundsätzliche Überlegungen und Praxisbeispiele aus dem Bereich Verbraucherfinanzen'] (2011) 59:10 *Österreichisches BankArchiv* 707–727; *id.*, 'New Old Consumer Principles: A Basis for Consumer Education?' ['Neue alte Verbraucherleitbilder: Basis für die Verbraucherbildung?'] (2013) HiBiFo *Haushalt in Bildung und Forschung* 44–60; Andreas Oehler and Lucia A. Reisch, 'Behavioral Economics – A New Approach for Consumer Policy?' ['Behavioral Economics – eine neue Grundlage für die Verbraucherpolitik?'] (2008) A study for vzbv Verbraucherzentrale Bundesverband, Berlin, <http://www.vzbv.de/sites/default/files/mediapics/studie_behavioral_economics_12_2008.pdf>, retrieved 15 May 2015.

ambiguity, which signifies a considerable lack of information regarding both potential outcomes and the probability of their occurrence.[2] In order to mitigate the lack of measurability of ambiguity, simplifying assumptions therefore allow corporate decision-makers, policy makers and regulators alike to measure and evaluate risk and to apply risk models based on statistical loss distributions. Based on these models and distributions specific risk adjustment strategies can be implemented and monitored. To date, the academic discussion has to a large extent been characterized by these simplifying assumptions as well.

Little attention has been paid to the risks that arise from the simplifying assumptions made in risk management. Our aim is to fill this gap in the literature. Specifically we focus on *model risk*, which follows either from (1) the use of a model that does not fit the situation (overoptimism), (2) the use of a model in a different way from or with a purpose other than that allowed (ignorance), or (3) the non-use of a model that would fit the situation (agnosticism).[3] Model risk is treated only occasionally in the literature.[4] However, in recent years, model risk has been discussed primarily in the context of financial institutions, such as banks, insurance companies and so on. With regard to the banking sector this development was fostered mainly in the context of supervision and regulatory measures included in the Basel accords (especially Basel II).[5] Recently, models and their appropriateness have received increased attention even beyond a particular economic focus, namely in the political discussion of the stability of system-relevant banks and politically enforced stress tests of allegedly system-relevant financial institutions.

---

[2] Andreas Oehler and Matthias Unser, *Financial Risk Management* [*Finanzwirtschaftliches Risikomanagement*] (2nd ed., Springer-Verlag 2002).

[3] Ottmar Bongers and Gerhard Stahl, 'Economic Capital and the Use Test' ['Ökonomisches Kapital und der Use Test'] in Andreas Oehler (ed.), *Risk Management for Investment Funds and Hedge Funds – Status Quo Vadis?* [*Risikomanagement für Investmentfonds und Hedge Fonds – Status Quo Vadis?*] (Springer 2007) 203–224.

[4] Office of the Comptroller of the Currency (OCC), *Supervisory Guidance on Model Risk Management* (2011) Office of the Comptroller of the Currency, <http://www.occ.treas.gov/news-issuances/bulletins/2011/bulletin-2011-12a.pdf>, retrieved 15 May 2015; KPMG, *A Guide to Model Risk and Control* (2006) KPMG International; KPMG, *Model Validation: Mitigating Model Risk* (2012) KPMG LLP.

[5] See Bongers and Stahl, *supra* note 3; Stefan Jaschke, Gerhard Stahl and Richard Stehle, 'Value at Risk Forecasts under Scrutiny – the German Experience' (2007) 7:6 *Quantitative Finance* 621–636.

In this chapter we analyse the causes of model risk and possible adverse consequences for stakeholders. Specifically, we focus on potentially inadequate decision-making and on illusion of control. In addition, we discuss possibilities to mitigate model risk on the basis of model risk management. Furthermore, we infer potential for further research on the adequacy of economic models.

The chapter is structured as follows. In Section II, we provide a brief overview of risk concepts applied in economics. In Section III, we explain the concept of a risk management cycle. Section IV analyses risks that arise from risk management itself, with particular focus on model risk. In Section V, we discuss the results and conclude.

II. RISK CONCEPTS AND RISK CATEGORIES IN ECONOMICS

Theoretical economic models are used to reduce complexity of reality by applying simplifying assumptions in order to help individuals on the corporate, political and regulatory levels to make decisions. In this section we discuss assumptions with respect to risk concepts and risk categories in the light of different economic paradigms. Both risk concepts and risk categories form the theoretical basis of risk models as well as risk management.

One crucial assumption covers potential future states of the nature and the probability of their occurrence in a given period of time. In this context, the most restrictive assumption – this is the assumption of certainty (or perfect foresight) – leads to a model where both the future and respective effects of decisions are deterministic. On the other hand, the least strong assumption represents full uncertainty or ambiguity. In fully uncertain or ambiguous situations decision-makers are not aware of all (possible) states of the nature and/or all alternatives. Instead, they only know some states or bundles of them and they can merely estimate some states' probabilities of occurrence. In situations, however, that are categorized as being risky, decision-makers *assume* to know all (possible) states of the nature, the respective (subjective) probabilities of their occurrence, and all alternatives to decide on.[6]

---

[6] See Oehler and Unser, *supra* note 2; Larry G. Epstein, 'A Definition of Uncertainty Aversion' (1999) 66:3 *The Review of Economic Studies* 579–608; Kip Smith, John Dickhaut, Kevin McCabe and José V. Pardo, 'Neuronal Substrates for Choice Under Ambiguity, Risk, Gains, and Losses' (2002) 48:6 *Management Science* 711–718.

In this context, risk can be generally defined as the probability that a particular (negative) event emerges during a given period of time or results from a particular challenge.[7] In order to quantify risk it is therefore necessary to determine the likelihood of occurrence and the potential negative outcomes or consequences in the case of occurrence.[8] Applying this idea to financial aspects leads to the definition of financial risks as the threat or danger which results from uncertainty that a financial variable deviates negatively from the respective financial target.[9] Financial variables include, for example, (future) cash flows, asset values, market values and returns as differences in absolute values. Target values may comprise the absolute value signed in a contract, the originally invested wealth, expected values or returns, the return of an alternative investment/project, current market values or benchmark values, or returns in a peer group. Financial risks mainly include market risk, credit risk, market liquidity risk, operational risk and legal risk.[10]

The economic literature treats risk and risk management in the context of different economic paradigms:

- *Neo-classical or traditional paradigm.* In this paradigm individuals are assumed to be clones of the idealized concept of a *Homo economicus*.[11] The *Homo economicus* is a perfectly informed individual that rationally decides upon transactions at any time in

---

[7] The Royal Society, *Risk: Analysis, Perception and Management* (The Royal Society 1992).

[8] Andy Bain and David Carson, *Professional Risk and Working with People: Decision-Making in Health, Social Care and Criminal Justice* (Jessica Kingsley Publishers 2008).

[9] Michael Bitz, 'Fundamentals of Financial Risk Management' ['Grundlagen des finanzwirtschaftlich orientierten Risikomanagements'] in Günther Gebhard, Wolfgang Gerke and Manfred Steiner (eds), *Handbook of Financial Management – Financial Instruments and Markets* [*Handbuch des Finanzmanagements – Instrumente und Märkte der Unternehmensfinanzierung*] (Verlag C.H. Beck 1993) 641–668.

[10] See Bitz, *supra* note 9; Oehler and Unser *supra* note 2; Frank J. Fabozzi and Pamela Peterson Drake, *Finance: Capital Markets, Financial Management, and Investment Management* (Wiley 2009).

[11] Andreas Oehler, 'Bank Rating and External Rating of Business Succession – Just Another Rating Approach in the Practice of Finance?' ['Banken- und externes Rating der Unternehmernachfolge – Nur ein weiterer Ratingansatz in der Praxis der Finanzwirtschaft?'] in Ann-Kristin Achleitner, Oliver Everling and Stefan Klemm (eds), *Successor Rating: Rating as a Chance for Company Succession* [*Nachfolgerating: Rating als Chance für die Unternehmensnachfolge*] (Gabler Verlag 2006) 297–312.

order to maximize its expected utility.[12] This means that all individuals decide rationally based on the identical economic model. In addition, the neo-classical paradigm assumes markets to be perfect. Perfect markets are characterized by perfect competition and exhibit the following three core elements: First, there are an infinite number of market participants, and each transaction only diminutively affects the market outcome; individuals are price takers, that is, they cannot influence the price of a certain good. Secondly, goods traded are standardized or homogeneous. Thirdly, there are no barriers to entering or leaving the market.[13] In addition, there exist no frictions, such as transaction costs or taxes, and every market participant has full information at all times.[14] In the neo-classical paradigm financial markets fulfil the criterion of completeness. In a complete financial market every cash flow or security can be traded irrespective of its uncertainty characteristic or maturity.[15] However, not every single individual needs to act fully rationally as long as there is a sufficiently large number of rational individuals to achieve rational market results (the 'as-if' approach).[16] In such an economic environment individuals are able to assess risks fully. In addition, since individuals can trade each arbitrary cash flow, they are able to offset every potential (financial) risk on their own. Hence, they are able to adjust their risk level to the level that fits their preferences. This means that corporate risk

---

[12] Andreas Oehler, 'Consumer Protection – a Holistic Approach from an Economic Perspective' ['Zur ganzheitlichen Konzeption des Verbraucherschutzes – eine ökonomische Perspektive'] (2006) 21:8 *Verbraucher und Recht* 294–300; *id.*, *supra* note 1 (2011) and (2013); Gebhard Kirchgässner, *Homo Oeconomicus – The Economic Model of Behaviour and Its Applications in Economics and Other Social Sciences* (Springer 2008).

[13] Robert E. Hall and Marc Liebermann, *Microeconomics: Principles and Applications* (4th ed., Cengage Learning 2007); Irvin B. Tucker, *Survey of Economics* (7th ed., Cengage Learning 2010); N. Gregory Mankiw, *Principles of Economics* (6th ed., Cengage Learning 2011).

[14] Oehler and Unser, *supra* note 2; Sergio M. Focardi and Frank J. Fabozzi, *The Mathematics of Financial Modeling and Investment Management* (Wiley 2004).

[15] Jonathan E. Ingersoll, *Theory of Financial Decision Making* (Rowman & Littlefield Publishers 1987); Oehler and Unser, *supra* note 2; Thomas S.Y. Ho and Sang Bin Lee, *The Oxford Guide to Financial Modeling: Applications for Capital Markets, Corporate Finance, Risk Management and Financial Institutions* (Oxford University Press 2003); Rose Anne Dana and Monique Jeanblanc, *Financial Markets in Continuous Time* (Springer 2007).

[16] Oehler, *supra* note 12 (2006); *id.*, *supra* note 1 (2011) and (2013).

management is typically not necessary. Following the ideas of neo-classical portfolio theory[17] and the capital asset pricing model,[18] individuals even simply need to hold a combination of a risk-free asset and the market portfolio to achieve their optimal risk position.

- *New institutional economics paradigm.* While the neo-classical paradigm focuses on market transactions, the new institutional economics paradigm combines managerial as well as micro-economic with macroeconomic elements.[19] Assuming transaction costs, including costs of searching, storing, processing and transmitting information, individuals do not possess full information and information is asymmetrically distributed among subjects.[20] As a consequence, it is only possible to write incomplete contracts and market mechanisms are not necessarily sufficient in order to reach expected economic outcomes. In addition, contract enforcement is not costless.[21] Besides informational asymmetries, this leads to asymmetries in decision-making power and in the distribution of economic results.[22] The asymmetries lead to agency conflicts among stakeholders. In order to mitigate these conflicts and to reduce agency costs (monitoring and bonding costs as well as the residual loss that persists despite any potential efforts to reduce

---

[17] Harry Markowitz, 'Portfolio Selection' (1952) 7:1 *The Journal of Finance* 77–91.

[18] William F. Sharpe, 'Capital Asset Prices: A Theory of Market Equilibrium under Conditions of Risk' (1964) 19:3 *The Journal of Finance* 425–442; John Lintner, 'The Valuation of Risky Assets and the Selection of Risky Investments in Stock Portfolios and Capital Budgets' (1965) 47:1 *The Review of Economics and Statistics* 13–37; Jan Mossin, 'Equilibrium in a Capital Market' (1966) 34:4 *Econometrica* 768–783.

[19] For an overview see Oehler and Unser, *supra* note 2; for fundamental explanations on institutional economics see Oliver E. Williamson, *The Economic Institutions of Capitalism: Firms, Markets, Relational Contracting* (Free Press 1985); Armen A. Alchian and Susan Woodward, 'The Firm is Dead; Long Live the Firm: A Review of Oliver E. Williamson's The Economic Institutions of Capitalism' (1988) 26 *Journal of Economic Literature* 65–79.

[20] For the fundamentals of transaction cost theory see Ronald H. Coase, 'The Nature of the Firm' (1937) 4:16 *Econometrica* 386–405.

[21] See Williamson, *supra* note 19 and Ronald H. Coase, *The Firm, the Market, and the Law* (University of Chicago Press 1988).

[22] Oehler and Unser, *supra* note 2.

agency conflicts),[23] institutional arrangements are necessary.[24] In this context, relevant risks include informational risks, delegation risks and risks with respect to asymmetric distribution of economic consequences which significantly depend on individual characteristics and behaviour.[25] These include uncertainty about both competences and intentions of contractual partners which leads to the risk of moral hazard and hold-up.[26] Furthermore, risks arise from the fact that individuals are not fully informed about the characteristics or the quality of goods and services. This information risk is particularly pronounced with respect to credence goods whose characteristics can neither be fully assessed after contract conclusion nor during or after the contract period.[27] Consequently, situations may arise in which individuals are unable to determine all potential consequences of specific decisions or the probabilities of

---

[23] Michael C. Jensen and William H. Meckling, 'Theory of the Firm: Managerial Behavior, Agency Costs and Ownership Structure' (1976) 3:4 *Journal of Financial Economics* 305–360.

[24] See Oehler, *supra* note 12 (2006) and *supra* note 1 (2011).

[25] Andreas Oehler, 'Functions of Banks and other Financial Intermediaries in Increasing International Financial Market Integration' ['Funktion von Banken und anderer Finanzintermediäre bei zunehmender internationaler Finanzmarktintegration unter der Perspektive ihrer gesellschaftlichen und nationalstaatlichen Bedeutung – Corporate Governance & Control in markt- und intermediärbasierten Finanzsystemen im Kontext von Personal- und Kapitalverflechtungen'] in Martin Heidenreich, Hans-W. Micklitz, Andreas Oehler, Hans Rattinger and Johannes Schwarze (eds), *Europe after the Eastern Expansion – Research on Europe at the University of Bamberg* [*Europa nach der Osterweiterung – Europaforschung an der Universität Bamberg*] (Kulturverlag Kadmos 2005) 212–223; Eirik G. Furubotn and Rudolf Richter, *Institutions and Economic Theory: The Contribution of the New Institutional Economics* (2nd ed., University of Michigan Press 2005).

[26] Oehler, *supra* note 11 (2006).

[27] Andreas Oehler, *Investor Protection in a Market and Intermediary-Based System* [*Anlegerschutz in einem markt- und intermediärbasierten System – Eine Analyse im Lichte der Neuen Institutionenökonomik, der Theorie der Finanzintermediation und der Behavioral Economics & Finance*] (2004) A study for the Scientific Advisory Board on Consumer and Food Policies at the Federal Ministry of Food, Agriculture and Consumer Protection; *id.*, 'Consumer Information as Driver of Quality Competition' ['Verbraucherinformation als Motor des Qualitätswettbewerbs'] in vzbv Verbraucherzentrale Bundesverband (ed.), *Economic Factor Consumer Information – the Importance of Information for Functioning Markets* [*Wirtschaftsfaktor Verbraucherinformation – Die Bedeutung von Information für funktionierende Märkte*] (BWV 2005) 28–50; *id.*, *supra* note 12 (2006).

the occurrence of these consequences. This means that in a new institutional economics setting, decision-making is typically characterized by a higher degree of ambiguity instead of risk.

- *Behavioural economics and finance paradigm.* This paradigm focuses on individuals' behaviour with respect to decision-making. Specifically, the individual behaviour with regard to gathering, perceiving and processing information and to forming decisions is analysed. Behavioural economics and finance is based on the concept of bounded rationality as introduced by Simon.[28] While the neo-classical concept of full rationality requires unlimited cognitive capabilities, bounded rationality characterizes individuals as having only limited cognitive capacity.[29] Even if individuals wish to act rationally, their real-life decision-making will be restricted by 'bounds' and it will not conform to the ideal of full rationality,[30] which leads to so-called 'anomalies', 'irrationalities' or 'biases' in decision-making, such as information overload, choice overload, customer confusion, home bias, overconfidence, hyperbolic discounting, framing effects and herding.[31] In this setting, individuals will not be able to identify and quantify all risks and their perceptions of risk will differ even in otherwise identical situations.

---

[28] Herbert A. Simon, 'A Behavioral Model of Rational Choice' (1955) 69:1 *Quarterly Journal of Economics* 99–118; *id.*, 'Rational Choice and the Structure of Environments' (1956) 63:2 *Psychological Review* 129–138.

[29] See also Daniel Kahnemann, 'Maps of Bounded Rationality' (2002) Nobel Lecture, Stockholm, 8 December 2002; Helmut Jungermann, Hans-Rüdiger Pfister and Katrin Fischer, *The Psychology of Decision: An Introduction* (2nd ed., Spektrum Akademischer Verlag 2005).

[30] Reinhard Selten, 'What is Bounded Rationality?' in Gerd Gigerenzer and Reinhard Selten (eds), *Bounded Rationality: The Adaptive Toolbox* (The MIT Press 2002) 13–36.

[31] Daniel Kahneman and Amos Tversky, 'On the Psychology of Prediction' (1973) 80:4 *Psychological Review* 237–251; Amos Tversky and Daniel Kahneman, 'Judgment under Uncertainty: Heuristics and Biases' (1974) 185:4157 *Science* 1124–1131; *id.*, 'The Framing of Decisions and the Psychology of Choice' (1981) 211:4481 *Science* 453–458; Andreas Oehler, '"Anomalies", "Irrationalities" or "Biases" of the Expected Utility Hypothesis and their Relevance for Financial Markets' ['"Anomalien", "Irrationalitäten" oder "Biases" der Erwartungsnutzentheorie und ihre Relevanz für Finanzmärkte'] (1992) 4 *Zeitschrift für Bankrecht und Bankwirtschaft* 97–124; *id.*, *Explaining the Behaviour of Private Investors – Theoretical Approach and Empirical Analyses* [*Die Erklärung des Verhaltens privater Anleger – Theoretischer Ansatz und empirische Analysen*] (Schäffer-Poeschel 1995); *id.*, *supra* note 1 (2013); Oehler and Reisch, *supra* note 1.

In addition, market outcomes will not be efficient in the neo-classical sense which influences the applicability of some market value-based financial variables and financial targets.

III. RISK MANAGEMENT CYCLE

Risk management follows the assumption that real-life situations are approximated by the concept of risk (instead of ambiguity). This section presents a standardized risk management process that is applicable to both the micro or firm level and macroeconomic considerations (with respect to regulation and policy making in the context of management of systemic risk). In the literature the risk management process is commonly set up as a cybernetic cycle in order to allow for the evaluation of the performance of risk management itself, to allow for adjustments over time and to reflect the dynamic evolution of internal and external conditions.[32]

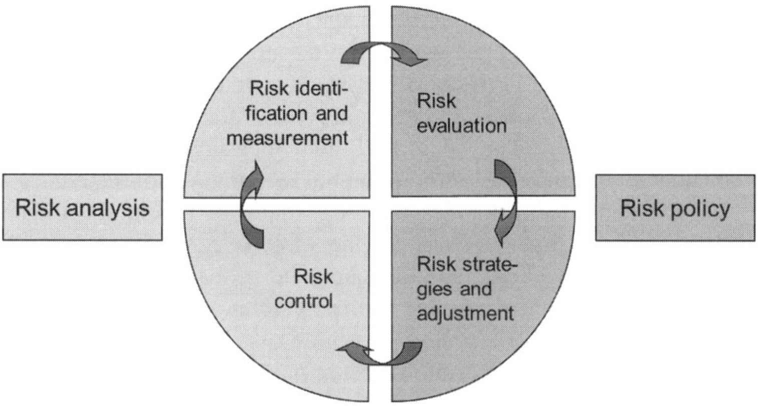

Source: Andreas Oehler and Matthias Unser, *Financial Risk Management* [*Finanzwirtschaftliches Risikomanagement*] (2nd ed., Springer-Verlag 2002).

Figure 2.1 Risk management as a cybernetic process

Figure 2.1 presents an exemplary risk management process set up as a cybernetic cycle.[33] In this process, risk analysis comprises identification

[32] Oehler and Unser, *supra* note 2.
[33] *Ibid.*

and measurement of risk as well as controlling risks; whereas risk policy includes both the risk evaluation and strategies to adjust the level of risk:[34]

- *Risk identification and measurement.* In the context of identifying and measuring risks all relevant risk categories should first be defined and determined. In order to compile a comprehensive listing of relevant risks a number of approaches can be applied, such as brainstorming, workshops and Delphi methods, and also checklists, SWOT and gap analyses, risk trees and flow charts.[35] However, as soon as deviations from the concept of a *Homo economicus* are considered, the relevance of risk categories might differ among stakeholders and is strongly influenced by current individual and firm-specific characteristics (regional and industry-specific features, product portfolio, etc.). After having identified relevant risks, risk managers need both micro and macro information in order to measure risk both quantitatively by applying shortfall or downside risk measures based on, for example, lower partial moments of the distribution of potential outcomes, such as the concept of Value at Risk or sensitivity measures, and qualitatively by, for example, conducting expert interviews. In addition, interdependencies between different risks and portfolio effects need to be detected in order to determine the overall risk position.
- *Risk evaluation.* The identified and measured risks should be evaluated in order to infer potential economic consequences for stakeholders. This includes the assessment of potential (financial) damage over time as well as the effectiveness of counteractive measures. Evaluation methods might be probability based or they might include sensitivity and scenario techniques.
- *Risk strategy and adjustment.* Given an overall risk strategy and the results of risk identification, measurement and evaluation, measures with respect to the adjustment of risk should be implemented. General risk adjustment strategies comprise hedging, insuring and diversification activities. Hedging means the reduction of the volatility of the distribution of potential outcomes by establishing a hedge position that offsets the original volatility, whereas insuring represents the risk transfer to a third party which has to be paid for

---

[34] For these and the following explanations see Oehler and Unser, *supra* note 2.

[35] Tobias Ibers and Andreas Hey, *Risk Management* [*Risikomanagement*] (Merkur-Verlag 2005).

with an insurance premium. While hedging in general offsets both positive and negative deviation from the expected result, insuring only offsets negative deviations at the cost of the insurance premium. Diversification means the combination of a number of single positions into a portfolio that exhibits the desired risk characteristics. In order to benefit from diversification effects, the single positions need to exhibit correlations between minus one and plus one; a correlation of minus one would represent a hedge as described above. Specific risk adjustment strategies include risk acceptance, risk reduction and risk avoidance. When risks are accepted the primary business activities remain unchanged, while risk reduction means that these activities are complemented by secondary activities, such as the conclusion of specific financial contracts. In order to achieve risk avoidance, the primary activities need to be adjusted or at the limit given up.

- *Risk control* covers the analysis of the performance of risk management itself. A gap between the actual and the target risk level and structure might be the result of either inadequate assumptions, changes in the external environment and in firm-specific conditions, or inappropriate application of risk adjustment strategies. From the results of the gap analysis, adjustments to the underlying assumptions need to be inferred as well as adjustments to risk measures and evaluation techniques if necessary. Subsequently, the risk adjustment strategies and their implementation might need revision in order to achieve the target risk level and structure.

IV. RISKS ARISING FROM THE USE OF MODELS IN ECONOMIC DECISION-MAKING

In order to handle the complexity and ambiguity of real-life situations decision-makers apply (typically quantitative) models which themselves exhibit different degrees of complexity. Not only is this reflected in models applied to risk management, but also in decision models, valuation models, forecasting models and models of economic or financial systems with respect to, for example, systemic risk or financial supervision.[36] Possible adverse consequences of decisions as a result of

[36] KPMG, *supra* note 4 (2012).

incorrect or misused models are subsumed in the concept of model risk.[37] Specifically, model risk arises in the following situations:[38]

- Decision-makers use a model which does not fit the situation (over-optimism); they consider the model to fit the situation although it does not.
- Decision-makers use a model in a different way from or with a purpose other than that allowed (ignorance).
- Decision-makers do not use a model which would fit the situation (agnosticism); they consider the model not to fit the situation although it does.

There are a number of factors that potentially lead to these situations. They relate to the assumptions underlying the models, input data quality, data processing within the model, and transfer of model estimates into information that is used in actual decision-making.[39]

The application of simplifying *assumptions* is inevitable to reduce the complexity of real-life situations and/or to focus on particularly important aspects depending on the intended model application.[40] Assumptions primarily reflect the theoretical paradigm upon which a model is implicitly or explicitly based (see Section II). Most models are set up in the context of the neo-classical paradigm. Since this paradigm – by relying on the concept of *Homo economicus* – fails to incorporate individual characteristics of subjects and relies heavily on the effectiveness and efficiency of market mechanisms, even otherwise well specified models will lead to estimates that significantly deviate from reality. Models based on the new institutional economics paradigm will lead to more realistic results since they incorporate informational asymmetries between individuals and allow individuals not to possess full information about all possible states of the nature and the probability of their occurrence. However, the informational paradigm implies that the reduction of informational asymmetries will lead to risk reduction. Given individuals' limited cognitive capacity to identify, quantify and assess risks, which is inherent in the behavioural concept of bounded rationality, (full) reduction of informational asymmetries is practically not achievable.[41] Instead, since the perception of risk among individuals differs

---

37 OCC, *supra* note 4.

38 Bongers and Stahl, *supra* note 3.

39 OCC, *supra* note 4.

40 *Ibid.*

41 Oehler, *supra* note 1 (2013).

even in identical situations, an appropriate set-up of risk models should also account for problems arising from information overload, choice overload, overconfidence, framing, and so on. Otherwise, risk models will heavily oversimplify reality.

Data quality influences (or even creates) model risk with respect to two dimensions. First, a model that would otherwise fit the situation might not yield sufficiently good estimates if it is fed with inappropriate data.[42] This is particularly obvious when historical or current data are used, which is typically the case. In particular in highly volatile and/or in quickly evolving environments, future developments probably differ significantly from historical developments which will lead to unrealistic model outcomes if only historical data are used. Second, backtesting of model validity either during the model development phase (before implementation) or regularly during model risk monitoring activities depends on data quality.[43] Inadequate or insufficient data in model validation may lead to an error of the first kind – that is, models that actually exhibit high validity are classified as being invalid – or an error of the second kind – that is, models with low validity are not detected but classified as providing highly valid results.

Data processing may be a source of model risk when mathematical calculation and quantification leads to erroneous estimates. This might result from programming errors, including incorrect implementation of algorithms,[44] and technical shortcomings such as insufficient computational capacity at single stages of the computational processes. However, in more complex model applications this might also arise due to insufficient interfaces between single stages of the computational processes or between computer systems. The *transfer of model estimates* into information that actual decisions are based upon leads to adverse consequences if estimates are not correctly understood and interpreted

---

[42] KPMG, *supra* note 4 (2012).

[43] For backtesting of credit risk models see, for example, Wolfgang Bühler, Christoph Engel, Olaf Korn and Gerhard Stahl, 'Backtesting of Credit Risk Models' ['Backtesting von Kreditrisikomodellen'] in Andreas Oehler (ed.), *Credit Risk Management: Core Areas, Supervision and Trends* [*Kreditrisikomanagement: Kernbereiche, Aufsicht und Entwicklungstendenzen*] (Schäffer-Poeschel 2002) 181–217; Gerhard Stahl, Uwe Traber and Thomas Dietz, 'Backtesting in Action' in Andreas Oehler (ed.), *Credit Risk Management: Core Areas, Supervision, and Trends* [*Kreditrisikomanagement: Kernbereiche, Aufsicht und Entwicklungstendenzen*] (Schäffer-Poeschel 2002) 219–241.

[44] KPMG, *supra* note 4 (2012).

given the modelling assumptions. This also includes situations in which some of the estimates are not considered while others are over-weighted.

Given these possible sources of model risk, decision-makers potentially use models in an overly optimistic, ignorant or agnostic way, either because they are not aware of model risk or because they deliberately decide to use them despite knowing about possible adverse consequences. The first effect will arise due to a lack of information and understanding of the model itself, about alternative models and/or due to information overload, choice overload or overconfidence when choosing a particular model. The second effect reflects, for example, the risk of moral hazard. Specifically, due to diverging interests, intentions and competences of individuals who develop, apply and take responsibility for the functioning of economic models and for the decisions based upon these models, situations arise in which model risk becomes particularly pronounced. In addition, however, decision-makers might be forced to use specific models by regulators and policy makers.

If decision-makers fail to take model risk into account, their decisions based on specific economic models will be characterized by the illusion of control.[45] This is why model risk management or modelling governance processes should be an integral part of risk management.[46] As for other types of risk, model risk management should include the identification of the sources of model risk and the assessment of its magnitude, including interactions and dependencies among different models applied. Based on the evaluation of the overall model risk position, potential strategies to mitigate model risk need to be implemented. These strategies cover the model development and implementation phase as well as the actual model use. With respect to the models themselves, rigorous model validation and backtesting procedures, as well as model revisions over time should be implemented, including the evaluation of conceptual soundness, ongoing monitoring and outcome analyses. These efforts should be complemented by governance, policies and controls in order to address the actual model application, including a clear definition of roles and responsibilities, limits on model use, reporting and documentation, and monitoring and supervision by internal and external controls.[47]

---

[45] Andreas Oehler, 'Credit Risk Management under Illusion of Control' ['Kreditrisikomanagement unter Kontrollillusion'] (2005) 53 *BankArchiv* 219–220.

[46] A detailed description of a model risk management approach is provided in OCC, *supra* note 4.

[47] OCC, *supra* note 4.

V. DISCUSSION AND CONCLUSION

In this chapter we have presented risk concepts and categories in the light of the neo-classical, the new institutional economics, and the behavioural economics and finance paradigms. In addition we have elaborated on a cybernetic approach to risk management. Based on these fundamental considerations we have focused on model risk and on model risk management.

In economic decision-making, models are typically applied in order to reduce the complexity of real-life situations. The benefits of reducing complexity, however, come at the cost of model risk. Generally, model risks arise due to oversimplifying assumptions, poor data quality, erroneous data processing, and insufficient transfer of model estimates into information that is used in decision-making. This results in situations where decision-makers use a model that does not fit the situation (over-optimism), use a model in a different way from or with a purpose other than that allowed (ignorance), or they do not use a model that would fit the situation (agnosticism). However, if decision-makers fail to take model risk into account, their decisions based on specific economic models will be characterized by the illusion of control.

Possibilities to mitigate model risk include, for example, model validation and backtesting procedures but also the introduction of governance and control procedures with respect to model use. On the other hand, other approaches such as scenario techniques might provide more realistic outcomes than historical data, which are particularly unsuitable when used in forecast models in volatile environments. Ideally, financial or economic risk management should therefore be complemented by model risk management with respect to model development, the choice of specific models and their implementation, the actual application of models and the interpretation of outcomes.

Completely avoiding models and model risk, however, would imply forgoing the benefits of models in reducing complexity. In addition, conclusions drawn purely by individual common sense and beliefs face the risk of being very misleading. On the other hand, insights and experience from real crises can lead to results and estimations which can be more worthwhile than those from simulated scenarios from synthetic models.[48] Future research should therefore focus on the question of how to balance model risk and risks arising from complexity. In addition,

[48] Bongers and Stahl, *supra* note 3.

further research is necessary in order to determine the effect of model risk on the adequacy of economic, political and regulatory decision-making when (re-)transferring modelling results to real life.

3. The social epistemology of risk observation and management – modern law and the transformation of its cognitive infrastructure

Karl-Heinz Ladeur

I. INTRODUCTION

This chapter ventures to demonstrate the existence of a much more intense inter-relationship between the law and the cognitive system of society than was previously assumed. 'Facts and norms' are not as clearly separated as the established mode of self-observation of the legal system maintains. The autonomy of the legal system which emerged in the late 19th century is dependent on the emergence of a new knowledge base of society, 'experience', which draws on a continuous practical processing of knowledge derived from the production systems that served non-local markets. The law draws on this process via a bridging concept, 'danger', which transfers knowledge into public decision-making procedures and allows for its integration into normative judgement. The chapter tries to explain the rise of the continental version of positivism as a self-description of the legal system on the continent, isolated from the transformation of society's knowledge system. It also seeks to demonstrate the interest taken by the state in the stabilisation and generalisation of knowledge which could be used for both private and public purposes of governance. An overview of a new type of group-based knowledge is given which relies upon rules of probability which imposed order on and allowed for recognition of patterns in phenomena which hitherto had been regarded as subject to blind chance. This reflection leads towards an understanding of the emerging postmodern regime of knowledge which takes on explicit forms, for example in standard-setting and public–private co-operation, when it comes to the development of high technology in a network society. The emerging model of knowledge creation has lost its stable frame of reference and undermines the functioning of the established modes of decision-making. A postmodern 'social epistemology' requires a more heterarchical mode of co-operation of state and society modelled on the patterns of fragmented knowledge generation and processing in private firms. This chapter tries to sketch an approach that focuses on a new 'paradigm' of a proactive relationship between 'facts and norms' in postmodernity, which should be understood as a functional equivalent to the active transformative relationship between law and experience in the past. Both in the past and in the future, the inter-relationship between the legal system and the societal knowledge base is a strategic one, and does not allow for a stable separation.

II. LEGAL POSITIVISM AND THE TRANSFORMATION OF SOCIAL KNOWLEDGE – THE ROLE OF PUBLIC AUTHORITIES IN THE RESTRUCTURING OF THE KNOWLEDGE GENERATION PROCESS

The abstraction process of the new 'positive' law which transcended the close relationships between normative and factual 'bindingness' does not abolish the dependence of the legal order on a cognitive and informational infrastructure that consists of a generative network of patterns of action, co-operative conventions, practices of co-ordination, common probability assumptions[1] and so on, within which it functions as a kind of 'knot'. The legal order and its continuous process of concretisation are linked to a set of rules of relevance[2] which, in a controlled manner, process the flow of information needed for the adaptation to new challenges. The autonomisation of the legal order seemed to have broken this link, but this was only a superficial observation of the transformation which had taken place. Legal norms can only produce their organisational and structuring effects by channelling thought and action on the basis of 'open-textured clusters of ideas'[3] which can be presupposed.

Looking back to the generative achievements of German legal positivism, one may assume that this inter-relationship between normativity and facts in the early 19th century was characterised by close-knit fragmented

---

[1] Scott Atran, *In Gods We Trust: The Evolutionary Landscapes of Religion* (OUP 2005) 235.

[2] Dan Sperber and Deirdre Wilson, *Relevance: Communication and Cognition* (Blackwell 1986).

[3] Atran, see note 1, 212, 251.

webs of local practices, while the new attitude of 'pure' legal self-construction of 'will relationships' beyond the binding forces of habits and conventions provoked a corresponding repercussion within the world of facts: a wave of abstractions and systematicity which intruded upon the knowledge base implied in everyday transactions between economic actors and industrial producers.[4] This co-evolution of the factual knowledge basis contributed to a process of interlocal exchange and generalisation of patterns of economic behaviour, technical knowledge, and rules of relevance for the evaluation of risks and pay-offs. When it comes to the evaluation of technical risks, a process of homogenisation and standardisation of the social knowledge infrastructure can be observed from a public law perspective. Not only did public law refer to practical experience in its definition of the limits to be imposed on technical industrial production, but the state actively intervened in the generation and stabilisation of the general knowledge base which might be used by private and public actors alike. In early processes of fragmented (proto-) industrial technical production, a network of knowledge had been generated on a practical case by case basis. This can be said both for the ways of manufacturing new products and the risks to be taken into consideration as side-effects of innovative ways of production. New information on promising methods of construction and ways to avoid losses and risks spread slowly and developed in a haphazard way, because production processes were locally based and thus experience was fragmented as well. In the process of early industrialisation, safety information did not easily reach small factories. In this period, for example, in Prussia, the state government initiated private self-organisation of industrial producers in order to raise the level of technical information by improving the exchange of knowledge and the formulation of standards of production and risk reduction.[5] Later on, the 'Technische Überwachungsvereine', a

---

[4] Karl-Heinz Ladeur, 'Coping with Uncertainty: Ecological Risk and the Concept of Self-Organization' in Gunther Teubner, Lindsay Farmer and Declan Murphy (eds), *Environmental Law and Ecological Responsibility* (Wiley 1999) 299.

[5] Ina vom Feld, 'Vertrauen ist gut – Kontrolle ist besser? Dampfkesselüberwachung in Preußen zwischen Fremdsteuerung und Selbststeuerung 1870–1914' in Birgit Feldner et al. (eds), *Ad fontes. Europäisches Forum Junger Rechtshistorikerinnen und Rechtshistoriker* (Peter Lang 2003) 121; Joel Mokyr, *The Gifts of Athena: Historical Origins of the Knowledge Economy* (Princeton University Press 2004).

private organisation for the control of technical risks,[6] which to this day still has a hybrid private and public function in the self-regulation of industries, was installed. It continued the public efforts in a more efficient way after the state had succeeded in breaking up the traditional limitations of society's knowledge base. The same is true for the spread of information on the building of houses, including safety rules and patterns of architectural design.[7] The knowledge generated in this field had also been restricted to regional information networks.

This public intervention – mainly by way of imposing organisational elements into private networks – stimulated an increase in technical, engineering and architectural knowledge which went far beyond the mere diffusion of existing knowledge; it provoked an immense take-off in private industry, which attained a much higher level of technical knowledge. This is a new version of public action which is often neglected because of the one-sided fixation on the 'public enlightenment' as a self-referential forum of rationality: this is the search for a practical private–public knowledge base for decision-making ('industrial enlightenment').[8] The universalisation of this knowledge base requires explicit standards instead of implicit rules of practice.[9]

In the long run, the roles had been completely changed: whereas, initially, it was the state which had access to the advanced regional levels of information and dominated the process of knowledge generation, later on it was the newly organised and spontaneously functioning private networks of knowledge which by far outweighed the informational potential of state bureaucracies and their creative function. Increasingly, the private organisations set up explicit private standards which replaced the spontaneous generation of patterns of 'normalisation'. But, at the same time, the receptive role of the state as a user of the privately generated knowledge in administrative decision-making became more important. Thus, the privately generated knowledge base was used by both public and private decision-makers.

---

[6] Milos Več, *Recht und Normierung in der industriellen Revolution* (Klostermann 2006).

[7] Robert Strecke, *Anfänge und Innovation der preußischen Bauverwaltung. Von D. Gilly zu F. Schinkel* (Böhlau 2000).

[8] Mokyr, note 5.

[9] Olivier Faverau, Olivier Biencourt and François Eymard-Duvernay, 'Where Do Markets Come From? From (Quality) Conventions!' in Olivier Favereau and Emmanuel Lazega (eds), *Conventions and Structures in Economic Organization: Markets, Networks and Hierarchies* (Edward Elgar 2002).

III. 'DANGER' AS THE BRIDGING CONCEPT BETWEEN THE NORMATIVE AND THE COGNITIVE DIMENSIONS OF THE LEGAL SYSTEM

As a 'bridging concept' which played a role as a rule of relevance in public law decision-making procedures, the concept of 'danger' (Gefahr) took a prominent role.[10] The limits which public law imposed on the dynamics of private industrial production were especially drawn up with this borderline concept in mind. 'Gefahr' referred even etymologically to 'Erfahrung' (experience); that is, to the set of private patterns of behaviour, expectations, standards of avoiding risk, and so on which no longer drew on local conventions but on more abstract general rules of practice which had been settled by the processes of exchange taking place at the regional or state level. 'Erfahrung' is, by itself, a typical hybrid concept which integrates informational, practical and normative elements.[11] Its role in public law can be compared to the rules defining 'negligence' in private law. It not only has a factual element of defining cause–effect chains, but it also implies a normative element inasmuch as risk alone must not prevent private action or impose limits on it by way of public intervention. 'Erfahrung' is drawn from practical action and aims to create practical rules of action for the future. The likelihood of the causation of harm alone was not a sufficient reason to interfere with private action and, in addition, a practical sense for pay-offs (immanent cost–benefit rules) had to be preserved. Abstract fears, for example of the risks involved in railway traffic, did not provide sufficient reason for public intervention. The same was true for the cumulative effects of individual actions. Experience defined a standard of 'normalcy' for goods and expectations to which public administrators could refer in decision-making procedures. The importance of this process of establishing stable links between public law and the societal knowledge base can be demonstrated by a comparative look at traditional police law

---

[10] Karl-Heinz Ladeur, 'Risikobewältigung durch Flexibilisierung und Prozeduralisierung des Recht. Rechtliche Bindung von Ungewißheit oder Selbstverunsicherung des Rechts?' in Alfons Bora (ed.), *Rechtliches Risikomanagement: Form, Funktion und Leistungsfähigkeit des Rechts in der Risikogesellschaft* (Duncker & Humblot 1999) 41; *id.*, note 4, 299.

[11] For a philosophical point of view, see Georg W. Bertram, *Hermeneutik und Dekonstruktion* (Fink 2002) 42; for a sociological perspective, see Anne Cauquelin, *L'art du lieu commun* (Seuil 1993) 29.

('policey'),[12] which came to a conclusion with the famous 'Kreuzberg judgment' of the Prussian High Court of Administrative Affairs (Preußisches Oberverwaltungsgericht)[13] which ruled out an administrative decision of the police prohibiting the construction of a building that would have disturbed the view of a memorial of the victorious war of 1870. According to the judges, the new building did not cause any harm to a concrete existing good, but was intended to protect an immaterial interest which had its value but was not part of a stable framework of 'normal' expectations. This example demonstrates the close link between the general law regulating the 'will' of the state and the public–private knowledge base defining the standards of 'normalcy' as opposed to the creation of new public interests that was a competency of the legislator but not of the administration.

This evolution of the new formal positive law developed in three stages: in a first step traditional norms and facts had been separated; at a later stage facts had to be mobilised and restructured according to abstract and universal rules of modern society; and in a third step both autonomous norms and restructured facts could be co-ordinated anew at a higher level of abstraction. The new form of co-operation presupposed the functioning of rules of relevance which steered the selective process of channelling cognitive openness and the normative closure of the legal system. The common experience which one might attribute to 'communities of practice'[14] is not based on a common project, but is incremental and remains implicit to a distributed process of trial and error.[15]

---

[12] Matthias Bohlender, 'Metamorphosen des Gemeinwohlp. Von der Herrschaft guter polizey zur Regierung durch Freiheit und Sicherheit' in Herfried Münkler and Harald Bluhm (eds), *Gemeinwohl und Gemeinsinn: Historische Semantiken politischer Leitbegriffe* (Akademie 2001) 247.

[13] Reports (Amtliche Sammlung) 9, 353 (14 June 1882).

[14] Paul Duguid, 'Community of Practice, Then and Now' in Ash Amin and Joanne Roberts (eds), *Community, Creativity, and Organization* (OUP 2008) 1, 8.

[15] For the relevance of implicit knowledge in the historical process of the European industrial take-off, cf. Mokyr, note 5.

IV. 'MANAGEMENT OF RULES' – THE COUPLING OF THE LEGAL SYSTEM AND SOCIAL RULES

A liberal legal order – which the positivistic doctrine also claimed to have established – has always had to presuppose and take into account that normativity, even if it has attained a more abstract level, is dependent on the societal processes of the normalisation of establishing practical conventions and behavioural patterns,[16] and, at the same time, intervenes in the processes going on in the networks of inter-relationships in which these norms are implied, as opposed to explicit legal norms. Normativity presupposes a 'precommitment',[17] which refers to the adaptation to constraints and expectations that are generated by private processes of co-operation and co-ordination and form a public–private knowledge base. Such a common knowledge base is needed in a society that uses norms and conventions in order to bind a new type of uncertainty which cannot be eliminated or reduced to chance. The new construction of an autonomous law which took its distance from the old intertwinement of facts and norms had, at the same time, to presuppose that the practical network of legal relationships and conventions implied in society[18] would be able to process a new, more abstract and more variable knowledge base ('experience') to be established beyond local fragmentation.[19] In addition, new rules of relevance which could reorganise the patterns of inter-relationships that impose connection constraints and possibilities in society had to be generated. The self-organisation of rules of practice which process new, practical possibilities of action determine the 'facts' to which the legal system has to refer in decision-making procedures, and which are, at the same time, reinforced by legal decisions. This is due to the fact that public and private action, even after the shift to a more

---

16 Christiane Chauviré, *Le moment anthropologique de Wittgenstein* (Editions Kimé 2004); Russell Hardin, *Indeterminacy and Society* (Princeton University Press 2003); *id.*, 'Street-Level Epistemology and Democratic Participation' in James S. Fishkin and Peter Lassett (eds), *Debating Deliberative Democracy* (Wiley and Blackwell 2003) 163.

17 Michael E. Bratman, *Faces of Intention* (Cambridge University Press 1999) 4; Atran, note 1, 234, 255.

18 Olivier Favereau, 'Règles, organisation et apprentissage collectif' in André Orléan (ed.), *Analyse économique des conventions* (Presses Universitaires de France 1994) 113; *id.*, Biencourt and Eymard-Duvernay, note 9, 213; for the conceptualisation of networks see Fritz B. Simon, *Einführung in die systemische Wirtschaftstheorie* (Carl Auer Systeme Verlag 2009) 89.

19 Lucien Jaume, *La liberté et la loi* (Fayard 2000) 181.

abstract legal order has taken place, always acts on the basis of linkages between past or future actions, in groups of actions ('plans') which have to bind uncertainty with reference to rules, conventions and expectations. Conventional and normative rules alike limit the recourse to 'good arguments' which seem to impose themselves by the apparently 'forceless force'[20] of reflection about each action taken in isolation. The legal system, in contrast, is not completely closed to moral or other arguments drawn from specific situations, but these arguments do have to fit into the 'rationality of rules'[21] which allows for a kind of 'management of rules', even with respect to non-legal patterns and conventions, and which also has to take precommitments and the stability of expectations into consideration. By fulfilling this function, the legal system can also take a cognitive role consisting in the establishment of patterns of action and rules of expectations. At the same time, practical rules of action and co-ordination create rules of relevance which contribute to the process of self-stabilisation of normativity. A liberal legal order regards the processing of inter-relationships within society as the real 'subject' of the law. Freedom, in this perspective, is the potential of individuals, by their continuous processing of decisions within networks of parallel and sequential strategies, to create and shape the 'landscape' within which they move.[22] This image might give an idea of what it means for society to create uncertainty by generating innovations which have, again and again, to be bound by new decisions and rules. Uncertainty, in this view, is not a lack of knowledge which can be remedied, but is instead the inescapable consequence of the process of the self-creation of society beyond tradition,[23] which has to be accepted as a precondition of societal operations.

---

[20] Jürgen Habermas, *Vorstudien und Ergänzungen zur Theorie des kommunikativen Handelns* (Suhrkamp 1984) 161.

[21] Edward F. McClennen, 'Rationality, Constitution and the Ethics of Rules' (1993) 4 *Constitutional Political Economy* 73; *id.*, 'Rationality and Rules' in Peter A. Danielson (ed.), *Modeling Rationality, Morality, and Evolution* (OUP 1998) 13.

[22] Peter M. Allen, 'Modelling the Coevolution of Communications and Socio-economic Structure' (1997) 15 *Prometheus: Critical Studies in Innovation* 83, 91; *id.*, 'Modelling Complex Economic Evolution' (1998) 9 *Selbstorganisation: Jahrbuch für Komplexität in den Natur-, Sozial- und Geisteswissenschaften* 47; W. Brian Arthur, *The Nature of Technology: What it is and How it Evolves* (Free Press 2009).

[23] Niklas Luhmann, *Erkenntnis als Konstruktion* (Benteli 1998).

V. THE EVOLUTION OF A NEW GROUP-BASED LOGIC FOR THE CO-ORDINATION OF NORMATIVE AND SOCIAL KNOWLEDGE – THE SECONDARY MODELLING OF THE LIBERAL LEGAL ORDER BY THE WELFARE STATE

The evolution of the welfare state which came to its culmination only after World War II led to new institutions and clearing procedures that established a new layer of co-ordination between public normativity and societal mechanisms of channelling cognitive and regulatory standards. The precondition of this evolution is to be seen in the organisational potential of big firms and in the standardised production processes which created new types of knowledge and provoked the rise of new 'meta-norms' that processed the exchange between facts and norms on the new layer of normativity devoted to collective phenomena. These processes of knowledge management found their repercussions in a set of pluralistic institutions of 'publicity' which established itself between the rules of society at large and the sphere of the state. In addition to this new evolutionary step of the legal system towards a 'secondary modelling' of the liberal order, a set of 'rules of conflict' for the management of the co-ordination of different types of rules (individualistic vs. collective) had to be introduced. There are, on the one hand, domains that underlie the rules of the liberal order or separate domains governed by collective rules and conventions; but, at the same time, there are overlapping domains for which co-ordination or priority rule have to be found (for example, within individualistic rules of liability, problems of the collective attribution of responsibility re-appear; this applies to product liability). New types of rules and judgements evolve which try to balance the liberal individualistic rationality against the new collective logic. However, taken together, the elements of this new paradigm for the management of rules form a functional equivalent to the prior model of the co-ordination of facts and norms which evolved in the 19th century; both establish complex models of exchange between legal norms and explicit and implicit types of knowledge which were linked to the rise of new collective actors and the collective phenomena that they had to manage. The knowledge base is increasingly processed and channelled by representative groups, organisations and a homogenising technical infrastructure beyond the open processes of self coordination among individuals and small organisations as used to be the case in the liberal order.[24] However, the linkage of normativity and facts is reproduced in a more reflexive form and on a higher level than before. The process of standardisation of knowledge and practices no longer follows a stable general domain of practices, but includes a more prospective proactive element which includes the harmonisation of competing interests.[25] This applies in particular to the process of collective bargaining in industrial relations. This type of co-operation not only follows a logic of collective distribution, but also includes a vital interest in the standardisation of work, payment methods, professional requirements, training on the job, and so on. In this respect, collective bargaining follows the logic of the co-ordination of facts and norms inasmuch as it generates the standardised elements which can become the object of normative stabilisation.

In the same vein, a process of standardisation takes place in economic relationships; for example, with reference to distribution of risks, liability for products marketed by big firms in particular. The judiciary also takes a more proactive role, especially in the formation and adaptation of, for example, liability rules and technical standards, which ex ante can only be determined in a general form without a stable form of reference to experience or rules of negligence because the process of knowledge generation has been accelerated. Big firms and the 'encompassing' representative organisations of employers and workers,[26] standardisation bodies, and so on, have introduced a more strategic element into the process of setting up conventions and rules of practice which might serve as a cognitive infrastructure for the legal system. The element of 'planning', comprising a whole set of inter-related actions, shall give orientation to the actors under conditions of rapid change.

---

[24] Eric Brousseau, 'Néo-institutionnalisme et Evolutionnisme: Quelles convergences?'(1999) 4 *Economies et sociétés* 5.

[25] Favereau et al., note 9.

[26] Cf. Mancur Olsen, *The Rise and Decline of Nations* (Yale University Press 1982).

VI. THE POSTMODERN TRANSFORMATION OF THE LINKS BETWEEN THE LEGAL SYSTEM AND ITS COGNITIVE INFRASTRUCTURE – THE NEW LOGIC OF INTRA- AND INTER-ORGANISATIONAL NETWORKS

Since the beginning of the new century, a new development has been observed which might be attributed to a new paradigm of co-ordination between cognitive and normative rules. One might talk about a 'tertiary re-modelling' of the liberal version of this intertwinement. The still increasing acceleration of the production and use of scientific information in complex technological environments has led to a new wave of transformations which curbs the hitherto attained level of stabilisation of the co-ordination with legal requirements. Once again, the representation of a clear separation of normative rule (which presupposes a stable concept of order[27]) and its concrete application is put to the test[28] and goes so far as to assume that the whole idea of the universality of public order has lost its sense; the crumbling of a universal order is reflected by the crisis of the idea of a unitary 'subject': such a 'subject' is no longer imaginable vis-à-vis the heterogeneity and fragmentation of the networks of inter-relationships that define the multiplicity of its positions as 'knots' to which changing legal values are attributed and can no longer be integrated into an overarching conception of a general law. Under these conditions, the state can neither be constructed as the representative of a stable idea of the common interest, as in the liberal order of the past, nor as the mediator of exchange processes among representative 'encompassing' groups and organisations with their own internal and external co-operative stable cognitive infrastructure. The groundbreaking transformation which takes place in postmodern societies can be characterised as the process of change of the 'great all-embracing order into several orders'[29] which, from the outset, have to be regarded as self-transcending, limited in their reach, with mobile and flexible limits which allow for disruptive change (as opposed to the continuous processes of accumulation of experience). It is not only the accelerating process of

[27] Cf. generally Bernhard Waldenfels, *Der Stachel des Fremden* (Suhrkamp 1990).

[28] Jean-Marie Guéhenno, *The End of the Nation State* (University of Minnesota Press 1995) 49; *id.*, 'Demokratie am Wendepunkt' (1998) 4 *Internationale Politik* 13.

[29] Waldenfels, note 27, 19

technological innovation which is at stake. The modes of production of knowledge themselves undergo a deep transformation: the knowledge-generating practical networks of the past were open and well distributed, did not aim at explicit goals, and their operations were incremental and evolutionary. This property allowed for a stable mode of coupling with normativity which could process its own self-observation by general doctrine ('Dogmatik'). The new versions of uncertainty generated by the dynamic of self-transformation of knowledge production can be characterised as being 'procedural' in the sense of H.A. Simon:[30] it is a type of uncertainty which, from the outset, is reproduced in a reflexive mode that does not suppress its self-transcending character in a paradoxical way. Uncertainty is, from the outset, integrated in the complex settings where it is produced and which have to be organised in a way which allows for productive operation with its phenomena by introducing new reflexive moments of design, of modelling of self-revision and of monitoring.[31] There the idea of the best decision no longer exists, only that of a satisfying decision. The knowledge generation itself is no longer incremental and continuous but goal-oriented and experimental. Knowledge 'gaps' cannot be filled, but they are an unavoidable element of the new experimental logic. Information processes can be disruptive inasmuch as they lead to breakdowns of the established technologies and the steep rise of new ones. Individuals are much more aware of the intertwinement of changing options and redesigning or transforming the whole option domain.[32] That is, individuals and organisations are operating far from equilibrium. Risk and ignorance of consequences of new technological 'paths' are no longer to be managed by incremental introduction of their use, but they have to be integrated into the process of decision-making and be processed by new decision techniques. At the same time, knowledge itself is pluralised; its hierarchical structure (based on the separation of general scientific 'laws' and specific technical application) is undermined by the parallel-processed multiplicity of experiments and

---

[30] Herbert A. Simon, 'From Substantive to Procedural Rationality' in *id., Models of Bounded Rationality* Vol. 2 (MIT Press 1982) 56.

[31] Luhmann, note 23, 10; Allen, note 22 (1997), 83, 88; cf. generally Georges Balandier, *Le désordre* (Fayard 1988); for the 'control' of financial markets in particular, see Elena Esposito, *Die Zukunft der Futures: Die Zeit des Geldes in Finanzwelt und Gesellschaft* (Carl Auer 2010) 272–276.

[32] Allen, note 22 (1997) 83, 88; Favereau, note 18; Brousseau, note 24; David Dequech, 'Fundamental Uncertainty and Ambiguity' (2000) 26 *Eastern Economic Journal* 41; *id.*, 'Bounded Rationality, Institutions, and Uncertainty' (2001) 35 *Journal of Economic Issues* 911.

modelling procedures and their consequences: an increasing set of specialised information which can no longer be systematised by general meta-rules.[33] This leads to the phenomenon that only those persons who produce the information (and have a practical interest in its use) have the professional capabilities to reflect the preconditions of its modellisation, while it is not accessible to researchers who take a more detached look at new ideas. Technical information itself disrupts option domains and does not only add a new option within a stable field of development. This evolution undermines even the relationship between implicit (practical)[34] and explicit (systematised and codified) knowledge.[35] New techniques have to be developed which systematically try to generate new explicit knowledge from implicit rules of practice using computer programs for different types of 'data-mining' or organisational management reform beyond stable separation between general management and the specific execution of programmes.

VII. THE NEW DYNAMIC OF STANDARD-SETTING UNDER CONDITIONS OF UNCERTAINTY

This process finds its repercussion in the procedures of standard-setting which also have a role to play in the stimulation and generation of new knowledge from implicit rules of practice and not just in the process of the systematisation of existing information.[36] The stable transformation formulae ('negligence' in private law/'danger' in public law) have turned out to convey too little flexibility once the process of knowledge generation has become extremely complex and diverse.[37] The information produced in technological production is too specialised to allow

---

[33] Guéhenno, note 28 (1998) 16.

[34] Michael Polanyi, *Personal Knowledge: Towards a Post-Critical Philosophy* (Routledge 1958).

[35] Patrick Cohendet, Francis Kern, Babak Mehmanpazir and Francis Munier, 'Routines, Structures of Governance and Knowledge Creating Processes' in Jacques Lesourne and André Orléan (eds), *Advances in Self-Organisation and Evolutionary Economics* (Economica 1998) 77; this evolution causes the devaluation of unqualified work, cf. Margherita Balconi, 'Tacitness, Codification of Technological Knowledge and the Organisation of Liberty' (2002) 31 *Research Policy* 357.

[36] Danièle Benezech, 'La norme. Une convention structurant les interrelations technologiques et industrielles' (1996) 75 *Revue d'économie industrielle* 27.

[37] Ladeur, note 10 (1999).

for general stable co-ordination of normativity and facts. This 'probléma-tique' is demonstrated by the rise of ex ante decision-making (public law) as opposed to ex post rules of liability (private law). Concrete strategies of steering risk management in production processes have to be based on specialised information and complex design of decisions in a long-term perspective. New transfer formulae that allow for a more flexible strategic intervention in private firms are put in place; the reference to the 'best available technologies' ('Stand der Technik') or the 'best available scientific knowledge' ('Stand der Wissenschaft') imposes much more complex procedural and proactive requirements for the co-ordination of public and private decision-making[38] than the traditional co-ordination of legal decision-making with 'experience'.[39] New types of knowledge and new procedures for the generation or transformation of technological information are needed. The legal system has had some difficulty in using these new 'bridging formulae': initially, science was expected to deliver clear answers to questions of safety and so on, which were expected to exclude any possible doubts. At the same time, the government had developed committees composed of researchers and administrators themselves which were to structure the new types of knowledge in anticipation of concrete decision problems. This new procedural element demonstrates the complexity of the new cognitive issues[40] which excluded simple answers. At a later stage, only theoretical doubts concerning safety were set aside, but once the element of theory (design and modelling using information produced by research) appeared within the practice itself, this was not a plausible answer to a complex question: this approach seemed to be able to replace 'experience' with a better type of knowledge ('science') and not a different one. However, the co-operation of science and the legal system is only possible if an intermediate layer is set up for the translation of scientific information into the normative regime of decision-making[41] which has to adapt to the unavoidable operation with uncertainty by introducing new proactive

---

[38] Olivier Godard, 'Social Decision-Making under Scientific Controversy, Expertise and the Principle of Precaution' in Christian Joerges, Karl-Heinz Ladeur and Ellen Vos (eds), *Integrating Scientific Expertise into Regulatory Decision-Making* (Nomos 1997) 39; *id.*, 'La politique des risques peut-elle être raisonnable?' (2012) 107 *Revue de Métaphysique et de Morale* 511.

[39] Bratman, note 17; *id.*, 'Reflection, Planning and Temporally Extended Agency' (2001) 114 *The Philosophical Review* 35.

[40] Simon, note 18, 56.

[41] Detlof von Winterfeldt, *Decision Analysis and Behavioral Research* (Cambridge University Press 1986).

management strategies. This approach has to include rules for the 're-codification' of scientific information into the selectivity of the law (for example, by introducing external stop rules defining the 'best available knowledge' against the openness of research processes) and rules for the stimulation of new knowledge within, for example, monitoring procedures. Rules of relevance for the coupling of norms and facts have to be redefined in order to be compatible with legal requirements.[42] Cognitive rationalities are transformed anew by legal intervention; this process requires the formulation of trans-scientific 'meta-rules' for the 'extraction' and re-formulation of information based on research so as to allow for its combination with legal procedures of decision-making.[43] These rules are part of a regime for the management of a kind of 'conflict of norms', which are part of the legal system, although they are oriented at the development of rules of mediation and co-operation between normativity and a world of facts. The rules of relevance determine the selection of the researchers to be included in committees;[44] they define the relevant questions to be answered or the methods to be used; they introduce the goals to be attained and where to stop questioning the reliability of 'available' knowledge. This interdependence demands transparency, but uncertainty as such cannot be avoided (for the relevance of uncertainty) in the evolution of the economic system.[45] We need more proactive rules for the management of uncertainty and the use of completely new types of knowledge. Such an approach would, for example, enable the differentiation of types of knowledge that may be used for the basic decision (concerning the acceptability of a new technology) and decision-making concerning limitations to be imposed on private firms which might be used for the generation of new knowledge beyond the 'availability' of the information required for the principled decision.

---

[42] Monika Böhm, *Der Normmensch* (Mohr 1996).

[43] von Winterfeldt, note 41.

[44] Christian Joerges and Ellen Vos (eds), *EU Committees: Social Regulation, Law and Politics* (Hart 1999).

[45] For the importance of uncertainty in the evolution of the economy cf. Douglass C. North, *Understanding the Process of Economic Change* (Princeton University Press 2010) 13.

VIII. THE 'DISAGGREGATING STATE' AND ITS NEW ROLE IN THE PROCESS OF KNOWLEDGE GENERATION

Beyond the logic of the group-based state, a new logic of networks develops, comprising both public and private spheres and based on the operation with a multiplicity of strategies and experimental design processes. As a consequence, the homogeneity of both spheres is questioned; it is supplanted by a plurality of overlapping 'arenas' in which heterogeneous types of knowledge are generated with a view to projects which, by themselves, transcend the disciplinary and organisational limits that were characteristic of the past ideologies.[46] Decision-making procedures which are relevant for the public are distributed over a variety of overlapping networks which may be interchangeable: they may be private, they may be public, or they may have a hybrid public–private form.[47] This is valid for the formulation of standards in particular.[48] The bridges between public and private cognitive and normative elements may also follow a variety of models, but there is only one thing which can be taken for granted: the clear separation between public and private elements has mainly lost its meaning.[49]

This evolution has important consequences for the organisation of the public sphere and for the law-making process in particular. In the past, the state could be regarded as a more or less homogeneous and unitary organisation whose logic was based on hierarchy. As a consequence, the autonomy of administrative bodies was limited. It was bound not only formally by the competencies of the legislator but also substantively by a shared conception of 'general' interests which defined the public goals. The logic of networks and the fragmentation of interests, of goals and of the common knowledge basis exposes the state to the pressure to grant more autonomy to the actors within the public realm. These actors begin to define more autonomous goals for themselves. Their compatibility with a sort of public interest can, in the long run, only be controlled by

---

[46] Bernard Conein, 'Communautés épistémiques et réseaux cognitifs' (2003) Special Number *Revue d'Economie Politique* 138; Cohendet *et al.*, note 35.

[47] Karl-Heinz Ladeur, 'Die Netzwerke des Rechts' in Michael Bommes and Veronika Tacke (eds), *Netzwerke in der functional differenzierten Gesellschaft* (VS Verlag 2010) 143.

[48] From an engineering point of view, see Jens Rasmussen, 'Risk Management Issues: Doing Things Safely with Words, Rules and Laws' in Christian Joerges, Karl-Heinz Ladeur and Ellen Vos (eds), note 38, 15.

[49] Guéhenno, note 28 (1995).

establishing a broad procedural framework aiming at transparency and by feedback from their 'customers' – the citizens are increasingly seen as 'customers' who expect the delivery of specific services. In the long run, it is only the 'disaggregating state'[50] which can profit from the new possibilities of experimenting with new options and of modelling complex decision-making processes under conditions of complexity, because the design of new option domains presupposes a loosening of the weight of stable normativity. External steering of public decision-making via general norms would not match open perspectives on strategies which have to be formulated bottom-up within project-based networks. The public managers have to accept the pressure from innovation to which public and private actors alike are exposed. They have to operate as mediators in learning processes and therefore have to claim more autonomy for themselves as well. The function of the state and its actors can no longer consist merely in the 'steering' of private learning processes, but has to design new meta-rules that are intended to stimulate experiments, to avoid the lock-ins of societal search processes, and ensure the preservation of diversity which might buffer the effects of complexity by presenting flexibility rather than fixed normative standards. An additional mode of private–public partnership in the field of standard-setting and its adaptation to a changing environment can be seen in the rise of exchangeable forms of regulation, deregulation and negotiated regulation.[51] They form the organisational basis for the flexible techniques of constructing 'loops' between facts and normativity.

In the liberal order, the paradigm of generality and the universality of legal norms had presupposed the existence and productivity of multiple 'practical communities' of producers, engineers, practitioners, and so on, which did not pursue a common project[52] but spontaneously contributed, by trial and error processes, to a common knowledge basis ('experience'). Its evolution is subject to generalisations of different types, such

---

[50] A.M. Slaughter, *A New World Order* (Princeton University Press 2005) 18.

[51] Jody Freeman, 'Collaborative Governance in the Contracting State' (1998) 45 *University of Los Angeles Law Review* 1; *id.*, 'The Contracting State'(2001) 28 *Florida State University Law Review* 155 (arguing that the rise of the contract 2003 in administrative action is a sign of a general transformation towards a more open type of 'governance' and not a symptom of decline of democratic legitimation of administrative agencies).

[52] Richard Arena, 'Relations inter-entreprises et communautés médiatisées – une analyse préliminaire' (2003) 113 Special Number *Revue d'Economie Politique* 209, 211; Patrick Cohendet and Patrick Llerena, 'Routines and Incentives: The Role of Communities in Firms' (2003) 12 *Industrial and Corporate Change* 271.

as cognitive (schools, universities) and organisational types (private conversation circles, standardisation, etc.). In contrast to their predecessors, the new 'epistemic communities' are goal-oriented, although, at the same time, they can no longer presuppose access to a broad general knowledge.[53] Projects are more complex than in the past; they have to generate and experiment with more possibilities. This is the basis for new paradoxical forms of co-operation between competitors who create research-oriented joint ventures with the prospect of sharing knowledge which, at a later stage, is used in different forms for competition. This form of co-operation demonstrates the new hybrid form of an intertwinement of general and specific knowledge in projects, a form which undermines the hierarchical separations characteristic of the knowledge systems of the past. Clearly, this approach creates not only new possibilities but also new risks, because these knowledge 'clusters' are less accessible to observation and evaluation from outside: 'control knowledge' can, in many respects, be generated only within such 'epistemic communities' and not be collected from detached expertise.[54] Many technological projects today can no longer be analysed in advance because it is only by practical development and not by observation from outside that the required knowledge can be accessed.

IX. LAW AND KNOWLEDGE GENERATION IN THE 'NETWORK ECONOMY'

This problem, which is linked to the changing character of knowledge generation, is exacerbated by the development of the 'network economy' that emerges as a result of the increasing importance of informational products and services. The 'epistemic communities'[55] which have evolved in this new domain are not only confronted with the problems of high technology in general, but are also confronted with the basic legal rules of separation between the knowledge which can be appropriated by private firms (patentable information) and the knowledge which has to become part of the general pool of variety accessible to everybody. This

---

[53] Patrick Cohendet and Frieder Meyer-Krahmer, 'The Theoretical and Policy Implications of Knowledge Codification' (2001) 30 *Research Policy* 1563.

[54] Philip E. Tetlock, *Expert Political Judgment: How Good Is It? How Can We Know?* (Princeton University Press 2005) 217; cf. for the construction of evaluation as 'second-order knowledge' Rudolf Stichweh, 'Wissensgesellschaft und Wissensystem' (2004) 30 *Schweizerische Zeitschrift für Soziologie* 147, 155.

[55] Conein, note 46.

problem also translates into customer relationships: on the one hand, the 'object' of selling cannot be defined clearly (copying); on the other hand, customers are increasingly integrated into the process of the development of software and other intelligent products whose use creates new information which can be reintroduced into the production processes.[56] At the same time the internal structures of the firm – beyond the traditional legal reference to responsibility in company law – are increasingly subject to legal rules, in particular with respect to the generation of risk knowledge, both in the technological sense and concerning economic risks.[57] In addition, producers have to bear in mind their contribution to and dependence on the social conditions of use of the new information technologies: there are no longer clear-cut technological evolutionary paths that limit the range of possibilities for the future.

> [T]he coming of novel technologies does not just disrupt the status quo by finding new combinations that are better versions of the goods and methods we use. It sets up a train of technological accommodations and of new problems, and in so doing it creates new opportunity niches that call forth fresh combinations which in turn introduce yet further technologies and further problems.[58]

The social and informational infrastructure of a society has to be open for the adoption of new products and services – this is a problem which goes far beyond the question of economic resources. Computerisation also changes the forms of co-operation with subsidiary firms: there is no longer the alternative of the exchange of products or the organisational integration of the producer. The internal and external relationships of firms are no longer clearly separated; relational long-term contracts allow for far-reaching integration by constructing overlapping networks for intense exchanges of information. The introduction of digital television and video also demonstrates the problems of flexibility for the definition of stable functions in the chain of distribution: the 'intelligence' can be shifted over different levels of the processing network. The roles of cable operators, producers of end-use devices, telecommunications providers,

---

[56] Ayse O. Costello and Thomas G. Costello, 'Defining Property Rights: The Case of Knowledge-Based Resources' (2005) 47 *California Management Review* 143.

[57] Michael Power, 'From Risk Society to Audit Society' (1997) 3 *Soziale Systeme 3; id., The Audit Society: Rituals of Verification* (OUP 1999); Bridget Hutter and Michael Power (eds), *Organizational Encounters with Risk* (Cambridge University Press 2005).

[58] Arthur, note 22, 199.

content providers and customers are no longer fixed from the outset. This evolution renders the process of standardisation much more complex than it was in the past and this creates a major problem for the formulation of an adequate role for public authorities.

M. Bourreau and M. Gensollen[59] have named the new emerging markets for complex information technology 'meta-markets', the institutional infrastructure of which is uncertain – beyond the 'normal' risks of market strategies. This is one of the phenomena of the network economy which undermines the stability of institutions in which the technologies are embedded. The same is true for the 'factory system' which once played a major role in the diffusion of knowledge in modern production systems.[60]

As far as technology is concerned we will face a new challenge once nanotechnology[61] plays a more important role, which is only a question of time: this new technology – if one may still speak of a technology at all – will make the relationship between science and technology even more complex: nanotechnology will not just provoke a new process of reframing of the relationship between science and technology but it will reverse the hitherto established hierarchy between both: technology no longer makes 'use' of science – it is rather technology that changes nature and creates new versions of 'objectivity'.[62] This new disruptive transformation will no longer allow for ex ante evaluations of risks and of risk management. Risk assessment technologies will, on the one hand, have to be integrated into the new technological trajectories and follow their evolution. On the other hand, there is the rise of 'smart systems' which can be used for the generation of a huge amount of risk information by the systematic observation of technological 'applications'. This new turn will demonstrate once more the importance of information technology and its ubiquitous presence in systems that generate artificial knowledge.

---

[59] Marc Bourreau and Michel Gensollen, 'Communautés d'expériences et concurrence entre sites de biens culturels' (2004) 114 *Revue d'Economie Politique* 61.

[60] Mokyr, note 5.

[61] Karl-Heinz Ladeur, 'Kommunikation über Risiken im Rechtssystem. Das Beispiel der Nanotechnologie' in Christian Büscher and Klaus Peter Japp (eds), *Ökologische Aufklärung*: 25 *Jahre 'Ökologische Kommunikation'* (VS Verlag 2010) 131.

[62] Lorraine Daston and Peter Galiston, *Objectivity* (Zone Books 2010).

4. Risk in three dimensions: the EU–US agreement on the processing and transfer of financial messaging data

Marise Cremona

I. INTRODUCTION

In this chapter we identify three different types of risk, and thus three different dimensions to the relationship between risk and the law, in the context of EU external relations: (i) legal risk, or the risks caused by legal uncertainty arising from different regulatory approaches to data protection, and the corresponding difficulty of reaching agreement and/or defending EU regulatory preferences; (ii) constitutional or political risk, or the risks inherent in attempting effective policy- and law-making in a complex institutional structure such as the EU, especially at a time of constitutional change; and (iii) the need to balance factual or real world risks – such as security risks – in the light of the EU's potentially conflicting policy priorities and constitutional norms. We will here explore these types of risk using as a case study the negotiation, renegotiation and eventual conclusion of the EU–US agreement on the transfer of financial messaging data (the SWIFT or TFTP agreement) and its impact on EU internal regulatory policy.[1]

[1] The story of the SWIFT agreement and its aftermath has already been the subject of analysis by more than one academic commentator, including Jörg Monar, 'The Rejection of the EU–US SWIFT Interim Agreement by the European Parliament – A Historic Vote and its Implications' (2010) 15 *European Law Rev* 143; Ariadna Ripoll Servent and Alex MacKenzie, 'The European Parliament as a Norm Taker? EU–US Relations after the SWIFT Agreement' (2012) 17 *European Foreign Affairs Rev* 71; Juan Santos Vara, 'The Role of the European Parliament in the Conclusion of the Transatlantic Agreements on the Transfer of Personal Data after Lisbon', CLEER Working Paper 2013/2. This

As well as the interplay between these different types of risk, we can also identify two further dynamics. The first is the interaction between internal and external policies and procedures: internal constitutional guarantees; internal security impacting on cooperation with third countries; internal regulatory regimes and their applicability to transnational commercial activity; the negotiation of external instruments and internal decision-making procedures. This dynamic adds another level of complexity to the relationship between risk and (constitutional) law in an external relations context. The second is the interplay between different interests: between different regulatory approaches (in this case in the US and the EU); between different (EU) institutional actors in the context of international action against terrorism where the EU needs to be seen as an effective actor and partner of the US; between public security, the needs of private commercial undertakings, and the interests of the individual in the requirements of data protection and privacy. It is arguable that one feature of the legal regulation of risk is this balancing of different interests with different perspectives on the balance of risk.

The proposal to conclude an agreement with the USA on the transfer of financial messaging data arose in the context of the EU's counter-terrorism strategy,[2] and in particular the international (including transatlantic) transfers of data for purposes of combating terrorism and organised crime, and the implications these pose for the protection of fundamental rights.[3] The Stockholm Programme for Justice and Home Affairs, adopted by the European Council in December 2009 in the midst of the second chapter of the 'SWIFT affair', emphasises the importance of its external dimension: it is, the Programme says, 'essential to address

---

chapter draws upon material in Marise Cremona, 'Justice and Home Affairs in a Globalised World: Ambitions and Reality in the Tale of the EU–US SWIFT Agreement', Austrian Academy of Sciences Institute for European Integration Research, Working Paper 04/2011.

[2] The promotion of international partnerships is one of the four dimensions of the EU Counter-Terrorism Strategy adopted in 2005; Council doc. 14469/4/05 REV 4.

[3] See generally Paul de Hert and Bart de Schutter, 'International Transfers of Data in the Field of JHA: The Lessons of Europol, PNR and SWIFT' in Bernd Martenczuk and Servaas van Thiel (eds), *Justice, Liberty, Security: New Challenges for EU External Relations* (VUB Press 2008); Vagelis Papakonstantinou and Paul de Hert, 'The PNR Agreement and Transatlantic Anti-terrorism Cooperation: No Firm Human Rights Framework on Either Side of the Atlantic' (2009) 46 *Common Market Law Rev* 885.

the key challenges we face' and is 'crucial to the successful implementation of the objectives of this programme'.[4] Indeed the area of freedom, security and justice has been one of the most active domains of EU external relations over the last decade.[5] The threats identified by the Internal Security Strategy (ISS) adopted in March 2010 – terrorism, serious and organised crime, cyber-crime, natural and man-made disasters – are not threats which respect the EU's external borders and it is not surprising that the ISS argues that the concept of internal security cannot exist without an external dimension.[6] External and internal dimensions of security are interdependent and a 'global security approach' with third countries is advocated.[7] In its Conclusions on the Commission's Action Plan for the ISS in February 2011, the Council summarised its view of the 'European Security Model':

> [T]he European Security Model, as defined by the Internal Security Strategy … should be based on a shared agenda for action, an appropriate balance between prevention and tackling the consequences of threats to security, the

---

4 The Stockholm Programme – an open and secure Europe serving and protecting the citizens, adopted by the European Council 11–12 December 2009, Council doc. 17024/09. The Programme covers 2010–2014. See also Commission Communication, A strategy on the external dimension of the area of Freedom, Security and Justice COM(2005) 491 of 12 October 2005; Council Strategy for the external dimension of the area of Freedom, Security and Justice, adopted December 2005, Council doc. 14366/3/05; Communication from the Commission to the European Parliament and the Council, An area of Freedom, Security and Justice serving the citizen COM(2009) 262, 10 June 2009.

5 On the external dimension of the area of freedom, security and justice generally, see Gilles de Kerchove and Anne Weyembergh (eds), *Securité et Justice: Enjeu de la Politique Exteriéure de l'Union Europeenne* (ULB 2003); Jörg Monar, 'The EU as an International Actor in the Domain of Justice and Home Affairs' (2004) 9 *European Foreign Affairs Rev* 395; Bernd Martenczuk and Servaas Van Thiel (eds), *Justice, Liberty, Security: New Challenges for EU External Relations* (VUB Press 2008); Sarah Wolff, Nicole Wichmann and Gregory Mournier (eds), 'Special Issue: The External Dimension of Justice and Home Affairs? A Different Security Agenda for the EU' (2009) 31 *Journal of European Integration*; Marise Cremona, Jörg Monar and Sara Poli (eds), *The External Dimension of the Area of Freedom, Security and Justice* (Peter Lang-P.I.E. 2011).

6 Internal Security Strategy for the European Union: *Towards a European Security Model* adopted by the European Council 25–26 March 2010, see Council doc. 7120/10.

7 Internal Security Strategy, note 6 above, 16. See also Commission Communication, Second Report on the implementation of the EU Internal Security Strategy, COM(2013) 179, 10 April 2013, section 3.2.

> development of security policies based on common values and a renewed effort to establish closer links between the external and internal aspects of EU security.[8]

The European Security Model promoted by the Internal Security Strategy, while thus designed to integrate the internal and external dimensions of 'mutually reinforcing' justice, freedom and security policies, is also committed to respect for fundamental rights, international protection, the rule of law and privacy.[9] In the case of SWIFT, the international dimension arose both from the EU's commitment to international cooperation on counter-terrorism and from the global nature of international financial data. The fundamental rights issue arose from the risk of non-compliance with EU data protection laws in a context of transnational transfers of data.

SWIFT is the Society for Worldwide Interbank Financial Telecommunication, a member-owned cooperative. According to its own information, more than 9000 banking organisations, securities institutions and corporate customers in 209 countries use SWIFT every day to exchange standardised financial messages. SWIFT is based in Belgium but has offices in 20 countries, including the USA. After 11 September 2001 and in response to UN Security Council Resolution 1373 (2001), the United States instituted the Terrorist Finance Tracking Program (TFTP). Under the TFTP, the US Treasury Department issued subpoenas for information on financial transactions to (among others) SWIFT's Operating Centre in the United States. The US Centre had servers which 'mirrored' (contained the same information as) the EU-based SWIFT servers and thus the US Treasury Department was able to order SWIFT in the USA to supply it with information on financial transfers between EU subjects.

II. REGULATORY RISK, LEGAL UNCERTAINTY AND THE NEED FOR AN EU RESPONSE

In June 2006, US newspapers revealed the existence of the TFTP and there was much comment about privacy. It was revealed that the SWIFT subpoenas covered European transactions and concerns were expressed in

---

[8] Council conclusions on the Commission communication on the European Union internal security strategy in action, 21 February 2011, Council doc. 6699/11.

[9] Internal Security Strategy, note 6 above, 9.

the European Parliament that EU data protection legislation (especially Directive 95/46/EC[10]) was not being complied with. Under the EU Data Protection Directive transfers of data to the US need to comply with EU Safe Harbour principles.[11] SWIFT itself was unhappy about the legal uncertainty in relation to its TFTP obligations and compliance with EU data protection laws, and with some reason: on 27 July 2006 the Belgian Data Protection Authority issued an opinion that SWIFT's activities were in breach of Belgian Data Protection Law, which implements the EU Data Protection Directive. In November 2006 the 'Article 29 Working Party' (the European Commission's independent advisory body on data protection and privacy) issued an opinion on the processing of personal data by SWIFT. Its view was that SWIFT was in breach of EU data protection law in transferring personal data to the US without ensuring adequate protection and without giving individuals information about how their data might be used.[12] For SWIFT and the financial institutions using its services, there was a significant legal risk as a result of a regulatory gap and legal uncertainty as to which regulatory regime should apply. The European Parliament adopted two Resolutions on SWIFT in 2006 and 2007, referring to the fact that 'businesses with operations on both sides of the Atlantic increasingly find themselves caught between the conflicting legal requirements of the US and EC jurisdictions', and calling for an agreement with the USA to resolve the existing legal uncertainty as to data protection guarantees.[13]

What was the response to this dilemma? Initially it was 'soft', in other words an attempt at reassurance over compliance with EU standards rather than a binding agreement. On 28 June 2007 the US Treasury sent the EU Council and Commission eight pages of 'Representations'

---

[10] Directive 95/46/EC of the European Parliament and of the Council on the protection of individuals with regard to the processing of personal data and on the free movement of such data [1995] OJ L281/31.

[11] Under the Commission Decision on Safe Harbour privacy principles, transfers to the US are compliant only if made to companies which agree to comply with the Safe Harbour principles: Commission Decision 2000/520/EC of 26 July pursuant to Directive 95/46/EC on the adequacy of the protection provided by the safe harbour privacy principles [2000] OJ L215/7.

[12] Article 29 Data Protection Working Party, Opinion 10/2006 on the processing of personal data by the Society for Worldwide Interbank Financial Telecommunication (SWIFT), 01935/06/EN, WP128, 22 November 2006.

[13] Resolution of 6 July 2006 on the interception of bank transfer data from the SWIFT system by the US secret services [2006] OJ C303 E, 843; Resolution of 14 February 2007 on SWIFT, the PNR agreement and the transatlantic dialogue on these issues [2007] OJ C287 E, 349.

outlining the operation of the TFTP and demonstrating that its demands of data from SWIFT and its handling of the data received met European data protection concerns.[14] It stressed the importance of financial information in tracking terrorism. It said the data were used only in connection with specific information on terrorist activity (no data-mining or general searches) and only in connection with terrorism (no other unlawful activity such as drug-trafficking or tax evasion); un-extracted data were deleted after five years. It set out the legal basis for the TFTP in US law. The US also agreed 'as a sign of our commitment and partnership in combating global terrorism' to the appointment of an 'eminent European person' to assess the TFTP controls. In December 2008 the Belgian data protection Authority issued a report confirming that in dealing with the TFTP subpoenas SWIFT now complied with Belgian data protection law. Judge Jean-Louis Bruguière, appointed by the Commission as the 'eminent European person', made an initial report in January 2009: this was reported to the European Parliament Civil Liberties, Justice and Home Affairs (LIBE) Committee in February 2009.[15] The report confirmed that the TFTP complied with the US Representations of June 2007. A second and final report was produced in early 2010.

At this stage, then, it was a matter of ensuring that the transfers within the USA made under subpoena by SWIFT to the US Treasury Department complied with the EU's data protection requirements, and in particular its Safe Harbour Principles. The results of the negotiations between the EU Commission and Council with the US Treasury were a series of undertakings on the US side, with some EU oversight of compliance.[16] However, this was not the end of the story.

From 1 January 2010 SWIFT altered its systems so that all the data concerning intra-European transactions is now held in two European sites and is no longer mirrored in the USA (the change having been first announced in October 2007 in the midst of the original 'SWIFT affair'). This meant that its EU-based data was no longer covered by US law (or the TFTP subpoenas) and transfers of EU data to the TFTP would no longer take place. The EU Council and Commission were concerned,

---

[14] See Terrorist Finance Tracking Program – representations of the United States Department of the Treasury [2007] OJ C166/18. For the Council's response to this, see Council doc. 11291/2/07 REV 2 (Presse 157), 28 June 2007.

[15] IP/09/264, 17 February 2009.

[16] Gloria González Fuster, Paul De Hert and Serge Gutwirth, 'SWIFT and the Vulnerability of Transatlantic Data Transfers' (2008) 22 *International Review of Law, Computers & Technology* 194.

both because they wanted to demonstrate cooperation with the US on counter-terrorism and because EU governments receive a substantial amount of information from the US TFTP, based on analysis of European records: since there is at present no EU equivalent to the TFTP the EU relies on the US processing of European data. In order to ensure that data would continue to be transferred from the EU to the US, on 27 July 2009 the Council thus authorised the Presidency, assisted by the Commission, to open negotiations for an agreement on financial messaging data between the EU and the USA (the so-called TFTP or SWIFT agreement). The agreement would allow the US Treasury Department to serve production orders on designated EU-based data providers, including SWIFT. The commercially driven action by SWIFT to relocate its data storage made a formal agreement between the EU and US necessary, an agreement which – it was envisaged – would both ensure data transfers from Europe to the US and meet EU data protection concerns.

III. CONSTITUTIONAL CHANGE AND LEGISLATIVE RISK

The proposed agreement was controversial and its history became linked to the coming into force of the Treaty of Lisbon and the changes that brought to decision-making in Justice and Home Affairs (JHA). It will be remembered that in 2007, following legal action by the European Parliament, an earlier agreement with the US on the transfer of air passenger name records (PNR) for law enforcement purposes had had to be renegotiated as a third pillar agreement.[17] In 2006, as we have seen, the SWIFT issue had been dealt with in the framework of the Data Protection Directive and the Commission's Safe Harbour Decision. This

---

[17] Joined Cases C-317/04 and C-318/04 *European Parliament v Council* [2006] ECR I-4721. The agreement had originally been concluded by the EC under internal market powers, but the Court held that this legal basis was inappropriate since data processing for purposes of 'public security, defence, State security and the activities of the State in areas of criminal law' was expressly excluded from the Data Protection Directive: Cases C-317/04 and C-318/04, paras 54–58, 67–69. Following the annulment of the Decision concluding the agreement, it was renegotiated and concluded by the EU under JHA powers. The current PNR agreement of 2012 was concluded on the basis of Articles 82(1)(d) and 87(2)(a) TFEU: Decision 2012/472/EU OJ 2012 L 215/4. See further Valsamis Mitsilegas, 'The European Union and the Globalisation of Criminal Law' (2009–2010) 12 *Cambridge Yearbook of European Legal Studies* 337, 374–379.

was possible, even in the light of the judgment in the PNR case,[18] since at this time the data were transferred from the EU to the USA by SWIFT for purely commercial purposes; the law enforcement requisition of the data took place within the USA. However, from 2010, when SWIFT no longer stored its EU data in the USA, the transfers to the US of EU data would be made solely for law enforcement purposes: hence it was now proposed that the EU–US TFTP agreement, as a law enforcement measure, would also be negotiated and concluded under the third pillar. But this was mid-2009 and the Treaty of Lisbon – which would abolish the third pillar – was to come into force on 1 December.

On 17 September 2009 the European Parliament passed a Resolution on the proposed TFTP agreement.[19] The Parliament commented on the fact that neither the negotiating directives nor the opinion of the Council's Legal Service on choice of legal basis were publicly available since they were classified as 'restricted', as well as on the fact that the proposed agreement would be fully provisionally applicable upon signature. While reaffirming its support for the fight against terrorism, it also mentioned 'the need to strike the right balance between security measures and the protection of civil liberties and fundamental rights, while ensuring the utmost respect for privacy and data protection', and the risk that the data could be 'misused for large-scale forms of economic and industrial espionage'. The Parliament asked why Article 4 of the EU–US agreement on mutual legal assistance,[20] which provides for the transfer of specific financial data on request, could not be used instead of an agreement on SWIFT, which provides for bulk transfers of data. It set out a series of minimum conditions with which the agreement should comply, including: that data are transferred and processed only for the purposes of fighting terrorism, as defined in the 2002 Framework Decision on combating terrorism,[21] and that they relate to individuals or terrorist organisations recognised as such by the EU; that the transfer requests are based on specific, targeted cases; that EU citizens and

---

[18] Cases C-317 and 318/94, note 17 above. Cf. also Case C-301/06 *Ireland v European Parliament and Council* [2009] ECR I-00593.

[19] P7_TA(2009)0016.

[20] Council Decision 2003/516/EC concerning the signature of the Agreements between the EU and the USA on extradition and mutual legal assistance in criminal matters [2003] OJ L/25. See further Valsamis Mitsilegas, 'The New EU–US Co-operation on Extradition, Mutual Legal Assistance and the Exchange of Police Data' (2003) 8 *European Foreign Affairs Rev* 515.

[21] Council Framework Decision 2002/475/JHA of 13 June 2002 on combating terrorism [2002] OJ L164/3.

enterprises are granted defence rights, procedural guarantees and rights of access to justice equivalent to those existing in the EU; a reciprocity mechanism, obliging the US authorities upon request to transfer relevant financial messaging data to the competent EU authorities; the inclusion of a sunset clause in the interim agreement; and the negotiation of a possible new agreement under the new EU legal framework that fully involved the European Parliament.

On 30 November 2009 – the day before the entry into force of the Treaty of Lisbon – the Council authorised the Presidency to sign an interim agreement between the European Union and the United States.[22] Like the 2007 PNR agreement, its legal basis was former Articles 24 and 38 TEU; it could therefore be signed by the Council alone without the European Parliament's consent.[23] The agreement was to have been applied provisionally (in other words, before its formal conclusion) from 1 February 2010. The agreement had a maximum duration of nine months and was to be replaced by a longer-term agreement. On 17 December 2009 the Commission adopted a proposal for a Council Decision concluding the agreement.[24] With the coming into force of the Lisbon Treaty, the legal bases changed and the new JHA legal bases specify the ordinary legislative procedure for the adoption of internal acts. As a result the consent of the European Parliament is required under Article 218 (6)(a)(v) TFEU.

In early February 2010 the LIBE Committee recommended the rejection of the agreement.[25] The LIBE Committee report was in favour

---

22 Council Decision 2010/16/CFSP/JHA of 30 November 2009 on the signing, on behalf of the European Union, of the Agreement between the European Union and the United States of America on the processing and transfer of Financial Messaging Data from the European Union to the United States for purposes of the Terrorist Finance Tracking Program [2010] OJ L8/9.

23 A particular feature of (then) Article 24 TEU, which formed the legal basis for the Decision authorising signature of the agreement, was that although the European Parliament was not involved, national parliaments might well be; under Article 24(5): 'No agreement shall be binding on a Member State whose representative in the Council states that it has to comply with the requirements of its own constitutional procedure; the other members of the Council may agree that the agreement shall nevertheless apply provisionally.'

24 COM(2009) 703. The legal bases proposed by the Commission were Articles 82(1)(d) and 87(2)(a) TFEU.

25 Committee on Civil Liberties, Justice and Home Affairs, Recommendation on the proposal for a Council decision on the conclusion of the Agreement between the European Union and the United States of America on the processing and transfer of Financial Messaging Data from the European Union to the United

of an agreement in principle, finding that the 'soft' guarantees in the US 'Representations' were not good enough. It was however unhappy that the agreement had effectively crystallised as a permanent arrangement something that was originally introduced as an emergency measure in the aftermath of 11 September 2001. It argued that the TFTP 'must be considered as a departure from European law and practice in how law enforcement agencies would acquire individuals' financial records for law enforcement activities, namely individual court-approved warrants or subpoenas to examine specific transactions instead of relying on broad administrative subpoenas for millions of records'. The debate was about 'the law enforcement use of data collected for commercial purposes' and 'accepting the proposed [agreement] (as it stands) could lead down the slippery slope of accepting other requests for commercial data with (f.e.) Skype, PayPal and other companies in the information-telecommunication field being potentially interesting for law enforcement purposes'. The Committee was concerned about mass transfers of data, about the absence of judicial authorisation, about the absence of controls over further onward transfers by the US to third countries, about the lack of information on the period for which extracted information was to be kept, the gaps in protection (access and redress) for European individuals and companies in the US, and the absence of true reciprocity (no EU access to US data). The Committee also complained of the failure to give the Parliament full information, including the Council's legal opinion and the reports by Judge Bruguière; it argued that this was a breach of the duty of sincere cooperation between EU institutions, now enshrined in the Treaties in Article 13(2) TFEU. It recommended that the Commission should propose a negotiating mandate for new agreements with the US on both financial messaging data for counter-terrorism investigations and privacy/personal data protection in the context of the exchange of information for law enforcement purposes (such as PNR).

The European Parliament was especially angry about the lack of consultation on the TFTP agreement. In February 2010 formal arrangements were not yet in place to implement Article 218(10) TFEU, which provides that '[t]he European Parliament shall be immediately and fully

---

States for purposes of the Terrorist Finance Tracking Program (05305/1/2010REV – C7-0004/2010 – 2009/0190(NLE)), Rapporteur: Jeanine Hennis-Plasschaert, 5 February 2010, A7-0013/2010.

informed at all stages of the [treaty negotiation] procedure'.[26] A new inter-institutional agreement, the Framework Agreement between the Parliament and the Commission, was agreed in October 2010 and covers parliamentary access to information relating to international negotiations.[27] According to this, Parliament is to be 'immediately and fully informed at all stages of the negotiation and conclusion of international agreements' in sufficient time for it to be able to express its views and for the Commission to take them into account, and the Commission and Parliament are to establish procedures and safeguards for the transmission of confidential information.[28] In cases where parliamentary consent is required, the Parliament is to be given the same information as the Council.[29] However, this agreement was still under negotiation in February 2010.

Alongside the inter-institutional arrangements, MEPs have also been prepared to seek access to information concerning proposed international agreements by way of the EU's general transparency procedures which cover access to documents by the general public, private individuals and non-governmental organisations.[30] In July 2009 MEP Sophie In 't Veld made a request under Regulation 1049/2001 for access to the opinion of the Council's Legal Service concerning the Commission's recommendation to the Council to authorise the opening of the TFTP negotiations. The request was refused; the Council argued both that disclosure would negatively impact the EU's negotiating position, thereby undermining 'the protection of the public interest as regards international relations' (Article 4(1)(a) of Regulation 1049/2001) and that the document contained legal advice on the sensitive issue of the legal basis and competence to conclude the agreement (Article 4(2) of Regulation 1049/2001).[31] In 't Veld brought an action before the Court challenging that

---

[26] Although the former Inter-institutional Agreement [2001] OJ C121/122 did in fact contain some provision for the Parliament to be kept informed during negotiations.

[27] Framework Agreement on relations between the European Parliament and the Commission, 20 October 2010, P7_TA(2010)0366; paras 23–27 and Annex 3 deal with international negotiations. Annex 2 deals with parliamentary access to classified information.

[28] *Ibid.*, paras 23–24.

[29] *Ibid.*, Annex 3, para. 5.

[30] Article 15(3) TFEU; Regulation 1049/2001 regarding public access to European Parliament, Council and Commission documents [2001] OJ L145/43; for the Commission's proposal to amend this Regulation see COM(2011) 137.

[31] The Council granted access only to the introductory paragraphs of the opinion which set out the context of the proposed agreement; see Council doc.

refusal. The General Court granted access to the document except insofar as the opinion revealed the specific content of the envisaged agreement or the negotiating mandate of the Council, which could have revealed the EU's strategic objectives.[32] In its view, disclosure of the arguments concerning the appropriate legal basis for the agreement would not have posed a threat to the EU's international relations interests. International negotiations fall in principle within the domain of the executive and the Council is not acting in its legislative capacity; thus public participation in the procedure 'is necessarily restricted, in view of the legitimate interest in not revealing strategic elements of the negotiations'. Nevertheless, the Court held that the principle of the transparency of the decision-making process of the European Union 'cannot be ruled out in international affairs', especially where the international agreement may have an impact on the EU's legislative activity.[33] In this particular case, where the agreement would have an impact on the protection of personal data, a fundamental right, the Court concluded:

> [t]here was an overriding public interest in the disclosure … since it would contribute to conferring greater legitimacy on the institutions and would increase EU citizens' confidence in those institutions by making it possible to have an open debate on the points where there was a divergence of opinion regarding … an agreement which, once concluded, would have an impact on the fundamental right to the protection of personal data.[34]

We have here in summary a more general issue facing the EU in its external relations: the need for public debate over international agreements which will have a quasi-legislative impact and may carry fundamental rights implications, and the difficulty in balancing this need with the traditional processes of international negotiations, seen as executive rather than legislative activity.[35]

11897/09 EXT 1, available in the Council's register of documents in this partially disclosed form.

[32] T-529/09 *In 't Veld v Council* [2012]. The Council has appealed (C-350/12P, pending). In 2010 In 't Veld also brought an action against a refusal, by the Commission this time, to grant her full access to the negotiating documents on the Anti-Counterfeiting Trade Agreement (ACTA): Case T-301/10 *In 't Veld v Commission* [2013].

[33] T-529/09 *In 't Veld v Council* [2012] para. 89.

[34] *Ibid.*, para. 93.

[35] See further Marise Cremona, 'International Regulatory Policy and Democratic Accountability: The EU and the ACTA' in Marise Cremona, Peter Hilpold, Nikos Lavranos, Stefan S. Schneider and Andreas R. Ziegler (eds), *Reflections*

Against the background of this debate, Home Affairs Commissioner Malmström spoke in the Parliament before the vote in February 2010, arguing that 'rejection of the Interim Agreement by this House would represent a serious blow to EU security', but this was not enough. In an unusual move, the Council issued a Declaration the day before the European Parliament vote, pointing out that the interim agreement was to last only nine months; that it contained many of the features called for in the Parliament's Resolution of 17 September 2009; that a longer-term agreement would be negotiated and requesting the Commission to adopt that very month a draft mandate for a new agreement; that the European Parliament would play a full part in those negotiations; that it recognised the need for the European Parliament to have access to restricted information; and committing itself to negotiating an inter-institutional agreement on this issue.[36]

Despite all these assurances, in a plenary vote in the European Parliament on 10 February 2010 the agreement was indeed rejected. The negative vote by the Parliament meant that the provisional application of the agreement was no longer possible. A letter from the Council Presidency was sent on 22 February to the US Secretary of State, stating that following the European Parliament vote the EU could not become a party to the interim agreement and terminating the provisional application of the agreement.

Here we have an example of what could be called legislative risk. The Council and Commission, faced with what they thought was an urgent need to get the agreement approved and the awkward transition to the new Treaty procedures, had adopted the risky strategy of trying to 'bounce' the European Parliament into approving the agreement by presenting it as a *fait accompli*, an agreement already signed and about to start being provisionally applied, and which therefore could not be renegotiated. They judged that – given a choice between accepting this and rejection, with all that implied in terms of transatlantic embarrassment and security risk – the European Parliament would reluctantly, and probably with much verbal protest, nevertheless agree. The strategy failed and as a result the legislative initiative failed too. Instead of an imperfect agreement there was no agreement. Two months after the coming into force of the Lisbon Treaty the Parliament had shown that it was serious

---

on the Constitutionalization of International Economic Law – Liber Amicorum Ernst-Ulrich Petersmann (Brill 2013).

[36] Council doc. 6265/10 (Presse 23) 9 February 2010. The inter-institutional agreement was agreed later in 2010; see note 27 above.

in exercising its new powers over external treaty-making and internal security policy.

IV. SECURITY RISKS AND FUNDAMENTAL RIGHTS

The rejection by the European Parliament provoked a storm of reaction, not least from the US.[37] The failure of the agreement brought to the fore the debate between the security risks which the data transfers were intended to combat, and the risks to the fundamental right to protection of personal data that – it was argued – the agreement represented and did not adequately meet. Before the vote Adam Szubin, the US Treasury Department official in charge of the TFTP, said that the failure of the agreement would be 'very damaging', stressing the amount of information given by the TFTP to EU governments, including Germany.[38] US National Security Advisor James Jones said that EU–US data transfer had 'prevented terrorist attacks and saved lives'.[39] Commissioner Malmström had argued in February that 'refusal of [parliamentary] consent risks to lead to both a data protection gap and a security gap'. In April she said:

> [T]his matter is very urgent. We know that there is a clear security gap since January of this year because TFTP data stored in Europe are no longer made available to the US Treasury Department, so the aim is to arrive at a signed agreement as soon as possible, preferably before the end of June.[40]

In fact the gap was limited, since in the absence of the agreement, specific (not bulk) transfers could be requested under the EU–US agreement on mutual legal assistance, together with the bilateral US–Member State agreements which the EU agreement supplements, and under the terms of national data protection law.[41]

---

[37] For a balanced and prescient assessment of the position after the February 2010 vote in the European Parliament, see Jörg Monar, 'The Rejection of the EU–US SWIFT Interim Agreement by the European Parliament: A Historic Vote and Its Implications' (2010) 15 *European Foreign Affairs Rev* 143.

[38] Interview available on Spiegel, 'Ahead of SWIFT Vote: US Urges European Parliament to Back Data Deal' *Spiegel Online* (Hamburg, 8 February 2010): http://www.spiegel.de/international/world/ahead-of-swift-vote-us-urges-european-parliament-to-back-data-deal-a-676524.html, last accessed 29 April 2015.

[39] *Ibid.*

[40] MEMO/10/149, 23 April 2010.

[41] See Monar, note 37 above, 149.

The Commission and Council moved quickly to negotiate a new agreement and this time they made sure to consult the European Parliament at every turn. A draft mandate was drawn up by the Commission on 24 March 2010 and agreed by the Council on 11 May. The legal bases were to be Articles 87(2)(a) and 88(2) TFEU (police cooperation). The Commission made a point of stressing how much useful information was passed by the US to EU governments, citing specific examples. There was a US charm offensive: MEPs were invited to Washington, and US Vice-President Joseph Biden made a speech on the SWIFT agreement to the European Parliament on 6 May.

The European Parliament adopted a Resolution on the Commission's draft negotiating mandate, welcoming 'the new spirit of cooperation demonstrated by the Commission and the Council and their willingness to engage with Parliament, taking into account their Treaty obligation to keep Parliament immediately and fully informed at all stages of the procedure'.[42] The Resolution highlighted the issues that were of most concern: bulk data transfers which, it said, 'mark a departure from the principles underpinning EU legislation and practice', and this departure could not simply be rectified by ex post controls and monitoring. It recommended a system based on public judicial oversight based in the EU and an EU-based monitoring authority. However, it also opened up the way for a compromise, suggesting a twin-track approach combining a TFTP agreement based on strict standards and EU oversight of the extraction process in the US with 'the fundamental longer-term policy decisions that the EU must address'. As far as the latter are concerned, the European Parliament argued that the best guarantee would be to carry out the extraction of data within the EU (in other words, to institute an EU TFTP).

The renegotiated agreement of 2010 contained some significant changes as compared with the rejected 2009 agreement. These include: an agreed definition of terrorism, based on the EU's 2002 Framework Decision;[43] verification by Europol – before the data are handed over – of whether the request meets the conditions in the agreement; appointment

---

42 European Parliament resolution of 5 May 2010 on the Recommendation from the Commission to the Council to authorise the opening of negotiations for an agreement between the European Union and the United States of America to make available to the United States Treasury Department financial messaging data to prevent and combat terrorism and terrorist financing P7_TA-PROV(2010)0143.

43 Council Framework Decision 2002/475/JHA on combating terrorism [2002] OJ L164, 3.

by the EU of an 'independent person' to monitor the use of data in the USA; more detail on judicial redress for EU citizens as well as better regulation of rights to rectification and erasure of data; and the regulation of onward transfer of data to third countries. The agreement is without doubt an attempt to balance security/law enforcement objectives with data protection. Within the EU, data protection rights for individuals have a higher visibility since the coming into force of the Lisbon Treaty. Not only has Article 8 of the Charter of Fundamental Rights on the protection of personal data acquired binding force; but also Article 16 TFEU reiterates the right to protection of personal data and establishes a competence to enact legislation on the processing of personal data by EU institutions and agencies, and by the Member States when acting within the scope of Union law, and rules relating to the free movement of such data. Nevertheless, as the opinion on the revised agreement by the European Data Protection Supervisor (EDPS) points out, Article 16 TFEU was not included as a legal basis for the decision concluding it, although to have done so would have served to emphasise that the agreement is designed to protect personal data as well as to facilitate their exchange.[44]

Although the EDPS recognised improvements in the new agreement, he also pointed to a number of remaining concerns. He was not convinced that a case had been made that the transfer of data is necessary – as opposed to merely useful – given existing frameworks for exchanges of data based on the mutual legal assistance agreement and arrangements between the US authorities and Europol and Eurojust. He was not convinced, he said, of the 'real added value' of this agreement. He was concerned that the bulk transfer of data does not meet the requirement of proportionality: the fact that the SWIFT system does not technically allow targeted searches does not per se render bulk transfers lawful. The negotiating mandate for the agreement had envisaged that a judicial public authority should have responsibility for receiving requests from the US Treasury and assessing compliance with the conditions for transfer. The agreement gives this task to Europol, which, as the EDPS points out, is not a 'judicial public authority'. In addition, since the agreement also allows Europol to itself request information from the US,

---

[44] Opinion of the European Data Protection Supervisor on the proposal for a Council Decision on the conclusion of the Agreement between the European Union and the United States of America on the processing and transfer of Financial Messaging Data from the European Union to the United States for purposes of the Terrorist Finance Tracking Program (TFTP II) [2010] OJ C355, 10.

'it is hard to reconcile this power of Europol, which may be important for the fulfilment of Europol's task and which requires good relations with the US Treasury, with the task of Europol to ensure independent oversight'.[45] With respect to the enforceability of data subjects' rights, the EDPS also had concerns.

The new agreement was signed on 28 June 2010. The LIBE Committee of the European Parliament issued a report on the new agreement on 5 July 2010, recommending consent.[46] A minority were opposed on the ground that some key demands, especially relating to bulk data transfer, had not been met. However, the European Parliament approved the revised agreement on 8 July 2010 and it came into force on 1 August 2010.[47] The Parliament's change of view no doubt reflected both the improvements it identified in the new agreement, and the fact that this time it had been kept informed and involved in the negotiations throughout. It might also be argued that a Parliament with real joint legislative power acts differently from a Parliament with only the power of expressing its opinion.[48]

Unusually, the Council Decision concluding the agreement makes a commitment towards developing the EU's own equivalent to the TFTP,[49] thus removing the need for bulk transfers of data, since the EU would be able to respond to specific requests – as the US authority now does to EU requests. However, until this happens bulk transfers will still take place. Of course, different views may be taken as to whether the agreement really offers 'added value' and whether the balance between security and

---

[45] *Ibid.*, para. 25.

[46] Recommendation on the draft Council decision on the conclusion of the Agreement between the European Union and the United States of America on the processing and transfer of Financial Messaging Data from the European Union to the United States for the purposes of the Terrorist Finance Tracking Program, A7-0224/2010.

[47] Council Decision 2010/412/EU on the conclusion of the Agreement between the European Union and the United States of America on the processing and transfer of Financial Messaging Data from the European Union to the United States for the purposes of the Terrorist Finance Tracking Program [2010] OJ L195/3. Both the UK and Ireland have chosen to participate in the agreement; for the UK's acceptance, see Council doc. 12024/10, for Ireland's acceptance, see Council doc. 5736/11.

[48] Ariadna Ripoll Servent and Alex MacKenzie, 'The European Parliament as a Norm Taker? EU–US Relations after the SWIFT Agreement' (2012) 17 *European Foreign Affairs Rev* 71, examine the processes that led the Parliament to accept the revised agreement; see especially 81–82.

[49] Decision 2010/412/EU, note 47 above, Article 2.

data protection was the best available at that time. Three reviews of the agreement and its implementation have been carried out, in 2011, 2012 and 2013, with generally positive conclusions in terms of compliance with the conditions established in the agreement.[50]

V. AFTER THE TFTP AGREEMENT

As the new TFTP agreement was approved, a number of initiatives concerning data protection, internal security and law enforcement were taking shape within the framework of the Internal Security Strategy approved by the JHA Council in February 2010.[51] The European Security Model presented in the ISS emphasises the importance of integrating respect for fundamental rights, the rule of law and privacy into the EU's justice, freedom and security policies, and ensuring an 'effective democratic and judicial supervision' of security activities by the European Parliament, national Parliaments and the European Court of Justice. The Commission's Action Plan for the implementation of the ISS, published on 22 November 2010, also emphasises the commitment to the protection of human rights – and indeed connects this to the interdependence of internal and external aspects of security:

> [I]nternal security cannot be achieved in isolation from the rest of the world, and it is therefore important to ensure coherence and complementarity between the internal and external aspects of EU security. The values and priorities in the Internal Security Strategy, including our commitment to promoting human rights, democracy, peace and stability in our neighbourhood

---

[50] Commission report on the joint review of the implementation of the Agreement between the European Union and the United States of America on the processing and transfer of Financial Messaging data from the European Union to the United States for the purposes of the Terrorist Finance Tracking Program, SEC (2011) 438 final, 30 March 2011; Commission Staff Working Document Report on the second joint review of the implementation of the Agreement between the European Union and the United States of America on the processing and transfer of Financial Messaging data from the European Union to the United States for the purposes of the Terrorist Finance Tracking Program, SWD (2012) 454 final, 14 December 2012; Communication from the Commission to the European Parliament and the Council on the Joint Report from the Commission and the US Treasury Department regarding the value of TFTP Provided Data, COM(2013) 843 final, 27 November 2013.

[51] Internal Security Strategy for the European Union: Towards a European Security Model, Council doc. 5842/2/2010. Among the 'significant common threats' identified by the ISS are terrorism and serious and organised crime.

> and beyond, are an integral component of the approach laid down in the European Security Strategy. As that Strategy recognises, relationships with our partners, in particular the United States, are of fundamental importance in the fight against serious and organised crime and terrorism.[52]

The Commission's Action Plan for the implementation of the Stockholm Programme, adopted in 2010, foresaw the adoption that year of a recommendation to authorise the opening of negotiations with the US for both an agreement on data protection for law enforcement purposes and a longer-term TFTP agreement,[53] and in 2011 of a Communication on the feasibility of a European Terrorist Finance Tracking Programme.[54] A Communication from the Commission in 2010 on establishing a new legislative framework for data protection[55] emphasised the limitations of the existing regulation of data protection in the area of police and judicial cooperation in criminal matters,[56] and the need to review procedures and guarantees when data are transferred to third countries:

> [T]he current legal instruments include no detailed, harmonized requirements as to which transfers can be considered lawful. This leads to practices which vary from Member State to Member State. … Moreover, international agreements concluded by the EU or its Member States often require the inclusion of data protection principles and specific provisions. This may result

---

[52] Commission Communication, The EU Internal Security Strategy in action: five steps towards a more secure Europe, COM(2010) 673, 3 (a footnote in the original text has been omitted).

[53] The Stockholm Programme, note 4 above; Commission Communication, Delivering an area of freedom, security and justice: action plan implementing the Stockholm Programme COM(2010) 171.

[54] The Communication was published in July 2011: see note 64 below.

[55] Commission Communication, A comprehensive approach on personal data protection in the European Union COM(2010) 609, 4 November 2010; see also JHA Council Conclusions on the Communication, 25 February 2011, Council doc. 5980/4/11 REV 4.

[56] The current instruments are Council Framework Decision 2008/977/JHA on the protection of personal data processed in the framework of police and judicial cooperation in criminal matters [2008] OJ L350/60, together with Council Decision 2008/615/JHA ('Prüm Decision') on the stepping up of cross-border cooperation, particularly in combating terrorism and cross-border crime [2008] OJ L210/1; and the Convention on Mutual Assistance in Criminal Matters between the Member States of the EU [2000] OJ C197/1. On the fragmentation of EU regulation of data protection in relation to JHA matters, and the resulting lack of coherence and clarity in the system, see de Hert and de Schutter, note 3 above, 314.

> in varying texts with inconsistent provisions and rights, and thus open to divergent interpretations.[57]

The 2008 Framework Decision on data protection in the framework of police and judicial cooperation in criminal matters, for example, leaves to the Member States the assessment of adequacy of data protection safeguards in relation to third countries to which data may be transferred.[58] In addition, Article 26 provides that 'This Framework Decision is without prejudice to any obligations and commitments incumbent upon Member States or upon the Union by virtue of bilateral and/or multilateral agreements with third States existing at the time of adoption of this Framework Decision.'

As a result transfers made under the TFTP agreement are subject to the safeguards contained in that agreement, not those in the Framework Decision.[59] A proposal for a replacement directive dealing with data protection in the context of criminal proceedings, published in January 2012 and still under debate at the time of writing, contains provisions for transfers of data to third countries designed to combine EU-level controls (adequacy decisions by the Commission) with the possibility of national derogations.[60]

In December 2010 the Council adopted a mandate for the negotiation of a new agreement between the EU and the US on personal data protection when cooperating to fight terrorism or crime.[61] This would provide the data protection regulatory context, including a supervisory mechanism, for specific agreements on data transfer, such as the TFTP agreement, or a new PNR agreement.[62]

---

[57] COM(2010) 609, note 55 above, 15.

[58] See note 56 above. See further Report from the Commission on the protection of personal data processed in the framework of police and judicial cooperation in criminal matters COM(2012) 12 final.

[59] See Valsamis Mitsilegas, *EU Criminal Law* (Hart Publishing 2009) 274.

[60] Proposal for a Directive of the European Parliament and of the Council on the protection of individuals with regard to the processing of personal data by competent authorities for the purposes of prevention, investigation, detection or prosecution of criminal offences or the execution of criminal penalties, and the free movement of such data, COM(2012)10 final, 25 January 2012, Arts 33–38; see also Art. 60 on prior international agreements entered into by Member States.

[61] JHA Council Conclusions, 2–3 December 2010, Council doc. 16918/10.

[62] The same Council meeting also agreed a negotiating mandate for PNR agreements with Australia, Canada and the USA: see note 66 below. See also Commission Communication on the global approach to transfers of Passenger Name Record (PNR) data to third countries, COM(2010) 492.

As we have seen, the Parliament had already expressed a preference for an EU-based TFTP which would avoid the transfer of bulk data to the US. The Council, in concluding the EU–US agreement, had invited the Commission to propose 'a legal and technical framework for the extraction of data on EU territory',[63] and the Commission's 2010 Action Plan for the Stockholm Programme includes the development of an EU TFTP.[64] On 13 July 2011, the Commission issued a Communication on the options available.[65] The two objectives of a Terrorist Finance Tracking System (TFTS) in the European Union would be (i) to provide 'an effective contribution to the fight against terrorism and its financing' within the EU; and (ii) to 'contribute to limiting the amount of personal data transferred to third countries'. This is not the place for an assessment of the Communication or the options proposed but it is worth noting the emphasis placed by the Commission on the need to comply with EU data protection standards and the need for any EU TFTS to have as its principal objective the security of EU citizens (rather than simply cooperation with US security objectives). The Communication has been discussed in the Council, with any final decision awaiting a detailed Impact Assessment, including a costs analysis and a better indication of the added value offered by the EU system; it would be important, in the view of the Council, that an EU system should not have any negative impact on cooperation with the US under the EU–US TFTP agreement.[66] In a follow-up Communication in November 2013 the Commission expressed doubts as to whether an EU TFTS is currently justified.

VI. CONCLUDING REMARKS

The three types of risk we have identified in this story represent three ways in which risk and law interact:

---

[63] See note 49 above. See also Article 11 of the US–EU TFTP (SWIFT) agreement.

[64] See note 53 above.

[65] Commission Communication, A European terrorist finance tracking system: available options, COM(2011) 429 final, 13 July 2011.

[66] See Presidency note to the Council on orientation of the ministerial debate on the TFTS, 15 September 2011, Council doc. 14207/11; Presidency note to the Council on state of play, 14 December 2011, Council doc. 18287/11.

i. Legal risk – the risks associated with legal uncertainty, uncertainty as to the applicable legal rules, either because of a gap in regulation or because of the interaction between different legal regimes.
ii. The political risks associated with the process of law-making, and the institutional framework through which issues of factual and legal risk may be addressed. This is not only a question of the uncertainties of the political and legislative process, but also achieving a balance between the need for an effective process and the risk of calling into question the legitimacy of the outcome.
iii. The factual or 'real world' risks which legal regimes and instruments seek both to minimise and to keep in balance: here, the balance between perceived security threats and the threat to fundamental rights caused by the response to those threats.

What does the EU–US TFTP agreement experience tell us about these different dimensions of the relationship between law and risk?

The law enforcement utility of personal data held by SWIFT, an international commercial enterprise, brought it into contact with competing and potentially conflicting regulatory and security regimes. The problem was exacerbated for both US and EU law enforcement authorities by SWIFT's decision to move its European data out of the US jurisdiction. For the EU, an internal data protection issue became an international security issue, requiring not only regulatory cooperation (the solution tried in 2006–2007) but ultimately an international agreement. The legal risk resulting from international commercial transactions interacting with different regulatory regimes, coupled with the EU's internal security policy, created a need for the EU to act at an international level. Thus the intra-EU police cooperation foreseen in the Treaty is extended to third countries, such as the USA.

The EU is keen to demonstrate that it is an effective actor in counter-terrorism, and an equal partner to the US. Here, it had serious difficulty over its ability to deliver what the Council and Commission had promised to the US – an agreement putting SWIFT transfers on a solid legal foundation. The irony is this: it is often claimed that the EU would be a more effective international actor if it were more supranational, more like a federal state, and less inter-governmental. Here, however, it was the increased powers granted to the European Parliament by the Treaty of Lisbon in the JHA field and in the procedure for concluding international agreements – that is, an increased level of supranationality – that created obstacles. By comparison, an agreement concluded under the former (inter-governmental) third pillar would not have posed these problems for the Council, which could have approved it under former Articles 24 and 38 TEU.[67]

The story of the TFTP agreement thus demonstrates the substantial shift brought about by the Treaty of Lisbon in the balance of power as regards international treaty-making by the EU: wherever agreements are concluded in a field where internal acts are to be adopted by the 'ordinary legislative procedure' (formerly known as co-decision), the Parliament must give its consent. If the Parliament must give its consent to the final text, it will in practice need to be involved by the Commission and the Council at earlier stages, even though Article 218 TFEU does not give the Parliament a formal role in the adoption of the negotiating mandate or the negotiation itself. As Monar points out, although this may result in an increased democratic legitimacy, the European Parliament is not subject to the same parliamentary majority-based disciplines as national Parliaments and the EU's executive cannot take its support for granted.[68] The 'pillar politics' epitomised by the PNR and SWIFT agreements has not disappeared with the removal of the pillar structure by the Treaty of Lisbon,[69] and the political risks associated with the parliamentary consent procedure are real. The Parliament is clearly determined to maximise its influence over counter-terrorism policy, both external and internal.[70]

---

[67] The history of the agreements on passenger name records with the USA and Australia is also illustrative of this point. Agreements were signed in 2007 and 2008 with the USA and Australia under former third pillar powers, and provisionally applied: see note 17 above. However, in May 2010 (following its first TFTP vote) the European Parliament decided to defer its consent to the conclusion of these agreements and in December 2010 the Council agreed a negotiating mandate for new agreements (for letters to the Council from the President of the Parliament, the rapporteur and the Chair of the LIBE Committee, expressing support for the new agreements but requesting to be kept fully informed of the progress of negotiations, see Council docs. 16972/10 and 17421/10). A new PNR agreement with Australia was accepted by the Parliament in 2011 (Council Decision 2012/381/EU [2012] OJ L186/3) and that with the USA in 2012 (Council Decision 2012/472/EU [2012] OJ L215/4).

[68] Monar, note 37 above, 148.

[69] On the inter-pillar dimension of JHA and the PNR case in particular, see Patryk Pawlak, 'The External Dimension of the Area of Freedom, Security and Justice: Hijacker or Hostage of Cross-pillarization?' (2009) 31 *Journal of European Integration* 25.

[70] Although see Juan Santos Vara, 'The Role of the European Parliament in the Conclusion of the Transatlantic Agreements on the Transfer of Personal Data after Lisbon' (2013) CLEER Working Paper 2013/2, arguing that the Parliament

International counter-terrorism policy-making requires a balance between security risks and safeguarding against risks to human rights and misuse of personal data. Although the EU has developed its own internal standards and monitoring mechanisms, including the European Data Protection Supervisor, the extension to third countries of these standards and safeguards, and the ability of individuals to enforce their rights, is not always straightforward. As de Hert and de Schutter point out, 'Controlling national actors is of course much easier than controlling actors outside the legal regime of the Member State of the data subjects.'[71] At the heart of the problem is the fragmentation of the EU's own internal regime for handling personal data in the context of law enforcement, and its uncertain balance between the principles of availability of data (making transfers possible under certain conditions and for specific purposes), and of adequacy of data protection. With respect to certain key partners, such as the USA, the EU has decided that an overall regulatory framework for transnational data protection is needed, and at the same time this must be compatible with its own internal standards. Here, then, we can see internal data protection objectives constraining and shaping external action: as the Internal Security Strategy puts it, 'Europe must consolidate a security model, based on the principles and values of the Union: respect for human rights and fundamental freedoms, the rule of law, democracy, dialogue, tolerance, transparency and solidarity.'[72]

There is much talk on all sides of the need to achieve an acceptable balance between security and law enforcement, and fundamental rights and data protection, between availability of data and adequacy of protection. But what is acceptable and how are the risks assessed? In practice objective criteria are difficult to identify, and the debate becomes a series of assertions by different actors: the US Treasury, the EU Commission, the Council, Member States, the European Parliament, not to mention commercial and other interest groups. This is perhaps inevitable but it suggests that the outcome of the debate over risk is in the end a political compromise rather than a technocratic solution. And the new EU Treaty architecture means that although the crafting of a compromise is in the hands of Commission and Council, the European Parliament will have the last word. It is perhaps too early to say whether,

---

has shown itself more concerned with asserting its role in the negotiation and conclusion of international agreements in the JHA field than in their content.

[71] Paul de Hert and Bart de Schutter, note 3 above, 306.

[72] Introduction to the Internal Security Strategy, Council doc. 7120/10.

in reaction to the much-discussed process of securitisation,[73] we will see a rebalancing and a re-politicisation of the debate over risk within EU Justice and Home Affairs, with corresponding attention to transparency and participation.[74]

In the case of SWIFT – as in the earlier case of PNR – EU policy appears primarily reactive: to both commercial pressure and to US requirements. There is a tendency for the EU to follow the US lead.[75] This is not the same as accepting US standards. The EU is unhappy sending bulk data to the US, but its response is to discuss whether to build its own version, an EU TFTP, which would involve EU-based authorities sifting through the bulk data, constrained by EU standards and controls. The ISS speaks of a European Security Model but it is not entirely clear what is specifically *European* about it. The EU's ambition is to be able to offer a Security Strategy that integrates internal security objectives with external instruments and policies, to use its key relationships, its neighbourhood policy and partnerships to promote its internal security-related priorities.[76] It also hopes to be able to integrate its fundamental values into its policies on justice and home affairs. The European Security Model represents the EU's own assessment of the balance of risk. We have looked at only one small example of the difficulty in doing just that when a strategic external partner's own

---

[73] See for example Jörg Monar, Wyn Rees and Valsamis Mitsilegas (eds), *The European Union and Internal Security: Guardian of the People?* (Palgrave Macmillan 2003).

[74] See for example the responses to the Commission's public consultation on the new TFTP agreement, available at: http://ec.europa.eu/dgs/home-affairs/what-is-new/public-consultation/2010/consulting_0005_en.htm, last accessed 29 April 2015.

[75] For a discussion of this tendency, using the EU–US PNR agreement as an example, see Javier Argomaniz, 'When the EU is the 'Norm-Taker': The Passenger Name Records Agreement and the EU's Internalization of US Border Security Norms' (2009) 31 *Journal of European Integration* 119. On the TFTP agreement, see Servent and MacKenzie, note 1 above.

[76] On the JHA and the EU's neighbourhood policy, see Thierry Balzacq (ed.), *The External Dimension of EU Justice and Home Affairs: Governance, Neighbours, Security* (Palgrave Macmillan 2009), and Sandra Lavenex and Nicole Wichmann, 'The External Governance of EU Internal Security' (2009) 31 *Journal of European Integration* 83; on the JHA and EU policy towards the Western Balkans, see Florian Trauner, 'Deconstructing the EU's Routes of Influence in Justice and Home Affairs in the Western Balkans' (2009) 31 *Journal of European Integration* 65.

security needs and different regulatory approaches come into the picture. But even this small example demonstrates the impact of an important new focus of EU external policy.

5. Managing the unmanageable: the European Union and terrorism

Jan Wouters and Sanderijn Duquet

1. INTRODUCTION

Over the years, public authorities have been struggling to anticipate and to respond to sudden, politically inspired, attacks that target citizens and society. The European Union ('EU' or 'Union'), the Member States of which have repeatedly suffered from terrorism in the past, is sensitive to the issue.[1] To protect European society, counterterrorism measures have been integrated across the Union's legal framework.[2] Following a surge of common counterterrorism action in the first few years of the 21st century, however, a sense of 'fatigue' in fighting terrorism was detectable in EU circles.[3] This is remarkable, as Europol's latest strategic analysis – the 2013 EU Terrorism Situation and Trend Report – shows that the terrorist threat remains high in Europe.[4] Statistics indicate that small

---

[1] One may recall major terrorist attacks that occurred on 11 March 2004 in Madrid and on 7 July 2005 in London. See for an analysis Jörg Monar, 'The EU's Externalization of Internal Security Objectives: Perspectives after Lisbon and Stockholm' (2010) 45 *The International Spectator* 23–39.

[2] Juan Santos Vara, 'The External Dimension of the Area of Freedom, Security and Justice in the Lisbon Treaty' (2008) 10 *European Journal of Law Reform* 585–586.

[3] In his November 2009 Discussion Paper, the EU Counterterrorism Coordinator, Gilles de Kerchove, noted the existence of this 'counterterrorism fatigue' in the Union, amid other global crises that require a close follow-up. See EU Counterterrorism Coordinator, EU Counter-Terrorism Strategy – discussion paper, 26 November 2009, available at: <http://register.consilium.europa.eu/pdf/en/09/st15/st15359-re01.en09.pdf> accessed 2 July 2013, 2. This criticism is echoed in the literature; see Oldrich Bures, *EU Counterterrorism Policy: A Paper Tiger?* (Ashgate 2013) 244.

[4] Europol, TE-SAT 2013: EU Terrorism Situation and Trend Report, 25 April 2013, <https://www.europol.europa.eu/sites/default/files/publications/europol_te-sat2013_lr_0.pdf> accessed 2 July 2013.

EU-based groups and solo terrorists are on the rise against the structured actions of larger groups and networks.[5] As a result, terrorist activities have become more varied than ever and thus more difficult to predict. In addition, terrorism-related activities are facilitated by modern technologies, such as the internet.[6] The changing nature of the threat of terrorism, and the risks that emerge from it, require the revitalisation of regulatory answers.

This chapter examines if and how the EU advances risk-oriented approaches in its counterterrorism management. It will be argued that it is necessary for the Union not only to focus on threats posed by terrorism, but, and even more prominently, also to decrease its vulnerability to terrorism through the further development of its legal framework. First, the chapter will provide a brief overview of the EU's counterterrorism strategy (Section 2). Subsequently, it will reflect on the use of the concept of risk as a parameter in counterterrorism regulation (Section 3). A final section concludes (Section 4).

2. THE EU'S COUNTERTERRORISM FRAMEWORK

The EU sees terrorism as a significant threat.[7] Securing Europe from it requires cooperative efforts by EU actors and Member States. In the first

---

[5] *Ibid*. This is confirmed in the media coverage of recent events in Europe, including deadly attacks on a British soldier in London in broad daylight in May 2013, on tourists at a Jewish Museum in Brussels in May 2014, and, recently, on journalists at the Paris Headquarters of the satirical magazine Charlie Hebdo in 2015. France has seen other incidents as well: in its Toulouse region, a jihadist shooter killed three soldiers and four bystanders outside a Jewish school in March 2012. In Paris, the police discovered bomb-making material, which resulted in the arrest of 12 suspects, all French citizens born in France, in the 1980s and 1990s (October 2012).

[6] See also the EU's 2010 Internal Security Strategy, stating that: 'The main crime-related risks and threats facing Europe today, such as terrorism, … adapt extremely quickly to changes in science and technology in their attempt to exploit illegally and undermine the values and prosperity of our open societies.' Council of the European Union, Internal Security Strategy for the European Union: *Towards a European Security Model*, March 2010, <www.consilium.europa.eu/uedocs/cms_data/librairie/PDF/QC3010313ENC.pdf> accessed 2 July 2013, 7.

[7] The 2003 European Security Strategy explains: 'Terrorism is a threat to all States and to all peoples. It poses a serious threat to the security of the European Union and the lives of its citizens. The EU remains determined to tackle this scourge. Doing so requires a comprehensive response.' See Council of the

few decades of the European integration process, counterterrorism action had strong intergovernmental features.[8] Even today, the EU's legal framework only allows for a certain degree of common action in the field. Supranational features are to be discerned whenever the European Treaties[9] allow for the application of the ordinary legislative procedure, in which the European Parliament and the Council adopt legislation together. The procedure applies when the EU drafts a framework for administrative measures with regard to the freezing of funds, financial assets or economic gains belonging to, or owned or held by, terrorists or terrorist groupings (Art. 75 TFEU); elaborates minimum rules concerning the definition and sanctioning of terrorism having a cross-border dimension (Art. 83 TFEU); and further determines Europol's mission in preventing and combating terrorism (Art. 88 TFEU). Counterterrorism action has been integrated both in the Area of Freedom, Security and Justice (AFSJ) and the Common Foreign and Security Policy.[10] Looking for comprehensive answers has proven to be complicated, as will be shown in the following section.

2.1 Counterterrorism Action in a Nutshell

An 'event driven' counterterrorism strategy has dominated the past 15 years of EU counterterrorism law-making.[11] The three major terrorist attacks that occurred on 11 September 2001 in the United States, 11 March 2004 in Madrid and 7 July 2005 in London were landmark

---

European Union, The European Union Strategy for Combating Radicalisation and Recruitment to Terrorism, Brussels, 24 November 2005, revised 14 November 2008, available at: <register.consilium.eu.int/pdf/en/05/st14/st14781-re01.en05.pdf> accessed 2 July 2013.

[8] Originally, cross-border crime and terrorism in a European context primarily were dealt with by the informal Trevi Group, established in 1975. The activities of the group were incorporated into the former intergovernmental third pillar on Justice and Home Affairs by the 1992 Maastricht Treaty, as further reformed by the 1997 Amsterdam Treaty; see Wouter Devroe and Jan Wouters, *De Europese Unie. Het Verdrag van Maastricht en zijn uitvoering* (Peeters 1996) 668; Patrizia De Cesari, 'The European Union' in Giuseppe Nesi (ed.), *International Cooperation in Counterterrorism* (Ashgate 2006) 208.

[9] Treaty on European Union [2012] OJ C326/13 [hereafter TEU]; Treaty on the Functioning of the European Union, [2012] OJ C326/47 [hereafter TFEU].

[10] See Ian Manners, 'European [Security] Union: Bordering and Governing a Secure Europe in a Better World?' (2013) 27:3 *Global Society.* Special Issue: Borders, Security and (Global) Governance, 398–416.

[11] See Rik Coolsaet, 'EU Counterterrorism Strategy: Value Added or Chimera?' (2010) 86 *International Affairs* 858.

moments. All three events caused disorder in Europe and (at least temporarily) led to a greater political will to address terrorism. This phenomenon is linked to national and European threat perceptions and is well documented in literature.[12]

Following the 9/11 attacks, a comprehensive EU Action Plan to Fight Terrorism was adopted within two weeks.[13] The Action Plan implemented parts of the 1999 Tampere Programme, which had until then received little support.[14] Furthermore, it served as the policy basis for legal instruments adopted in the course of the following months. The most significant were the two Council Framework Decisions of 13 June 2002 on Combating Terrorism,[15] and the European Arrest Warrant.[16]

---

[12] See, amongst others, Jan Wouters and Frederik Naert, 'The European Union and "September 11"'(2003) 13 *Ind. Int'l & Comp. L. Rev* 721; Javier Argomaniz, *The EU and Counter-Terrorism: Politics, Polity and Policies After 9/11* (Routledge 2011) 200; Christina Eckes, 'The Legal Framework of the European Union's Counter-Terrorist Policies' in Christina Eckes and Theodore Konstadinides (eds), *Crime within the Area of Freedom, Security and Justice: A European Public Order* (Cambridge University Press 2011) 127–158.

[13] Extraordinary European Council, Conclusions, 21 September 2001, Brussels, <http://www.consilium.europa.eu/uedocs/cms_data/docs/pressdata/en/ec/140.en.pdf> accessed 2 July 2013. See also European Parliament Resolution on the Extraordinary European Council Meeting in Brussels on 21 September 2001, 4 October 2001.

[14] The goal of the Tampere Programme was to construct an Area of Freedom, Security and Justice across the Union. The programme's implementation was far from fully realised by 2001; Tampere European Council 15 and 16 October 1999, Presidency Conclusions, <http://www.europarl.europa.eu/summits/tam_en.htm> accessed 2 July 2013. For further reading, see Javier Argomaniz, 'Post-9/11 Institutionalisation of European Union Counter-terrorism: Emergence, Acceleration and Inertia' (2009) 18:2 *European Security* 151–172.

[15] Council Framework Decision of 13 June 2002 on combating terrorism (2002/475/JHA) [2002] OJ L164/3. In this, a definition of terrorism was introduced and terrorism was recognised to be a special offence in all EU Member States. In 2008, three more offences linked to terrorism were added to this list: public provocation, recruitment and training for terrorism. See Council Framework Decision 2008/919/JHA of 28 November 2008 amending Framework Decision 2002/475/JHA on combating terrorism, [2008] OJ L330/21. For further reading, see Eugenia Dumitriu, 'The E.U.'s Definition of Terrorism: The Council Framework Decision on Combating Terrorism' (2004) 5 *German Law Journal* 585–601.

[16] Council Framework Decision 2002/584 on the European Arrest Warrant and the Surrender Procedures between Member States, [2002] OJ L190/1; Jan Wouters and Frederik Naert, 'Of Arrest Warrants, Terrorist Offences and Extradition Deals: An Appraisal of the EU's Main Criminal Law Measures against

Internally, specialist anti-terrorist teams within Europol and Eurojust were established.[17] External action in the field of law enforcement cooperation with third countries was also strengthened, including with the United States in the form of a Europol–US Agreement on the exchange of personal data[18] as the most notable example of cooperation, along with the EU–US Agreements on extradition[19] and mutual legal assistance.[20,21] The 9/11 attacks received significant follow-up in the EU. Remarkably enough, by 2003 the Council had had to face the reluctance of Member States in implementing common counterterrorism tools.[22] The interest of national policy-makers to regulate had gradually declined in contrast to the risks the Union still faced, as demonstrated by the large-scale attacks that took place within the Union's borders in 2004 and 2005.

The Madrid March 2004 attack re-invigorated the political will to adapt the legal framework on counterterrorism. On 25 March 2004, the

---

Terrorism After "11 September"' (2004) 41:4 *Common Market Law Review* 909–935.

17 Jürgen Storbeck and Mascia Toussaint, 'Outline of a Balanced and Effective Internal Security Strategy for the EU' (2004) 12 *European Journal of Crime, Criminal Law and Criminal Justice* 3.

18 Agreement between the United States of America and the European Police Office, Council Doc. 13359/01 Europol 82, 31 October 2001; Supplemental Agreement between the United States of America and the European Police Office on the Exchange of Personal Data and Related Information, Council Doc. 15231/02 Europol 104, 5 December 2002; Agreement between the United States of America and the European Union on the use and transfer of Passenger Name Records to the United States Department of Homeland Security, [2012] OJ L215/5.

19 Agreement on extradition between the European Union and the United States of America, [2003] OJ L181/27.

20 Agreement on mutual legal assistance between the European Union and the United States of America, [2003] OJ L181/34.

21 Later on, a Terrorist Finance Tracking Program was also launched; see the Agreement between the European Union and the United States of America on the processing and transfer of Financial Messaging Data from the European Union to the United States for the purposes of the Terrorist Finance Tracking Program, [2010] OJ L195/5. For further reading, consult Christian Kaunert, 'The External Dimension of EU Counter-terrorism Relations: Competences, Interests, and Institutions' (2009) 22:1 *Terrorism and Political Violence* 54–57.

22 Council of the European Union, *European Security Strategy: A Secure Europe in a Better World*, 12 December 2003, <http://www.consilium.europa.eu/uedocs/cmsUpload/78367.pdf> accessed 2 July 2013. See also Asle Toje, 'The EU Security Strategy Revised: Europe Hedging its Bets' (2010) 15 *European Foreign Affairs Review* 181.

European Council adopted a Declaration on Combating Terrorism,[23] which contained a 'Declaration on solidarity against terrorism' in which Member States and acceding States stated their political commitment to act jointly in the event of a terrorist attack.[24] In order to facilitate inter-State police and judicial cooperation, mutual assistance and recognition frameworks were developed and extradition and arrest warrant procedures were simplified.[25] In November 2004, the 1999 Tampere Programme was replaced by the Hague Programme. The latter called for a more integrated and coherent approach. These aspirations have been embodied in a newly created bridging function within the EU institutions dedicated to maintaining an overview of the many counterterrorism instruments:[26] Gijs de Vries was appointed the first EU Counterterrorism Coordinator within the Council Secretariat 'while paying due regard to the responsibilities of the Commission'.[27]

In July 2005, the city of London was under attack. A fresh political momentum was built to speed up on-going regulatory work.[28] This resulted in the adoption of the EU Counterterrorism Strategy ('CTS' or 'Strategy'), proposed by the UK, which held the rotating presidency at the time.[29] The development of the CTS was crucial for the Union. Both internal and external counterterrorism initiatives had multiplied in the era that followed 9/11. Counterterrorism action suffered from a lack of coherence and it was clear that the mere creation of a coordinating

---

23 European Council, Declaration on Combating Terrorism, 25 March 2004, <www.consilium.europa.eu/uedocs/cms_data/docs/pressdata/en/ec/79637.pdf> accessed 2 July 2013.

24 Article I-43 of the Treaty establishing a Constitution for Europe, [2004] OJ C310/1, signed in Rome on 29 October 2004 also contained a solidarity clause. The Lisbon Treaty would take over this clause literally. See *infra*, section 3.2.2. on the Solidarity Clause. For further reading, see Steven Blockmans and Ramses A. Wessel, 'The European Union and Crisis Management: Will the Lisbon Treaty make the EU More Effective?' (2009) 14:2 *Journal of Conflict and Security Law* 303.

25 The European Arrest Warrant is not a measure specific to terrorism, yet it was deployed as a tool in the fight against terrorism; Wouters and Naert, *supra* note 16.

26 Declaration on Combating Terrorism, *supra* note 23, 13.

27 *Ibid.*, 13. Since 2007, the position has been held by Gilles de Kerchove.

28 Argomaniz, *supra* note 14, 160.

29 Council of the European Union, The European Union Counter-Terrorism Strategy, 30 November 2005, <register.consilium.eu.int/pdf/en/05/st14/st14469-re04.en05.pdf> accessed 2 July 2013.

function would not suffice.[30] Based on the British internal strategy combating terrorism, the CTS served the purpose of creating order in the existing regulatory chaos.[31] For the first time, a strategic and multifaceted approach was introduced, allowing for a more substantial common response to a new kind of terrorist threat.

2.2 The 2005 EU Counterterrorism Strategy: Introducing Risk-Based Governance

Along with the development of a more comprehensive approach to counterterrorism, the CTS added risk parameters to the Union's counter-terrorism management. The Strategy's structure reflects the idea that threats should be tackled at different stages and thereto introduces four pillars ('Prevent', 'Protect', 'Pursue' and 'Respond'). As a result, the Strategy cautiously introduced risk prevention[32] as well as risk responses[33] to the Union.

Throughout, however, the CTS struggled to define what exactly constitutes the common threat of terrorism. Some remarks are in order concerning its description of a 'terrorism threat'. The Strategy presents an inclusive definition.[34] First, it is all-encompassing with regard to the origins of the threat: no particular groups, internal or external, are named. The Strategy merely states that all forms of terrorism bring about risks.[35] Yet, in its proposals to counter this, the Strategy focuses on the internal aspects of the terrorism threats. Motivational and structural factors underpinning radicalisation and terrorist recruitment, or, in other words, the threats posed by home-grown terrorism, have been singled out to be prioritised in regulatory choices.[36] Follow-up to the Strategy was indeed provided for in the EU's Strategy for Combating Radicalisation and

[30] See Argomaniz, *supra* note 14, 155–156.

[31] Coolsaet, *supra* note 11, 860.

[32] One such proposed measure under the 'Protect' pillar has been to develop risk analyses through Frontex, the European border agency, in relation to the EU's external borders; see the EU Counter-Terrorism Strategy, *supra* note 29, 21, 35.

[33] *Ibid.*, 32, referring for example to the risk-based approach to capability assessment under the 'Respond' pillar.

[34] Monar refers to this as the diversification of the EU's threat definition. See Jörg Monar, 'Common Threat and Common Response? The European Union's Counter-terrorism Strategy and its Problems' (2007) 42 *Government and Opposition* 297.

[35] EU Counter-Terrorism Strategy, *supra* note 29, 1–2.

[36] *Ibid.*, 6–13; Argomaniz, *supra* note 14, 160–161

Recruitment to Terrorism ('Radicalisation Strategy').[37] Secondly, the Strategy is all-encompassing with regard to the addressees of the threat: European citizens and infrastructure, as well as the EU's security, values, rights and freedoms are at stake. The Union as a whole being an addressee of terrorism makes it vulnerable. A factor recurrently singled out as adding to that vulnerability concerns the risk brought about by the single market. The threat is at least partially due to the Union's specific openness: terrorists may abuse the free movement of people across borders and the freedoms of the internal market.[38] The Union's design and openness consequently added new elements that needed to be reflected in the Union's counterterrorism management. The CTS successes lie in streamlining counterterrorism initiatives while also integrating the concept of risk in the EU's strategic approach. In the years that followed, however, political intentions needed to be reflected in legislative action.

3. THE CONCEPT OF RISK IN THE EU'S COUNTERTERRORISM FRAMEWORK

The previous section showed that, in particular after 2005, strategic thinking grounded in risk analysis slowly found its entrance in the EU. However, the implementation of the presented concepts has often occurred in an uncoordinated way. Legal and policy instruments adopted on the basis of the CTS have, to different extents, defined and employed risk analyses. Moreover, a theoretical framework that allows for a risk-based approach in counterterrorism policies is still lacking. While the four stages of the Strategy have introduced risk-based approaches and have given input to certain initiatives, they have failed to establish a comprehensive framework across the EU's various policy fields. This section proposes such a twin track framework. It will differentiate between laws and policies designed to manage threats posed by terrorism, on the one hand, and laws and policies designed to manage the vulnerability of the Union, its Member States and its citizens, on the other. The first set of laws and policies acknowledges the potential

---

[37] EU Strategy for Combating Radicalisation and Recruitment to Terrorism, *supra* note 7.

[38] The EU's internal market with its four freedoms stretches out over the territories of 28 Member States, covers over 500 million EU citizens and is characterised by an increasing mobility: EU Counter-Terrorism Strategy, *supra* note 29, 2.

danger of terrorism both within and outside of the Union's borders and focuses on the reduction of threats that can be quantified and analysed. The starting point of the second set of laws and policies is different: it emphasises the enhancement of the legal framework to make the Union less vulnerable in case a terrorist attack occurs. Rather than centralising external threats (focus on the 'other') it stresses the protection of European citizens via the refinement of EU laws on terrorism (focus on the 'self').

3.1 Reducing the Threat of Terrorism

To reduce the threat posed by terrorism, the Union relies on criminal investigation methods and measures preventing radicalisation. Both the activities of intelligence services and general deterrence strategies are considered important components of modern criminal policy and necessary in the fight against terrorism.[39] Due to its limited powers in criminal law-making, the EU is prevented from assuming a meaningful, leading role in the field: the Treaties spell out that safeguarding the territory from terrorist acts constitutes an essential corollary of a State's sovereignty.[40] States bear the primary responsibility for assessing the risk of terrorism and the EU lacks the necessary competences and operational capacity in criminal matters and intelligence-gathering.[41] However, as will be explained below, the EU did contribute to threat reduction by playing a supportive and coordinating role. Gradually building common tools to analyse terrorist threats, legal and policy instruments have been developed under the 'Prevent' and 'Pursue' pillars of the CTS.

3.1.1 Preventing people from turning to terrorism

Since 2005, prevention has been a constitutive part of the EU's counter-terrorism strategy. The Union combats radicalisation as well as the

---

39 Mareile Kaufmann, *Ethnic Profiling and Counter Terrorism: Examples of European Practice and Possible Repercussions* (46 Hamburger Studien Zur Kriminologie Und Kriminalpolitik, LIT Verlag 2010) 39.

40 Article 4(2) TEU labels security to be an essential State function.

41 The further implementation of Art. 82 and 83 TFEU, however, opens up possibilities of further harmonisation and for stretching the boundaries of these competences; see Ester Herlin-Karnell, 'EU Competence in Criminal Law after Lisbon' in Andrea Biondi, Piet Eeckhout and Stephanie Ripley (eds), *EU Law after Lisbon* (OUP 2012) 331–346.

recruitment of terrorists,[42] mainly by focusing on the disruption of factors that draw people into terrorism.[43] This approach requires the alignment of internal and external policies.

Radicalisation reduction measures have been integrated throughout the EU's external action instruments. As an example, we can refer to the EU's neighbourhood policy (ENP), which has seen the setting up of inter-cultural dialogues, research analyses exchanges, and the promotion of principles of good governance, democracy, education and economic prosperity – all with the broader aim to prevent radicalisation.[44] Moreover, similar topics are addressed in the EU's political dialogues with third countries, to raise the issue of prevention and suppression of terrorism, in particular in those countries that represent a potential threat to international peace and security. These efforts are backed by the 2004 Guidelines for a Common Approach to the Fight Against Terrorism, which serve as a tool for consistency on external counterterrorism action.[45] Furthermore, providing technical assistance in police and law enforcement work, improving border management capacities, and institutional and judicial capacity-building are preferred modes of operation in third countries. The Association Agreements concluded with Mediterranean partners, for example, contain provisions on cooperation in the field of justice and home affairs.[46] In addition, these agreements commit the EU and Mediterranean countries to countering terrorism in international networks.[47] The operation mode at the external plane to prevent terrorism

---

[42] EU Strategy for Combating Radicalisation and Recruitment to Terrorism, *supra* note 7.

[43] Extremist behaviour can be spotted, for example, through the monitoring of communication. *Ibid*., 8–9.

[44] Such assistance focuses on areas in which the EU has a comparative advantage, for example, geographically (for example, ENP). The main EU instruments for funding technical assistance are: (i) the Instrument for Stability, (ii) the European Neighbourhood and Partnership Instrument, (iii) the European Instrument for Democracy and Human Rights and (iv) the Development Cooperation Instrument. See Peter Wennerholm, Erik Brattberg and Mark Rhinard, 'The EU as a Counter-terrorism Actor Abroad: Finding Opportunities, Overcoming Constraints' (2010) 60 *EPC Issue Paper*.

[45] Council of the European Union, *Guidelines for a Common Approach to the Fight Against Terrorism*, 19 March 2004, partial declassification 22 May 2008.

[46] Wyn Rees, 'The External Face of Internal Security' in Christopher Hill and Michael Smith (eds), *International Relations and the EU* (OUP 2011) 226–245.

[47] See Article 61 Euro-Mediterranean Agreement establishing an association between the European Communities and their Member States, of the one part,

cannot be deemed a concrete format to reduce actual threats.[48] Rather, it should be judged as an open acknowledgement of the limited competences of the EU in the field and a component of the Union's long-term democratisation policies.[49]

Internal anti-radicalisation measures differ considerably from external action. Building on what was agreed upon in the CTS, the 2010 Internal Security Strategy commits to eradicating terrorism at its source.[50] To this end, a Radicalisation Awareness Network was established by the Commission in partnership with the Committee of the Regions.[51] The network reaches out to actors in the Member States by pooling the expertise of policy-makers, law enforcement and security officials, prosecutors, local authorities, academics, field experts and civil society organisations. It has been referred to as a 'network of networks',[52] in which the EU's role focuses on the facilitation of contacts. The inexistence of a more established common mechanism to fight radicalisation can be attributed to the firm grip taken on the issue by Member States. Radicalisation is considered best to be addressed at a level closest to the susceptible individuals.[53] Member States are the preferred actors to deal with people who are attracted to terrorist activities, since they have the knowledge to assess the risks involved. It also draws on the general preference of Member States not to transfer policing competences to the Union.

---

and the Republic of Morocco, of the other part, [2000] OJ L70/2, that refers to cooperation through the Financial Action Task Force, a body originally set up by the G-7 to review terrorist financing and to implement counter-measures.

48 But see EU Counter-Terrorism Coordinator, EU Counter-Terrorism Strategy – Discussion Paper, May 2012, <http://register.consilium.europa.eu/pdf/en/12/st09/st09990.en12.pdf> accessed 2 July 2013: 'Another key ingredient to success is to develop partnerships with individuals and civil society groups in our own countries that have particular connections to regions of concern. Their socioeconomic and political ties to their countries of origin can help us to better make the link between domestic and overseas prevent work and to act more effectively'.

49 See for further reading: Anne Wetzel and Jan Orbie, 'Promoting Embedded Democracy? Researching the Substance of EU Democracy Promotion' (2011) 16 *European Foreign Affairs Review* 565–588.

50 Internal Security Strategy for the EU, *supra* note 6.

51 See Communication from the Commission to the European Parliament and the Council, *The EU Internal Security Strategy in Action: Five Steps towards a More Secure Europe Council of the European Union*, 22 November 2010, COM(2010) 673 final, 7.

52 Charter of Principles Governing the EU Radicalisation Awareness Network, 20 December 2012, 2.

53 *Ibid.*

3.1.2 Pursuing terrorists: criminal investigation methods

Threat assessments are an indispensable tool in national intelligence-led policing. Domestic intelligence agencies thereto identify and analyse the methods, communications and instruments used by terrorists. The EU embraces such efforts and builds on them in its own counterterrorism activities. Its focal concern is to coordinate between national intelligence services. As a result, Union initiatives have focused on the streamlining of Member States' and EU agencies' ability to access each other's databases and to store data.[54] To a certain extent, however, EU actors also analyse scientific data to determine risks while remaining dependent on the expertise and raw intelligence of the Member States. The European Police Office (Europol) and the EU Intelligence Analysis Centre (IntCen) are the main actors involved in dealing with statistics on internal as well as external threats posed.

The mandate of the EU's law enforcement agency, Europol, includes the fight against terrorism in the Union.[55] More specifically, the 2009 Council Decision establishing Europol spells out the Agency's competence over terrorist activities when affecting two or more Member States:[56] Europol is tasked to 'collect, store, process, analyse, and exchange information and intelligence'.[57] In a second phase, data are used as a basis for risk assessments which Europol conducts itself. This type of assessment identifies terrorism trends and determines terrorism rates for Member States. Here, the Agency makes an original contribution to the EU's risk-based activities, even if it does not gather data directly. Results are published in the Terrorism Situation and Trend Report by Europol annually, collating the information received from Member States' or third parties' authorities as well as Europol's analyses of them.[58]

IntCen is the intelligence actor in the European external security action. Previously located within the Council Secretariat, IntCen has been integrated in the structure of the European External Action Service (EEAS). A specific counterterrorism group within the centre produces

[54] European Council, The Stockholm Programme: An Open and Secure Europe Serving and Protecting Citizens, 4 May 2010.

[55] See generally Oldrich Bures, 'Europol's Fledgling Counterterrorism Role' (2009) 20:4 *Terrorism and Political Violence* 498–517.

[56] Arts. 3 and 4, Council Decision of 6 April 2009 establishing the European Police Office (Europol), 2009/371/JHA, [2009] OJ L121/37.

[57] *Ibid.*, Art. 5(1)(a).

[58] Gregory Mounier, 'Europol: A New Player in the EU External Policy Field?' (2009) 10:4 *Perspectives on European Politics and Society* 585.

and exchanges sensitive information with Member States and third countries.[59] Strategic intelligence planning is conducted on the basis of risk assessments.[60] In addition to producing intelligence analyses, IntCen has been particularly active in providing early warning and situational awareness information. Annually, 200 strategic situation assessments and 50 special reports and briefings are produced by its staff of around 70 people.[61]

3.1.3 Interim conclusion

The Union's activities to reduce the threat of terrorism focus on the prevention of the radicalisation of people and the gathering and analysis of intelligence on those who may radicalise or who have already radicalised. Intelligence assessments are predictive in nature. In a first step, threat assessments are provided by competent law enforcement authorities and statistical experts in Member States. The EU's role lies primarily in collecting and sharing information, or, in other words, the storing and dissemination of terrorism intelligence. In a second phase, these data may be used for the purpose of threat recognition and threat assessment, which requires law- and policy-makers to cooperate. Union actors facilitate such contacts.

The above findings would suggest that, in the EU context, legal instruments are of secondary importance as tools to reduce terrorism threats. Admittedly, this is due to the nature of the functions performed by intelligence services in general and the absence of a common criminal legal framework. To strengthen its legal capacity in the field and to further a counterterrorism framework the EU has to focus, as will be explained in the following section, on the reinforcement of its substantive and procedural legislation on criminal justice and joint Member State action in the field.

---

[59] John D. Occhipinti, 'Availability by Stealth? EU Information Sharing in Transatlantic Perspective' in Christian Kaunert and Sarah Leonard (eds), *European Security, Terrorism and Intelligence: Tackling New Security Challenges in Europe* (Palgrave Macmillan 2013) 160.

[60] IntCen is referred to as the EEAS' 'intelligence hub' in a Joint answer given by High Representative/Vice-President Ashton on behalf of the Commission on 16 August 2012 in reply to written parliamentary questions E-006018/12, E-006020/12.

[61] *Ibid.* and Answer given by High Representative/Vice-President Ashton on behalf of the Commission on 13 December 2012 in reply to written parliamentary question E-006017/2012.

3.2 Reducing Vulnerability

Taking a risk-based approach to counterterrorism goes beyond analysing and diminishing potential threats. Prospective targets also have to be made less vulnerable to terrorism. To reduce its vulnerability, it is submitted that the Union must prioritise the elaboration of its legal framework. The protection of the Union and its citizens depends on the development and implementation of legal tools. These may, but should not necessarily, be specific to terrorism. Investigation, prosecution and assistance procedures have to be up and running and bear the capacity to be activated instantly. The rationale is that a well-developed legal framework serves as an important defence mechanism if a terrorist attack occurs. In EU policy terms, vulnerability reduction should, to a larger extent, be made part of the 'Protect' and 'Respond' pillars of the CTS.

In contrast to the threat reduction measures discussed above, vulnerability reduction is less context-specific and dependent on data (collected through Member States). The risk of occurrence of a terrorist attack should not influence the decision to improve the Union's legal framework. Vulnerability reduction is a legal obligation for the EU. Article 196 TFEU on civil protection requires the Union 'to encourage cooperation between Member States in order to improve the effectiveness of systems for preventing and protecting against terrorism'. Vulnerability reduction efforts of the EU via cooperative efforts, as well as the development of common legal instruments, require closer analysis.

3.2.1 Protecting citizens via improved legal cooperation

Citizens of the Union have to be protected from, and defended by their government against, terrorist attacks. Given that terrorism often assumes a transnational character, the protection of citizens demands the improvement of cooperative and coordinative efforts in the criminal sphere, both between the Member States and with third countries. Intergovernmental cooperation in the area of security and police affairs in countering terrorism was installed from the early days of European integration onwards and continues to be a key element in the EU's counterterrorism strategy. Furthermore, the Union seeks to adopt a holistic approach of improved security of borders, transport and critical infrastructure.[62] In the current set-up of the Treaties, these activities have been integrated in AFSJ, an assortment of EU policies designed to address sensitive issues

---

[62] EU Counter-Terrorism Strategy, *supra* note 29. See also: Council Directive 2008/114/EC of 8 December 2008 on the identification and designation of European Critical Infrastructures, [2008] OJ L345/75.

related to border checks, asylum and immigration, judicial cooperation in civil matters, and police and judicial cooperation in criminal matters.

Setting up a framework for Member States to act jointly against terrorists and terrorist groups is not, in itself, a new initiative[63] nor is it reserved to the Union alone.[64] In the past 15 years, progress has been made in the EU on the traditionally sensitive subject of the approximation of criminal laws.[65] Article 1 of the Framework Decision on Terrorism successfully introduced a common definition of terrorism. From that point onwards, the Member States were obliged to criminalise terrorist offences in their territories.[66] The flurry of counterterrorism actions post-9/11 also gave positive impulses to the development of mutual assistance and recognition frameworks.[67] In addition, Europe witnessed the coming into being of measures of a more general nature, such as the European Arrest Warrant and simplified extradition procedures, which have been used in the fight against terrorism.

The contours of the EU's judicial cooperation strategy for the period 2010–2014 are laid down in the Stockholm Programme. The programme made the increase in efficiency in judicial cooperation in criminal affairs an objective.[68] It did not, however, put forward benchmarks for the approximation of substantive and procedural criminal laws. The Treaty provisions on this matter, as introduced by the Treaty of Lisbon, are not particularly innovative either. According to Article 83(1) TFEU, 'the European Parliament and the Council may, by means of directives

---

[63] See for example, the efforts made by Member States since the establishment of the above mentioned Trevi Group. Activities were multiplied with the coming into force of the Treaties of Maastricht and Amsterdam.

[64] Early initiatives to cooperate in the fight against terrorism were also conducted within the intergovernmental settings of NATO, the Western European Union and the Council of Europe. The latter is still particularly active in improving cooperation on extradition (see the 1977 Convention on the Suppression of Terrorism, CETS No. 090, Strasbourg, 27 January 1977 and its 2003 amending Protocol), terrorism prevention (Convention on the Prevention of Terrorism, CETS No. 196, Warsaw, 16 May 2005) and terrorism financing (Convention on Laundering, Search, Seizure and Confiscation of the Proceeds from Crime and on the Financing of Terrorism, CETS No. 198, Warsaw, 16 May 2005).

[65] Anne Weyembergh, 'Approximation of Criminal Laws, the Constitutional Treaty and the Hague Programme', 42 *Common Market Law Review* (2005) 1567–1597.

[66] Art. 1, Framework Decision on combating terrorism, *supra* note 15.

[67] Wouters and Naert, *supra* note 16.

[68] The Stockholm Programme, *supra* note 54, at 3.1.1.

adopted in accordance with the ordinary legislative procedure, establish minimum rules concerning the definition of criminal offences and sanctions' in the area of terrorism. The restrictive formulation of this provision precludes the Parliament and the Council from approximating criminal laws beyond defining constituent elements of criminal acts and penalties. In counterterrorism legislation, both elements have already been covered[69] as was originally provided for in the Treaty of Amsterdam.[70]

Throughout the development of a counterterrorism framework, however, a growing need was felt to go beyond cooperation and coordination and to move on to forms of integration. Shortly after 9/11, approximation activities were carried out via framework decisions, binding upon the Member States as to the result to be achieved. This operation mode has been criticised for exceeding the legal basis. With the abolition of framework decisions as legal instruments by the Lisbon Treaty,[71] the understanding grew that proceeding approximation efforts in counterterrorism without a clear legal mandate was not a preferred way of moving forward. In more recent years, the political climate never again seemed ripe to agree upon going beyond the established minimalist harmonisation of national criminal law.[72] Currently, Member States are divided on the further development of police and criminal justice regulations. The position of the UK stands out. Protocol 36 to the EU Treaties entitled the UK to opt out from legislation in the field of police cooperation and judicial cooperation in criminal matters adopted prior to

---

[69] See the Framework Decision of 2002, *supra* note 16 and the EU's sanctions regime. For further reading on sanctions, see Christina Eckes, 'EU Counter-terrorist Sanctions Against Individuals: Problems and Perils' (2002) 17 *European Foreign Affairs Review* (2012) 133–156.

[70] See the approximation principle the Treaty of Amsterdam introduced in Article 31(e) TEU: 'Common action on judicial cooperation in criminal matters shall include … measures establishing minimum rules relating to the constituent elements of criminal acts and to penalties in the fields of organized crime, terrorism and illicit drug trafficking.' This provision constituted the clearest legal basis for approximation of the laws and regulations of the Member States within the former third pillar; Framework Decisions were considered the preferred instruments for this purpose.

[71] Before, the European Court of Justice had ruled on the effect of Framework Decisions. National courts are required to interpret national law in the light of the wording and purpose of the Framework Decision, but this could never lead to an interpretation *contra legem*. See ECJ, Case C-105/03, Criminal proceedings against Maria Pupino [2005] ECR I-05285.

[72] Monar, *supra* note 34, 309.

entry into force of the Treaty of Lisbon.[73] However, other Member States may opt to increase efforts in this domain. It may thus be that, in the near future, the further approximation of national counterterrorism laws will be developed in a 'two speed' Europe.[74]

3.2.2 Responding to terrorism: the implementation of vulnerability reduction tools

In contrast to the rather restrictive provisions on the approximation of substantive counterterrorism laws, the Lisbon Treaty did provide the EU with a new set of reactive common counterterrorism tools, some of which need to be implemented. A first tool is the potential establishment of a European Public Prosecutor's Office (Art. 86 TFEU). The main task of this Office, to be linked with Eurojust, would be to combat crimes affecting the financial interests of the EU. While the fight against terrorism is not directly among the core tasks of this yet-to-be-established Office, Art. 86(4) TFEU includes the possibility for the European Council to adopt a decision to extend the powers of the Prosecutor's Office to include serious crimes having a cross-border dimension. Despite the efforts of Spain and Belgium, which successively held the

---

[73] See Art. 10 of Protocol No. 36 on transitional provisions, [2008] OJ C115/322. The UK Government announced its decision to opt out of all the pre-Lisbon measures on 9 July 2013 so that these will cease to apply to the UK as from 1 December 2014. See UK Government, Decision pursuant to Article 10 of Protocol 36 to The Treaty on the Functioning of the European Union, 9 July 2013 (Cm 8671), <http://www.official-documents.gov.uk/document/cm86/8671/8671.pdf> accessed 4 October 2013. Simultaneously, the Government published a list of 35 measures, considered 'in the national interest', for which it would seek to negotiate to opt back in. Among the list of 35 are important measures in the fight against terrorism, such as the Council Decision 2002/187/JHA of 28 February 2002 setting up Eurojust, Council Decision 2009/371/JHA establishing Europol, the earlier referred to Council Framework Decision on the European arrest warrant, and a variety of Framework Decisions adopted to enhance mutual recognition. For a complete list, consult <www.parliament.uk/briefing-papers/SN06684.pdf> accessed 4 October 2013. Following the Government's announcement, a Friends of Presidency Group was activated to assist the Permanent Representatives Committee to examine 'issues linked to the end of applicability of the relevant acts to the United Kingdom and to the possibility for the United Kingdom to notify its wish to participate in such acts, according to Article 10(5) of the Protocol, including the requirements of practical operability and coherence'. See: Council of the European Union, Application of Article 10 of Protocol 36 to the Treaties, Brussels, 10 March 2014.

[74] Ester Herlin-Karnell, 'Treaty of Lisbon and the Criminal Law: Anything New under the Sun' (2008) 10 *European Journal of Law Reform* 328.

rotating presidency of the Council in 2010 and pushed Member States to find agreement, the implementation of Art. 86 continued to be hindered by the lack of a political agreement on the matter.[75] In July 2013, the Commission presented its proposal for a Council Regulation to establish the Office.[76] In accordance with the 'yellow card procedure' introduced by the Lisbon Treaty (Article 7(2) of Protocol No. 2 TFEU on the application of the principles of subsidiarity and proportionality), national Parliaments asked the Commission to reconsider the proposal. Fourteen reasoned opinions were issued by chambers of Parliaments of the Member States for non-compliance with the principle of subsidiarity. Despite this opposition, the Commission decided to maintain the proposal.[77] Recently, the European Parliament's Committee on Civil Liberties, Justice and Home Affairs voted in favour of an interim report on the creation of the Office,[78] sending a clear signal to national governments on the importance of going forward with this proposal.[79] By virtue of

---

[75] The 2010 Spanish presidency supported operationalising the Prosecutor's Office and argued in favour of holding a debate at the JHA Council of April 2010 on its establishment. One reason for such debate was to discuss whether it would be appropriate to consider the possibility provided for in Art. 86(4) – including terrorism in the Prosecutor's mandate – from the start of the procedure. See Council of the European Union, Spanish presidency, The European Public Prosecutor's Office in the European judicial area, 15 April 2010, <http://register.consilium.europa.eu/pdf/en/10/st08/st08614.en10.pdf> accessed 2 July 2013. The Belgian presidency indicated that the major objection among Member States was the overriding power of the Prosecutor to the disadvantage of national investigators: Valentina Pop, 'Belgian Presidency in Push for EU Prosecutor's Office' (*EU Observer*, 22 September 2010) <http://euobserver.com/9/30855> accessed 2 July 2013.

[76] Commission, Proposal for a Council Regulation on the establishment of the European Public Prosecutor's Office, 17 July 2013, COM(2013) 534 final. The Prosecutor's Office will be located in 'Europe's judicial capital', Luxembourg.

[77] Communication from the Commission to the European Parliament, the Council and the National Parliaments on the review of the proposal for a Council Regulation on the establishment of the European Public Prosecutor's Office with regard to the principle of subsidiarity, in accordance with Protocol No. 2, COM/2013/0851 final.

[78] Interim report on the proposal for a Council regulation on the establishment of the European Public Prosecutor's Office, COM(2013)0534 – 2013/0255(APP), 29 April 2015.

[79] If the Member States, acting in the Council, do not reach unanimity, the Treaties foresee that a group of at least nine Member States may still proceed to establish the Office by entering into an enhanced cooperation (Art. 86(1) TFEU).

specific protocols to the EU Treaties, Denmark, the United Kingdom and Ireland will not participate automatically.[80]

The proposal seeks to set up the Office and to define its competences and procedures. These competences exclusively comprise crimes affecting the EU's budget. The proposal does not make use of Art. 86(4)'s possibility to extend the Office's powers to the prosecution of terrorism.[81] According to the Commission's 2013 proposal, it will be considered in the longer term. The fight against terrorism is referred to only once: the European Public Prosecutor may authorise the transfer of personal data to third countries, international organisations or Interpol if the transfer of the data is 'absolutely necessary in the interests of preventing imminent danger associated with crime or terrorist offences'.[82] On this ground, the EU Prosecutor most likely will not play a significant role in the fight against terrorism.

A second tool that may be used to decrease the Union's vulnerability to terrorist attacks can be found in Art. 222 TFEU. This provision introduced a solidarity clause in the Union's legal framework.[83] Solidarity as a constitutional principle consists of a legal obligation for the Union and its Member States to assist each other in the event of terrorist attacks if requested to do so.[84] Pursuant to Art. 222(1), 'The Union shall

---

[80] See Protocol No. 22 on the position of Denmark, [2010] OJ C83/299; Protocol No. 21 on the position of the United Kingdom and Ireland in respect of the area of freedom, security and justice, [2010] OJ C83/295. Under these protocols, the UK and Ireland may decide to participate in measures adopted under the criminal law provisions in Title V of the TFEU, as well as in the amendments of existing binding measures. Denmark does not have the possibility to opt in. Danish citizens, however, will be granted the opportunity to do away with the opt-out on JHA cooperation altogether in a referendum that has yet to be organised.

[81] This option will be considered in the medium term. Art. 74 of the Proposal tasks the Commission to present a report five years after the start of application of the proposed Regulation, containing its findings 'on the feasibility and advisability of extending the competence of the European Public Prosecutor's Office to other criminal offences in accordance with Article 86(4) of the Treaty'.

[82] European Public Prosecutor's Office proposal, *supra* note 76, Art. 61(2)(b).

[83] This concept had already been introduced in the EU in the 2004 Declaration on combating terrorism, see *supra* note 23.

[84] The very broad wording and terminology of Art. 222 theoretically enables States to use the clause in response to, for example, a cyber-attack or the blocking of energy supplies by a third country. However, Declaration No. 37 on Art. 222 of the TFEU, appended to the Lisbon Treaty, qualifies the strong

mobilise all the instruments at its disposal, including the military resources made available by the Member States', a provision which can be interpreted in different ways.[85] The article seems to distinguish common security and defence capabilities[86] (assistance from Member States is required) from other instruments at the Union's disposal, such as those developed to facilitate police and judicial cooperation[87] and civil protection.[88] The implementation of the solidarity clause did not go off without a hitch: it took joint efforts of Union actors and Member States to push for a legislative proposal on the matter.[89] The Commission picked up the issue in a Communication in November 2010 when it presented its objective to make full use of the solidarity clause.[90] At the end of 2012, the efforts were integrated in a joint proposal by the Commission and the

wording of the provision and indicates that Member States have the choice to apply the 'most appropriate means' to comply with the solidarity obligation. See also Nicolai von Ondarza and Roderick Parkes, 'The EU in the Face of Disaster: Implementing the Lisbon's Solidarity Clause' (2010) *Stiftung Wissenschaft und Politik Comments* <http://www.swp-berlin.org/en/products/swp-comments-en/swp-aktuelle-details/article/implementing_the_eus_solidarity_clause.html> accessed 2 July 2013.

[85] M. Fuchs-Dropier, 'The European Union's Solidarity Clause in the Event of a Terrorist Attack: Towards Solidarity or Maintaining Sovereignty?' (2011) 19 *JCCM* 87.

[86] Art. 222 TFEU (containing a minimum of internal security commitments) is to be distinguished from the mutual defence clause contained in Art. 42(7) TEU (on external security). However, as Konstadinides argues, an erosion of the 'schism between internal and external security' is to be observed as well since international security clearly affects the internal situation as well. See for further reading on the relationship between the two Treaty articles: T. Konstadinides, 'Civil Protection in EU Law: Is There Room for Solidarity to Wriggle Past?', (2013) 19 *European Law Journal* 267–282.

[87] Title V, Chapters 4–5 TFEU.

[88] Title XXIII, Art. 196 TFEU.

[89] EU Counter-Terrorism Coordinator, EU Counter-Terrorism Strategy – Discussion paper, 10 May 2010, 2 < http://register.consilium.europa.eu/pdf/en/10/st09/st09685.en10.pdf> accessed 6 October 2010. The Belgian presidency of 2010 also strongly pushed for this.

[90] 'Through the implementation of this clause the EU aims to be better organised and more efficient in managing crises, in terms of both prevention and response. On the basis of a cross cutting proposal by the Commission and the High Representative – to be presented in 2011 – the EU's collective task will be to put the solidarity clause into practice'; see Communication on the EU Internal Security Strategy in Action, *supra* note 51, 13.

High Representative,[91] and in 2014, the Council adopted a decision on the rules and procedures for the implementation of the solidarity clause.[92] Unlike the proposal on the competences of the Prosecutor's Office, the Decision on the solidarity clause explicitly includes terrorist attacks in its scope, as foreseen in the Treaties.[93] Moreover, it embraces the idea that Europe must have tools in place to deal with attacks.

As discussed, the Union has few structures in place that deal exclusively with terrorism. When implementing the Solidarity Clause, it will be necessary for the Union to list and mobilise all the instruments it has at hand to be employed in case a terrorist attack occurs. Such exercise would contribute to the further identification of gaps in the EU's civil protection system. EU initiatives worth mentioning here are the Integrated Political Crisis Response arrangements (IPCR) and the Emergency Response Centre (ERC).[94] The ERC is linked to the Commission's Union Civil Protection Mechanism and ensures a 24/7 operational capacity.[95] When a Member State is the object of an actual or imminent terrorist attack it should, following Art. 4 of the Decision on the Solidarity Clause, address its request for assistance to the Presidency of the Council while simultaneously addressing the invocation to the President of the European Commission through the ERC. The ERC adds to the preparedness of the Union in relation to terrorist activities.

3.2.3 Interim conclusion

Neither the EU, nor its Member States, can eliminate all threats posed by terrorism. However, mechanisms can be created that better deal with challenges that relate to the prosecution of terrorists and the protection of citizens, society and critical infrastructure. The legal basis provided for by the Treaty of Lisbon limits the further harmonisation of national

---

[91] Joint Proposal by the Commission and the High Representative of the Union for Foreign Affairs and Security Policy for a Council Decision on the arrangements for the implementation by the Union of the Solidarity clause, 21 December 2012, JOIN/2012/039 final.

[92] Council Decision on the arrangements for the implementation by the Union of the solidarity clause, OJ 2014, L 192/53, 1 July 2014.

[93] *Ibid.* Art. 2.

[94] The ERCC was launched in May 2013 as a part of the existing Crisis Room for humanitarian crises and the Monitoring and Information Centre for civil protection. See press release: 'Emergency Response Centre: For a Faster and More Efficient European Response to Disasters', 15 May 2013 <http://europa.eu/rapid/press-release_IP-13-422_en.htm> accessed 5 October 2013.

[95] Proposal for a Decision of the European Parliament and of the Council on a Union Civil Protection Mechanism, 20 December 2011, COM(2011) 934 final.

criminal laws to the establishment of common minimal rules on the definition and sanctioning of terrorism. As a result, Member States retain the possibility to criminalise other terrorism-related conduct. In this sense, it reflects the political reality that there has been a slowdown in harmonisation exercises. The Treaty has been more innovative in presenting common instruments in the fight against terrorism. In particular, it opened up new perspectives on reducing the vulnerability of the EU. Yet, these novelties have yet to be implemented coherently and should be used to a greater extent in the fight against terrorism.

4. CONCLUDING REMARKS

This chapter has assessed the embedding of risk regulation in the EU's counterterrorism strategy. It was found that, in the aftermath of the major terrorist attacks in the 2000s and driven by public shock, political momentum was created in the Union, often leading to hasty decision-making. Since 2005, strategic thinking grounded in the analysis of actual risks posed has quietly found its way into European law- and policy-making. However, as counterterrorism remains a highly fragmented policy field, no single approach that links risk to terrorism could be discerned. The chapter proposed an evaluation of the existing framework based on two different, yet interrelated, concepts in risk regulation: the reduction of threats within and outside of the Union and the reduction of the vulnerability of the Union. It is conceded that an accurate and cohesive counterterrorism framework in the EU requires both. Moreover, both components of risk regulation demand an increase in the possibilities of action of the Union and in the political will of the Member States to jointly address terrorism. The most pressing issues identified in this chapter are: (i) continuing the implementation of the Lisbon Treaty; (ii) improving Member State cooperation in criminal affairs; and (iii) streamlining counterterrorism tools and instruments across policy fields. The threat of terrorism has become common for the Union and its Member States. More can be done, however, to also commonly address the risks involved.

6. EU risk regulation: the role of science in political and judicial decision-making

Marjolein B.A. van Asselt and Ellen Vos

1. INTRODUCTION

The major institutional shortcomings of European Union (EU) (and national) decision-making that were revealed by the BSE (or 'mad cow') and other food crises made clear that the EU is faced with a predominant concern as to how to make decisions in situations of risks and uncertainty.[1] These crises forced the EU to drastically reform both its foundations and its institutional arrangements pertaining to food safety and more generally risk regulation.[2] Without doubt, they emphasized and made visible that governance of uncertain risks is difficult, and inherently political. New approaches introduced by the EU in the aftermath of these crises have therefore sought to repair alleged deficiencies in EU risk regulation. The reforms thus introduced a clearer separation between risk assessment and risk management, particularly expressed by the creation

[1] For further discussion on the concepts of risk and uncertainty, see Marjolein B.A. van Asselt, 'The Complex Significance of Uncertainty in a Risk Era: Logics, Manners and Strategies in Use'(2005) 5:2/3/4 *International Journal for Risk Assessment and Management* (special issue on uncertainty) 125–158; Marjolein B.A. van Asselt and Ortwin Renn, 'Risk Governance' (2011) 14(4) *Journal of Risk Research*, Special issue 'Uncertainty, Precaution and Risk Governance' 431–449; Gerard de Vries, Imrat Verhoeven and Martin Boeckhout, 'Taming Uncertainty: The WRR Approach to Risk Governance' (2011) 14.4 *Journal of Risk Research* 485–499; Marjolein B.A. van Asselt, Peter de Goede, V.C. Karin Ammerlaan and Jelle van Aanholt, *Physical Safety. A Matter of Balancing Responsibilities* (Scientific Council for Government Policy (WRR), Amsterdam University Press 2012).

[2] See for an overview of EU food regulation pre-BSE, Ellen Vos, 'EU Food Safety Regulation in the Aftermath of the BSE Crisis' (2000) *Journal of Consumer Policy* 227–255.

of the European Food Safety Authority (EFSA), and a clarification of the distinct roles of scientists and decision-makers, the precautionary principle, and increased transparency and participation in the science-based decision-making on food.[3]

How to deal responsibly with situations in which there are suspicions that hazards may exist, although (sufficient) scientific or historical evidence for them is lacking, is in fact the key question that can be derived from Ulrich Beck's agenda-setting critique and provoking notion of 'organized irresponsibility'.[4] Over time, his plea has been reinforced by interdisciplinary risk research.[5] Not surprisingly therefore, prominent risk scholars have indicated that dealing with 'uncertain risks' is a major challenge in contemporary societies.[6] Such uncertain risks concern

---

[3] Marjolein B.A. van Asselt, Michelle Everson and Ellen Vos, 'Trade versus Health and the Environment?' in Marjolein B.A. van Asselt, Michelle Everson and Ellen Vos (eds), *Trade, Health and the Environment: The EU Put to the Test* (Earthscan, Routledge 2014) 3–8. See also Christopher K. Ansell and David Vogel (eds), *What's the Beef? The Contested Governance of European Food Safety* (MIT Press 2006); Elizabeth Fisher, *Risk Regulation and Administrative Constitutionalism* (Hart Publishing 2009); Paul Harremoës *et al.*, *The Precautionary Principle in the 20th Century: Late Lessons from Early Warnings* (Earthscan, Routledge 2002); Joakim Zander, *The Application of the Precautionary Principle in Practice: Comparative Dimensions* (Cambridge University Press 2010).

[4] See Ulrich Beck, *Risk Society: Towards a New Modernity* (Sage 1986); *id.*, *World Risk Society* (Polity Press 1999).

[5] See Brian Wynne, *Rationality and Ritual: The Windscale Inquiry and Nuclear Decisions in Britain* (British Society for the History of Science 1982); *id.*, 'Creating Public Alienation: Expert Cultures of Risk and Ethics' (2001) 10 *Science as Culture* 445–481; Sheila Jasanoff, 'Bridging the Two Cultures of Risk Analysis' (1993) 13 *Risk Analysis* 123–129; Maarten A. Hajer, *The Politics of Environmental Discourse: Ecological Modernization and the Policy Process* (Clarendon Press 1995); Jerome R. Ravetz, *Scientific Knowledge and its Social Problems* (Transaction Publishers 1996); Andreas Klinke and Ortwin Renn, 'A New Approach to Risk Evaluation and Management: Risk-Based, Precaution-Based, and Discourse-Based Strategies' (2000) 22 *Risk Analysis* 1071–1094; Sheila Jasanoff, *Designs on Nature: Science and Democracy in Europe and the United States* (Princeton University Press 2005); Ragnar E. Löfstedt, *Risk Management in Post-Trust Societies* (Palgrave Macmillan 2005).

[6] See for example Brian Wynne, 'Technology Assessment and Reflexive Social Learning: Observations from the Risk Field' in Arie Rip, Thomas J. Misa and Johan Schot (eds), *Managing Technology in Society: The Approach of Constructive Technology Assessment* (Pinter Publishers 1995); Jerry R. Ravetz, 'Models of Risk: An Exploration' in Matthijs Hisschemöller, Rob Hoppe, William N. Dunn and Jerry R. Ravetz (eds), *Knowledge, Power and Participation*

situations of suspected, potential hazards, which are usually associated with complex causalities, large-scale, long-term and transboundary processes. They are generally difficult to control and also transcend human sensory capacities. In such cases of uncertain risks, since scientific knowledge is presented as limited, experts, stakeholders or the public have or create doubts about the possibility or severity of hazards. Faced with these queries, paradoxically, regulators tend to turn to science and experts in order to justify their decisions. This situation we term the 'uncertainty paradox'.[7] This interaction pattern raises important questions about the role of science and scientific expertise in the regulation of innovation, trade and risks.

For example, in the field of food we may observe that the focus on science by both the new legislative framework and the regulatory authorities tends to lead to a scientification of EU food regulation.[8] This may be problematic as the question of how to deal with uncertain risk is not merely one of how to assure that the science used in EU governance is sound, but also encompasses the manner in which scientific opinions are balanced against far wider ethical and social values. This chapter seeks therefore to identify how the EU can overcome the various difficulties the EU encounters in uncertain risk regulation by examining critically the role of science and scientific expertise in both EU political and judicial decision-making. To this end, it will first examine the role of science in political decision-making (section 2). In particular it will discuss the role of EFSA and reveal how the European Commission as a risk manager and the 'driver of the food safety car'[9] tends to follow, if not to rubberstamp, the opinions of EFSA, as 'the indications-giving passenger'.[10] To better understand the regulation of food risks, it will hereby examine the nature and scope of risk assessment. As judicial review of decisions involving scientific uncertainty and complexity is

---

in Environmental Policy Analysis (Transaction Books 2001) 471–492; Harremoës *et al.*, *supra* note 3; Ortwin Renn, *Risk Governance: Towards an Integrative Approach*, IRGC White Paper No. 1, International Risk Governance Council (IRGC 2006).

[7] See Marjolein B.A. van Asselt and Ellen Vos, 'The Precautionary Principle and the Uncertainty Paradox' (2006) 9 *Journal of Risk Research* 313–336.

[8] Michelle Everson and Ellen Vos, 'The Scientification of Politics and the Politicisation of Science' in Michelle Everson and Ellen Vos (eds), *Uncertain Risks Regulated* (Routledge/Cavendish Publishing 2009) 1–17.

[9] See Ellen Vos, 'The EU Regulatory System on Food Safety: Between Trust and Safety' in Everson and Vos (eds), *ibid.*, 249–267.

[10] *Ibid.*

co-shaping the governance of uncertain risks, it will subsequently examine the difficulties EU Courts have in reviewing science-based measures (section 3). In conclusion, it will suggest how the role of risk assessment could be reconsidered (sections 4 and 5).

2. THE ROLE OF SCIENCE IN POLITICAL DECISION-MAKING BY THE EU INSTITUTIONS

2.1 Scientification of Food Regulation

The creation of EFSA in response to the BSE crisis and the resulting crisis of confidence in EU science-based decision-making has been quite a common answer to crises in the EU setting. We may observe this institutional response also in the aftermath of various other crises such as the crisis with the oil tanker *Erika*, which led to the creation of the European Maritime Agency. The creation of EFSA was indeed foremost a reaction to the problem of confidence: it aimed to offer a new institutional structure to guarantee greater independence, excellence and transparency, whilst also strengthening the scientific basis of food safety regulation. The creation of EFSA, however, also addressed other problems of a more practical nature, namely to support the data collection and preparation of scientific opinion through its own scientific staff. Moreover, through the creation of EFSA, the problem of fragmentation that existed under the old, pre-BSE committee model was addressed, thus offering a more coherent common basis for food safety. Ultimately, EFSA's creation can be understood as yet another step towards the Europeanization of science and the scientific underpinning of EU food safety regulation.[11]

Over the years EFSA has obtained a central role as science provider for EU decision-making on food issues. This is substantiated by the impressive number of tasks the European legislator has assigned EFSA. Hereby the carrying out of a risk assessment, as an obligatory and pivotal basis for EU food regulation, is key. In addition to the formulation of scientific opinions, EFSA will *inter alia* need to provide the Commission with scientific and technical support, promote and co-ordinate the development of uniform risk assessment methodologies, commission scientific studies, collect scientific and technical data, set up networks, identify

---

[11] Vos, *supra* note 9.

emerging risks and assist the Commission in crisis management.[12] With the allocation of this broad range of tasks to EFSA, the EU institutions undoubtedly indicated their desire to take science as a critical resource in food regulation. They deliberately designed EFSA as a networked agency, instead of following the example of its American counterpart, the Food and Drug Administration. Moreover, the Commission tends to closely follow EFSA's scientific opinions; with regard to the authorization of genetically modified organisms (GMOs), for example, the Commission has never departed from EFSA's opinions.[13] This dependency has been depicted by comparing the relationship between the Commission and EFSA to that of two people driving a car: a blind driver (the Commission) and a direction-giving passenger (EFSA).[14] In practice we thus observe that the strict formal separation between risk assessment and management tends to become blurred.[15]

Together this has resulted in what we have called the 'scientification' of food, and more generally risk, regulation, revealing a tendency by regulators to perceive and/or use science as an objective and neutral source to validate their decisions. And the scientific experts try to behave accordingly, although in practice they cannot live up to this classical image of science providing truth to power.[16] This scientification process, that is, the strong reliance on regulatory science as the basis for decisions, seems to be upheld even where scientific uncertainty is

---

[12] Article 23, Regulation (EC) No. 178/2002 of the European Parliament and of the Council of 28 January 2002 laying down the general principles and requirements of food law, establishing the European Food Safety Authority and laying down procedures in matters of food safety [2002] OJ L31/1.

[13] Vessela Hristova, 'Between Politics and Science: Accommodating National Diversity in GMO Regulation' in Marjolein B.A. van Asselt, Esther Versluis and Ellen Vos (eds), *Balancing between Trade and Risk: Integrating Legal and Social Science Perspectives* (Routledge 2013) 107–127; Jinhee Kim, Christoph Klika and Esther Versluis, 'Agencies as Risk Managers? Exploring the Role of EU Agencies in Authorization Procedures' in van Asselt, Versluis and Vos (eds), above, 175–196; and Madjar Navah, Esther Versluis and Marjolein B.A. van Asselt, 'The Politics of Risk Decision-Making: The Voting Behavior of the EU Member States on GMOs' in van Asselt, Versluis and Vos (eds), *supra* note 13, 128–146.

[14] Ellen Vos and Frank Wendler (eds), *Food Safety Regulation in Europe: A Comparative Institutional Analysis* (62 Ius Commune Europaeum, Intersentia 2007).

[15] Marjolein B.A. van Asselt and Ellen Vos, 'Wrestling with Uncertain Risks: EU Regulation of GMOs and the Uncertainty Paradox' (2008) 11 *Journal of Risk Research* 281–300 and Kim *et al.*, *supra* note 13.

[16] Everson and Vos, *supra* note 8.

increasingly ascertained, especially as regards the use of innovative technologies.[17]

2.2 Science as a Neutral Arbiter in Free Trade

The position of science as 'neutral arbiter' has solidified particularly in the context of the free movement of goods (including food) and trade. Internal market and free trade concerns are becoming increasingly intermingled with health and other concerns that can create barriers to free trade. In the EU and World Trade Organization (WTO) context, both Member States and the EU are increasingly being required to provide a scientific justification for any deviations from free trade in favour of interests relating to the protection of health, the environment or ethical concerns. This obligation to justify political decisions in terms of science and scientific evidence has been introduced as a means to ensure that measures adopted are inspired by genuine non-trade rather than protectionist motives and intentions. The majority of controversial cases in the ambit of the free trade versus protection of human health and the environment dilemma involve high levels of scientific uncertainty.[18] However, decision-making on controversial and/or high technology and products raises not only risk concerns, but also ethical and socio-economic questions. It is helpful to recall here the classical Wildavsky view that the regulation of innovation is always about balancing potential advantages and disadvantages in the broadest sense of the word.[19] The discourse of risk, which was once liberating as it allowed society to raise concerns pertaining to human health and in a later stage environmental health, can also be narrowing, as it masks other important societal diversity.[20] The question therefore arises whether the controversies surrounding innovation and trade can be sufficiently captured in terms of risk, or whether one needs to reframe the issue at stake.

---

[17] Van Asselt and Vos, *supra* note 15; M. Weimer, 'Risk Regulation, GMOs, and the Challenges to Deliberation in EU Governance – Politicisation and Scientification as Co-producing Trends' in Christian Joerges and Carola Glinski (eds), *The European Crisis and the Transformation of Transnational Governance* (Hart Publishing, 2014).

[18] Van Asselt, Everson and Vos, *supra* note 3.

[19] Aaron B. Wildavsky, *Searching for Safety* (Transaction 1998).

[20] Marjolein B.A. van Asselt, Tessa Fox, Esther Versluis and Ellen Vos, 'Regulating Innovation, Trade and Uncertain Risks' in van Asselt, Versluis and Vos (eds), *supra* note 13, 247–275.

2.3 The Example of GMOs

This scientification of risk regulation and the presence of the uncertainty paradox are clearly visible in various fields of risk regulation, such as GMOs and nanotechnology. For example, a case study we carried out on the authorization process of three genetically modified organisms demonstrated the central position of EFSA and scientific opinions in the decision-making process,[21] which has been confirmed by follow-up research.[22] In the three cases we examined, we observed that regulatory deadlocks occurred because no agreement pro or against import was reached in the relevant comitology committees and/or the Council (under the old comitology procedures). To avoid procedural standstill, the relevant legislative provisions ultimately empowered the Commission to adopt a decision. Despite the resistance of several Member States, the Commission could issue consents for the placing on the market of three GMOs under Directive 2001/18, merely rubberstamping EFSA's opinions.[23]

In view of the societal and political controversies in the EU pertaining to genetic modification,[24] it is striking that notwithstanding the political controversy about possible authorization of the three GMOs that we investigated, the decisions about import were ultimately taken in a technocratic manner: the Commission, following EFSA, simply authorized these products. Our analysis confirms the findings of Susanna Borrás that scientific experts continue to have a central, undisputed

---

[21] Van Asselt and Vos, *supra* note 15.

[22] See Kim *et al.*, *supra* note 13; Navah *et al.*, *supra* note 13; Laura Drott *et al.*, 'Accountability and Risk Governance: A Scenario-Informed Reflection on European Regulation of GMOs' (2013) *Journal of Risk Research* 1123–1140.

[23] Marjolein B.A. van Asselt, Ellen Vos and Bram Rooijackers, 'Science, Knowledge and Uncertainty in EU Risk Regulation' in Everson and Vos (eds), *supra* note 8, 359–388.

[24] See for example George Gaskell *et al.*, 'Biotechnology and the European Public' (2000) 18(9) *Nature Biotechnology* 935–938; George Gaskell, 'GM Foods and the Misperception of Risk Perception' (2004) 24(1) *Risk Analysis* 183–192; Les Levidow, 'Genetically Modified Crops: What Transboundary Harmonization in Europe?' in Joanne Linnerooth-Bayer, Ragnar E. Löfstedt and Gunnar Sjöstedt (eds), *Transboundary Risk Management* (Earthscan 2001) 59–90; Wynne, *supra* note 5, 445–481; Jasanoff, *supra* note 5, Les Levidow, Joseph Murphy and Susan Carr, 'Recasting Substantial Equivalence: Transatlantic Governance of GM Food' (2007) 32(1) *Science, Technology and Human Values* 26–64; Tom Horlick Jones *et al.*, *The GM Debate: Risk, Politics and Public Engagement* (Routledge 2007); Maria Lee, *EU Regulation of GMOs: Law, Decision-Making and New Technology* (Edward Elgar 2008).

position in actual EU regulation of GMOs, notwithstanding rhetoric and institutional changes after the BSE crisis.[25] It thus endorses the trend of scientification of politics and confirms the existence of the uncertainty paradox. It is exactly such technocratic division of responsibility, and associated credibility and legitimacy questions, which were the main political concern after the BSE crisis and the *raison d'être* of EFSA. In these cases the regulatory provisions sustained or even reinforced the uncertainty paradox. We argue, therefore, that the current regulatory model which evolved in the EU in the aftermath of the BSE crisis and is reinvigorated by WTO law's quest for a scientific underpinning of health or environment protection measures, privileges processes of scientification.[26] This critical reliance on science in both political and judicial decision-making, also referred to as the 'meta-legal authority of science' by Christian Joerges,[27] is commonly agreed upon by both risk regulation practitioners and scholars.

In the debate on EU GMO regulation, it is interesting to observe that most critics continue to frame EFSA's role in terms of the uncertainty paradox: EFSA is expected to resolve diverging scientific opinions and is still cast as 'a body responsible for supplying *unimpeachable* scientific advice and guidance'.[28] It is not recognized that the problems arise from the great burden placed on science as the basis for decisions.[29] Surely, we must stress that in the context of GMOs, the new approach for GMO cultivation that the Commission launched in 2010 addresses the political sensitivities of Member States that do not want to cultivate GMOs on their territory. The Commission's proposal also explicitly recognizes the need to balance between maintaining the EU system of authorizations

[25] Susanna Borrás, 'Legitimate Governance of Risk at the EU Level? The Case of Genetically Modified Organisms' (2006) 73 *Technological Forecasting and Social Change* 61–75.

[26] Van Asselt, Everson and Vos, *supra* note 3.

[27] Christian Joerges, 'Scientific Expertise in Social Regulation and the European Court of Justice: Legal Framework for Denationalised Governance Structures' in Christian Joerges, Karl-Heinz Ladeur and Ellen Vos (eds), *Integrating Scientific Expertise into Regulatory Decision-Making: National Experiences and European Innovations* (Nomos 1997) 320.

[28] Ed Randall, 'Not that Soft or Informal: A Response to Eberlein and Grande's Account of Regulatory Governance in the EU with Special Reference to the European Food Safety Authority (EFSA)' (2006) 13:3 *Journal of European Public Policy* 413, emphasis added.

[29] Les Levidow, Susan Carr and David Wield, 'European Union Regulation of Agri-biotechnology: Precautionary Links between Science, Expertise and Policy' (2005) 32:4 *Science and Public Policy* 261–276.

based on scientific assessment of health and environmental risks and the freedom of Member States to address specific national, regional or local issues raised by the cultivation of GMOs.[30] It may be wondered, though, whether this proposal is truly motivated by the recognition of the fundamental problems raised by the uncertainty paradox and hence the desire to shatter the uncertainty paradox. It does not seem coincidental that the proposed approach would free the EU institutions from being challenged before the WTO courts and confer unambiguously upon Member States themselves the responsibility to justify possible trade barriers before the WTO. Whilst today a new compromise on the proposed derogation possibility has been reached, some Member States continue to doubt the legal compatibility of this provision with both WTO law and EU internal market rules.[31]

The emphasis on science in decision-making on nanotechnology poses similar problems.[32] Although the EU regulatory provisions on nanotechnology expressly include ethical and other concerns as concerns to be taken into account in the decision-making, in practice, according to Maria Lee, this has not led to the inclusion of ethical concerns in chemicals or cosmetics regulation, and even in respect of food, decisions are framed largely around risk and safety.[33] She underlines that regulatory innovations 'fail to grapple with the basic issue, which is that conventionally we regulate only on the basis of risk. Superficial changes go nowhere when the decision is so heavily constrained by the regulatory context, dominated by a narrow approach to risk assessment.' This leads

---

30 See COM(2010) 0375 final, Proposal for a Regulation Of The European Parliament And Of The Council amending Directive 2001/18/EC as regards the possibility for the Member States to restrict or prohibit the cultivation of GMOs in their territory.

31 See for the text of the presidency compromise proposal of 14 February 2014: Council document 6528/14. See also draft minutes of the 3297th Council meeting of 3 March 2014. See also Press release 3152nd Council meeting, 9 March 2012.

32 See for similar problems regarding trade in cloned food, Maria Weimer, 'EU Risk Governance of Cloned Food: Regulatory Uncertainty between Trade and Non-trade' in van Asselt, Versluis and Vos (eds), *supra* note 13, 33–58.

33 See Maria Lee, 'Beyond Safety? The Broadening Scope of Risk Regulation' in Colm O'Cinneide (ed.), *Current Legal Problems 2009* (OUP 2010) 820.

to serious problems of accountability as decisions are taken with reference to science and risk when they are actually political.[34] This underlines the need to revisit the role of science in decision-making. We will come back to this below.

3. THE ROLE OF SCIENCE IN JUDICIAL DECISION-MAKING BY THE EU COURTS

The scientification of risk regulation is not only problematic in terms of political decision-making but also echoes in the EU court room.[35] When looking at the case law of the EU Courts,[36] we observe that these Courts treat science with the same authority that the legal frameworks prescribe and decision-makers do. Another observation is that the EU Courts, just like their counterpart courts elsewhere,[37] visibly struggle with the (scientific) technicalities of such cases. These issues are at times so complex that the question arises as to whether the EU Courts (and courts in general) have the necessary expertise and hence legitimacy to deal with such issues.[38] This therefore raises the question of how the Courts should review cases which involve (scientific) uncertainty and uncertain risks.[39]

Without doubt, the standard of review applied by the Courts when reviewing measures is of utmost importance, as it determines the allocation of regulatory powers on science-related matters. Analysis of the Court's case law on EU measures reveals that, in sharp contrast to its approach towards measures adopted by Member States, the Court has

---

[34] *Ibid.*

[35] See van Asselt and Vos, *supra* note 7; Anne-May Janssen and Marjolein B.A. van Asselt, 'The Precautionary Principle in Court: An Analysis of Post-Pfizer Case Law' in van Asselt, Versluis and Vos (eds), *supra* note 13.

[36] In this chapter we will refer to the EU Court, European Court or the Courts as encompassing both the General Court and the Court of Justice of the European Union, unless otherwise specified.

[37] Caroline E. Foster, *Science and the Precautionary Principle in International Courts and Tribunals: Expert Evidence, Burden of Proof and Finality* (Cambridge University Press 2011); Stephanie Tai, 'Uncertainty About Uncertainty: The Impact of Judicial Decisions on Assessing Scientific Uncertainty' (2008) 11:3 *Journal of Constitutional Law* 671–727.

[38] Eric Barbier de la Serre and Anne-Lise Sibony, 'Expert Evidence before the EC Courts' (2008) 45:4 *Common Market Law Review* 941.

[39] See Ellen Vos, 'EU Risk Regulation Reviewed by the European Courts' in van Asselt, Everson and Vos (eds), *supra* note 3, 213–232.

been habitually respectful of the discretionary powers of the EU institutions and has demonstrated a deferential approach towards measures adopted by them.[40] Today, notwithstanding the Court's insistence on the limits of its review of measures involving (scientific) uncertainty, as it is 'not entitled to substitute its assessment of the facts for that of the Community institutions',[41] it increasingly pays attention to the science underlying the decision-making.[42] We can thus observe a change in the Court's behaviour from a rather deferential to a more proactive, 'modern'[43] approach to setting the standard of review, paying much more attention to the question of whether authorities relied on a sufficiently rigorous assessment and applying the established grounds for review with much more intensity than before.[44]

This has resulted in the Court stretching its review also to include the adequacy and quality of the informational basis of science-based measures, although formally still upholding the same wording and examining whether the exercise of discretionary powers by the EU institutions 'is

---

[40] Joanne Scott and Ellen Vos, 'The Juridification of Uncertainty: Observations on the Ambivalence of the Precautionary Principle within the EU and the WTO' in Christian Joerges and Renaud Dehousse (eds), *Good Governance in Europe's Integrated Market* (OUP 2002) 253–286. This would link up with the view of McNelis who, in her comparison of the WTO and EU Courts, argues that the 'real standard of review lies in the relationship between judging entity and the actor "judged"'. See Natalie McNelis, 'The Role of the Judge in the EU and WTO: Lessons from the BSE and Hormone Cases' in Thomas Cottier and Petros C. Mavroidis (eds), *The Role of the Judge in International Trade Regulation* (University of Michigan Press 2003) 234. See Janssen and van Asselt, *supra* note 35.

[41] Case C-269/90 *Technische Universität München v Hauptzollampt München-Mitte* [1991] ECR I-5469; Case T-13/99 *Pfizer Animal Health SA v Council* [2002] ECR II-03305, para. 169.

[42] See, for instance, Case C-331/88 *The Queen v The Minister for Agriculture, Fisheries and Food and the Secretary of State for Health, ex parte: Fedesa and other (Fedesa)* [1990] ECR I-4023; Case C-405/92 *Établissements Armand Mondiet SA v Armement Islais SARL (Mondiet)* [1993] ECR I-6133; Case C-280/93 *Germany v Council* [1994] ECR I-4973. See Elen Stokes, 'The EC Courts' Contribution in Refining the Parameters of Precaution' (2008) 11:4 *Journal of Risk Research* 491–507.

[43] Paul P. Craig, *EU Administrative Law* (OUP 2006) 446–447.

[44] Damian Chalmers, Gareth Davies and Giorgio Monti, *European Union Law* (Cambridge University Press 2010) 898.

vitiated by a manifest error or a misuse of power'.[45] This new or modern approach of the Court, we argue, is very much to be applauded. Yet, cases like *Pfizer* provoke concerns as to whether the Court is not going beyond the limits of its judicial function, by judging also on the science. In *Pfizer* the Court had to rule on the validity of the EU ban on the use of four antibiotics as growth promoters in feedingstuffs.[46] Upholding the EU ban, the Court arguably went further in this case than beyond its role of informational catalyst and immersed itself in the scientific merits of the case, acting as a kind of 'super-expert', herewith clearly overstepping its mandate.[47]

As Elen Stokes[48] argues, as a consequence the Court is increasingly dictating the parameters of science and risk assessment. *Pfizer* illustrates the resonance of the scientification of EU risk regulation in the judicial review of relevant measures. Whilst the Court's more intense standard of review is to be welcomed, as set forth above, we argue against a role as a 'super-expert' for the Court and its becoming immersed in the quagmires of scientific uncertainty and complexity that may surround a dispute. It cannot, and should not want to, play this role.

Scott and Sturm's re-conceptualization of the Court's role as an informational catalyst would be of great importance in the formulation of a normative framework for how the Court should operate in the face of uncertainty and complexity, and hence review cases that involve the regulation of uncertain risks.[49] This would suggest that Courts need to actively engage in normatively motivated and accountable inquiry, which forces decision-makers to reveal and motivate all (science-based) reasoning in their decisions. This would stimulate a development towards better-informed and motivated decisions which do not escape judicial scrutiny. Such an informational catalyst function of Courts thus could circumvent situations whereby regulators would, through a light judicial review, be encouraged to support scientification of political decisions. Proper explanation of reasons for the adoption of a decision would allow that science-based reasons can also be challenged, both in the political or

---

45 See for example Case C-157/96 *National Farmers' Union and Others* [1998] ECR I-2211, para. 39, referring to a classic case in this respect, ECJ, Case 98/78 *Racke v Hauptzollamt Mainz* [1979] ECR 69, para. 5.

46 Case T-13/99, *supra* note 41.

47 Van Asselt and Vos, *supra* note 7.

48 See Stokes, *supra* note 42, 491–507.

49 Joanne Scott and Susan P. Sturm, 'Courts as Catalysts: Rethinking the Judicial Role in New Governance' (2007) 13:3 *Columbia Journal of European Law* 565–594.

judicial process,[50] because, as the Court acknowledged in *Pfizer*, 'scientific legitimacy is not a sufficient basis for the exercise of public authority'.[51]

As Courts need to actively engage in normatively motivated and accountable inquiry on the decision-making process, including the scientific underpinning, it seems necessary that the judges (better) understand science.[52] The question therefore arises as to whether Courts need to be assisted by Court-appointed experts or whether there is a need for specialized Courts in order to better understand the underlying science, but not to adjudicate it.[53] Until now the Courts have been reluctant to use Court-appointed experts in cases of scientific uncertainty and complexity as they fear relinquishing power to external experts and the delegation of adjudication to experts.[54] However, 'since, by definition, the EC Courts do not master the technical discipline at issue, there could be no guarantee that their opinion on the existence of a manifest error is not purely arbitrary'.[55] This, together with findings in the literature that the case law of the Courts, especially in trade mark cases, is full of examples of verdicts based on the EU judges' personal experience,[56] would argue in favour of having such experts informing the EU Courts. Yet, the use of Court-appointed experts would further encourage a scientification of judicial review and might give rise to a 'battle of experts', outcomes which have surely to be avoided.[57] These questions therefore still beg further reflection.

---

50 Lee, *supra* note 33, 276–277.

51 Case T-13/99, *supra* note 41, para. 201.

52 Scallen and Wiethoff emphasize the importance of an expert's ethos whereby 'analyzing and understanding the conceptual frameworks within which expert witnesses express their opinions is as essential as evaluating the basic reliability of any scientific theories on which they rely'. Eileen A. Scallen and William E. Wiethoff, 'The Ethos of Expert Witnesses: Confusing the Admissibility, Sufficiency and Credibility of Expert Testimony' (1998) 49 *Hastings Law Journal* 1168.

53 See for a discussion Barbier de la Serre and Sibony, *supra* note 38.

54 *Ibid.*, *supra* note 38, 949. In an American study amongst 108 judges, all 108 judges disfavoured court-appointed experts. See 'The 1997 Forum for State Court Judge' (1998) *The Roscoe Pound Foundation*, Washington.

55 Barbier de la Serre and Sibony, *supra* note 38, 957.

56 *Ibid.*, 959.

57 See Vos, *supra* note 3.

4. THE ROLE OF RISK ASSESSMENT REVISITED

The above made clear that the view of science as 'neutral arbiter' or 'the meta-legal authority of science' in legal frameworks, political decision-making and judicial review is problematic, particularly in cases of scientific uncertainty. For it is clear that science cannot provide answers to the problems and/or conflicts which have arisen in situations where the science is uncertain.[58] In order to defeat the uncertainty paradox, it is therefore necessary to revisit the role of risk assessment in the whole process. To this end we need to reflect on different political dimensions of risk assessment and to determine who carries out the risk assessment, what precisely is assessed and how the risk assessment is carried out.[59] Although these queries may look technical or institutional at first sight, they appear to be highly politically significant issues in practice. Hereby it should be realized that the decision on which risk assessment approach is taken determines which risk aspects and concerns are assessed.[60] Tessa Fox *et al.*, for example, have indicated that issues pertaining to the relevance of dosage as a measure of risk and to the interactions of chemicals also raise questions about which risk assessment approach is adequate.[61] A related question is what information will be used in the risk assessment. In a multi-actor context, different types of evidence are brought to the fore, and the evaluation of what counts as evidence may differ significantly. It is clear that those risk concerns that are, or are not, dealt with in the risk assessment frame the political debate.[62] It seems therefore appropriate to consider risk assessment, providing for the scientific basis of any EU risk management measure, in various cases where the EU is required to act upon risk, to be a rather political act.[63]

---

[58] See for example the various contributions to van Asselt, Versluis and Vos (eds), *supra* note 13.

[59] Marjolein B.A. van Asselt, Tessa Fox, Esther Versluis and Ellen Vos, 'Regulating Innovation, Trade and Uncertain Risks' in van Asselt, Versluis and Vos (eds), *supra* note 13, 247–275.

[60] *Ibid.*

[61] Tessa Fox, Esther Versluis and Marjolein B.A. van Asselt, 'Regulating the use of Bisphenol A in Baby and Children's Products in the European Union: Trade Implications of an Uncertain Risk' in van Asselt, Versluis and Vos (eds), *supra* note 13, 147–172.

[62] *Ibid.*

[63] Marjolein B.A. van Asselt, Tessa Fox, Esther Versluis and Ellen Vos, 'Regulating Innovation, Trade and Uncertain Risks' in van Asselt, Versluis and Vos (eds), *supra* note 13, 247–275.

This is the more so in view of the fact that agencies like EFSA at times do more than a mere risk assessment[64] and that there is no recognized risk assessment approach in the EU legal order (if this is at all possible).[65] Moreover, legal authorities and regimes tend to favour positivistic assessment approaches: the risk is defined as a function of probability and effect, and both dimensions are considered to be calculable on the basis of statistics. As a consequence, today risk assessment tends to be past-based instead of future-oriented. Yet the presence of uncertainty requires that the focus should shift 'from the question of probability of the occurrence to a known hazard to the question of defining a potential hazard and its nature in the first place'.[66] In such instances, risk assessment should be more future-oriented, which requires an implicit or explicit scenario approach.[67] Whether or not a particular risk dossier is qualified as uncertain should thus have consequences for which risk assessments are accepted in the policy and legal arenas. How uncertainty is addressed in the risk assessment is critically important in the political and legal arenas.[68] Where scientific experts, for example, do not discuss uncertainties when mapping the decision situation[69] the Commission will not be adequately informed and hence will not be able to formulate a viable response to the problem. Hence the legally required risk assessment carried out in the initial decision-making stage is of critical political importance.[70] Janssen and Van Asselt even argue that as

---

64 Van Asselt and Vos, *supra* note 7.

65 Nicolas de Sadeleer, 'The Precautionary Principle in European Community Health and Environment Law: Sword or Shield for the Nordic Countries?' in Nicolas de Sadeleer (ed.), *Implementing the Precautionary Principle: Approaches from the Nordic Countries, EU and USA* (Earthscan 2007). See also Janssen and van Asselt, *supra* note 35.

66 See Weimer, *supra* note 32.

67 See Marjolein B.A. van Asselt, Susan A. van 't Klooster, Philip W.F. van Notten and Livia A. Smits, *Foresight in Action: Developing Policy-Oriented Scenarios* (Earthscan 2010).

68 See the various contributions to van Asselt, Versluis and Vos (eds), *supra* note 13.

69 Harrie F.J. Van Dijk, Eric van Rongen, Gilbert Eggermont, Erik Lebret, Wiebe E. Bijker and Daniëlle R.M. Timmermans, 'The Role of Scientific Advisory Bodies in Precaution-Based Risk Governance Illustrated with the Issue of Uncertain Health Effects of Electromagnetic Fields' (2001) 14:4 *Journal of Risk Research*, special issue 'Uncertainty, Precaution and Risk Management', 451–466.

70 Boryana Ivanova and Marjolein B.A. van Asselt, 'Pre-empting Precaution: GMO Trade Conflicts, Uncertainty Intolerant Risk Assessment and Precaution-Based Management' in van Asselt, Versluis and Vos (eds), *supra* note 13, 81–104

soon as formal regulatory experts write 'something' down on the risk issue at stake in a particular policy-making phase, it will be treated and accepted as a risk assessment in the policy and legal realm. 'The fact that experts have been asked to consider the risks seems to be sufficient [to qualify it] as … risk assessment.'[71]

Moreover, it is vital to understand that 'scientific evaluation is just the starting point for a reflective discourse'.[72] We therefore suggest that risk assessment should be recognized as one of the elements of regulatory decisions in addition to the 'other legitimate factors' such as social, ethical and political concerns, at the national, European or WTO level. As pointed out above, in the EU (and WTO) legal frameworks, the requirement of risk assessment serves to guarantee that measures to protect 'public goods' are not used as disguised discriminatory restrictions to trade. The underlying assumption hereby is that risk assessment can serve as an objective arbiter or, as Motta phrased it, 'science [is assigned] the role of mediating between … economy and politics'.[73] Above we pointed out that this is rather illusionary. The obligation to carry out a risk assessment and the ways in which it is currently satisfied and endorsed make it more difficult to respond to societal concerns and therefore also to accommodate diversity in decisions pertaining to traded products and technology. Therefore, whilst it is true that risk assessment and, more generally, scientific expertise can, in Sheila Jasanoff's terms, 'inject much needed competence and critical intelligence into a regulatory system that otherwise seems all too vulnerable to the demands of politics',[74] we will need to rethink its role in the legislative frameworks, legal requirements and standards of review.

5. CONCLUDING REMARKS

Today we can observe an ongoing trend of scientification of both risk regulation and judicial review of science-based measures. We have documented the scientification of risk regulation in a number of policy

---

[71] Janssen and van Asselt, *supra* note 35.

[72] Frank Rodrigues, 'The Scientification of Participation' in van Asselt, Versluis and Vos (eds), *supra* note 13, 233.

[73] Renata C. Motta, 'Risky Politics: A Sociological Analysis of the WTO Panel on Biotechnological Products' in van Asselt, Versluis and Vos (eds), *supra* note 13, 59–80.

[74] Sheila Jasanoff, *The Fifth Branch: Science Advisers as Policymakers* (Harvard University Press 1990) 209.

areas, in particular relating to the free movement of goods, such as foods, GMOs and products involving nanotechnology. This trend is problematic as, we argue, science alone cannot provide answers to the problems and/or conflicts which arise in situations where the science is uncertain. This chapter has emphasized the need to take other factors into account.[75] We argue that in order to defy the uncertainty paradox, it is necessary to recognize that risk assessment is an act of a political nature, whilst at the same time to understand that risk assessment is one (though very important) element in decision-making. In the current regulatory arrangements, both at the EU and the WTO level, risk assessment is an institutionalized necessary step before regulators can engage in risk management: risk management measures need to be preceded by a risk assessment. This also holds for the risk assessments by EFSA on GMOs, as we set forth above. The risk management phase is often reduced to rubberstamping the risk assessment, even if the political support for the decision is lacking. The recognition that science is not a monolithic kind of activity and that a risk assessment is not neutral, but is a social construct and has political dimensions, is also critical for the reflection on the role of EU court rooms when reviewing EU measures involving scientific uncertainty. Hereby, it is important to take into account that the EU Courts should respect the discretionary powers of the EU decision-makers and make sure that they remain Courts and do not become institutions of science.

Above we have observed that the legal frameworks put in place determine the role and position of science and the room for uncertainty in risk regulation. The recognition of the political dimensions of risk assessment, in our view, will increase the opportunities in the political and legal realms to be (more) responsive to uncertainty. We suggest that the role of experts in risk assessment should be understood in that they provide information about uncertainty, which might help non-experts to understand uncertainty and to evaluate the impact of uncertainty on decisions as well as the political importance of uncertainty. Importantly, this needs further reflection and necessitates further interdisciplinary legal and social sciences research into EU risk regulation.

---

[75] Discussion on the need to change participatory structure falls beyond the scope of this chapter. Surely also appropriate participatory structures would be put into place. See on that issue, for example, Rodrigues, *supra* note 72.

7. The emergence of EU lifestyle risk regulation: new trends in evidence, proportionality and judicial review

Alberto Alemanno and Amandine Garde

I. INTRODUCTION

The EU has over the last two decades witnessed the enactment of a vast body of legislation to protect the environment as well as individuals' health and safety.[1] The growing involvement of the EU in the government of risk reflects the powers it derives from the EU Treaties in the field of both environmental protection and public health, and the ensuing Treaty-sanctioned imperatives to ensure a 'high level of protection' in both these policy areas.[2]

There is an emerging area of risk policy intervention in which both the EU and its Member States are increasingly interested in taking action: lifestyle risks.[3] As a global consensus has emerged on the urgency to

[1] Alberto Alemanno, 'The Shaping of Risk Regulation by Community Courts' (2008) 18 *The Jean Monnet Working Papers*. It is notable that Joerges and Dehousse in their pioneering works have also discussed this phenomenon in terms of 'social regulation': Christian Joerges, 'Scientific Expertise in Social Regulation and the European Court of Justice' in Christian Joerges, Karl-Heinz Ladeur and Ellen Vos (eds), *Integrating Scientific Expertise into Regulatory Decision-Making* (Nomos 1997) 296; Christian Joerges and Ernst-Ulrich Petersmann, *Constitutionalism, Multilevel Trade Governance and Social Regulation* (Hart 2006) 491 *et seq*.

[2] Articles 9, 11, 114(3) and 168(1) TFEU.

[3] For an introduction to this notion, see Simon Planzer and Alberto Alemanno, 'Lifestyle Risks: Conceptualizing an Emerging Category of Research' (2010) 4 *European Journal of Risk Regulation* 337. For a detailed analysis and systematisation of the emerging EU lifestyle risk policy, see Alberto Alemanno and Amandine Garde, 'The Emergence of an EU Lifestyle Policy – the Case of Alcohol, Tobacco and Unhealthy Diets' (2013) 50:6 *Common Market Law Review* 1475.

tackle non-communicable diseases (NCDs) such as diabetes, heart disease and stroke, chronic respiratory disease and cancer,[4] the need to regulate the major lifestyle risk factors associated with these largely preventable diseases has been acknowledged by both the EU and its Member States.[5] The four main risk factors are: tobacco consumption, the harmful use of alcohol, unhealthy diets and physical inactivity. Despite the fact that NCDs account for nearly 86 per cent of deaths and 77 per cent of the disease burden in Europe,[6] the EU's awareness of the threat posed by their growing burden on the EU's economy and the well-being[7] of its citizens is relatively recent. After having promoted the free movement of tobacco, alcohol and food, the EU's stance towards these products is shifting to meet another policy objective: eradicating their consumption (for tobacco) or limiting their excessive consumption (for alcoholic beverages and food high in fat, sugar or salt). The move away from a free movement rationale to meet public health concerns raises questions regarding the new frontiers of EU risk regulatory action.[8] As a result of the legal, as well as the ethical and legitimacy issues that it raises,[9] this emerging policy of lifestyle risk regulation is likely to be particularly contested and, as a result, lead the EU Courts to delineate the boundaries of legitimate EU (and national) action. This is particularly so given the marked shift in recent case law towards more engagement with

---

[4] See the Political Declaration of the High Level Meeting on the Prevention and Control of NCDs (A/66/L.1) which the UN General Assembly adopted unanimously on 19–20 September 2011: <http://www.un.org/ga/search/view_doc.asp?symbol=A/66/L.1> (all websites in this chapter were accessed 15 May 2015).

[5] Council of the European Union, Council Conclusions: *Closing Health Gaps within the EU through Concerted Action to Promote Healthy Lifestyle Behaviours* (2011) 1–2 December.

[6] WHO, *Global Status Report on Non-Communicable Diseases* (2011) Geneva.

[7] Under Article 3(1), 'the Union's aim is to promote peace, its values and the well-being of its peoples'.

[8] Alberto Alemanno and Amandine Garde, 'The Prevention of Non-communicable Diseases in the European Union' in Tania Voon, Andrew Mitchell and Jonathan Liberman, *Regulating Tobacco, Alcohol and Unhealthy Foods: The Legal Issues* (Routledge 2014).

[9] See, for example, Riccardo Rebonato, *Taking Liberties – A Critical Examination of Libertarian Paternalism* (Palgrave Macmillan 2012).

standards of proof, as opposed to the deference traditionally granted in the past to both EU and national policymakers.[10]

This chapter aims to sketch out and discuss some of the major legal challenges raised by the emerging EU lifestyle risk policy. After briefly reconstructing the evolution of this policy and how it has interacted with the lifestyle policies of Member States (section II), it focuses on the proportionality review applied to both EU and national measures by examining in particular the role of evidence in lifestyle intervention (section III). As both EU and Member State lifestyle interventions are subject to a proportionality scrutiny, this chapter aims to identify the evidence required to have measures adopted at EU or national level upheld under EU law. In so doing, it will not only distinguish the evidence burden imposed on the EU and its Member States, but it will also discuss how this comes into play in relation to both *ex ante* (standard-setting) and *ex post* (judicial review) scenarios.

II. THE EVOLUTION OF THE EU'S LIFESTYLE RISK POLICY AND ITS CONSTITUTIONAL LIMITS

In the last decade, the EU has adopted several measures aimed at reducing the impact of the four main NCD risk factors: smoking, excessive alcohol consumption, unhealthy diets and physical inactivity. In line with World Health Organization (WHO) recommendations, these measures recognize that NCDs can only be dealt with effectively if a broad range of sectors that impact on the different aspects of our daily lives are involved in the NCD agenda. After contextualizing the EU's intervention to prevent and control NCDs within the recommendations of the WHO (1), the discussion will focus on how EU intervention has interacted with the intervention of Member States in this field of risk regulation (2).

---

[10] For some recent illustrations, see Niamh Nic Shuibhne and Marsela Maci, 'Proving Public Interest: The Growing Impact of Evidence in Free Movement Case Law' (2013) 50:4 *Common Market Law Review* 965–1005; Alberto Alemanno, 'Case C-79/09, *Gowan Comércio Internacional e Serviços Lda v Ministero Della Salute*, Judgment of the Court of Justice (Second Chamber) of 22 December 2010' (2011) 48:4 *CMLR* 1329; Ittai Bar-Siman-Tov, 'The Puzzling Resistance to Judicial Review of the Legislative Process' (2001) 91 *Boston University Law Review* 1915; Alberto Alemanno, 'The Evidence-Based Judicial Reflex: A Response to Bar-Siman-Tov's Semiprocedural Review' (2013) 1:2 *Theory and Practice of Legislation* 327–340.

1. Towards an EU Policy on Lifestyle Risk Regulation?

a. Developments at global level

In September 2011, the UN General Assembly adopted a Political Declaration on the Prevention and Control of NCDs which recommended the adoption of a 'regulatory mix' of cost-effective, population-wide interventions to reduce the impact of the main NCD risk factors.[11] The UN Political Declaration significantly increased the momentum initiated by the 2008–2013 WHO NCD Action Plan to adopt a more transversal approach covering all four major NCD risk factors.[12] In May 2013, the Sixty-sixth World Health Assembly unanimously approved the Global Action Plan for the prevention and control of NCDs for 2013–2020 which the WHO had developed in consultation with Member States.[13] The NCD Global Action Plan complements WHO strategies on NCD risk factors: tobacco, with the adoption in 2003 of the first International health law treaty, the Framework Convention on Tobacco Control (FCTC);[14] unhealthy diets and physical inactivity, with the adoption of the global strategy on diet and physical activity in 2004[15] and the adoption of a set of recommendations on the marketing of food and non-alcoholic beverages to children in 2010;[16] and alcohol abuse, with the adoption of the global strategy to reduce the harmful use of alcohol also in 2010.[17]

These documents, which collectively contribute to the emergence of a global policy for NCD prevention and control, share important features. First, they highlight that a preventive approach has the potential to reverse existing NCD trends in the longer term by influencing the population's lifestyle through the creation of a supportive environment. This is particularly true not only for children but also in general in relation to all addictive habits (not least tobacco, alcohol and perhaps even sugar). Secondly, NCD prevention and control policies must be

---

11 <http://www.who.int/entity/nmh/events/un_ncd_summit2011/political_declaration_en.pdf>. This was only the second time in UN history that the General Assembly had met to discuss a health issue (the previous issue discussed being AIDS in 2001).

12 <http://www.who.int/nmh/publications/9789241597418/en/>.

13 The Global Action Plan includes a Global Monitoring Framework which lays down specific targets to be met by 2025: <http://www.who.int/nmh/en/>.

14 <http://www.who.int/fctc/en/>.

15 <http://www.who.int/dietphysicalactivity/en/>.

16 <http://www.who.int/dietphysicalactivity/marketing-food-to-children/en/>.

17 <http://www.who.int/substance_abuse/activities/gsrhua/en/>

based on sound, reliable evidence. Consequently, governments and other relevant stakeholders should continue to build on the foundations laid down by previous research findings and continue to finance research supporting intervention at all stages of the policy cycle, from policy development to policy implementation to policy monitoring and policy evaluation. Thirdly, emphasis is placed on the need to adopt multi-sectoral, multi-level and multi-stakeholder strategies. This vocabulary has become a common feature of the thinking on NCD prevention and control. The multi-sectoral component of NCD prevention and control strategies recognizes that tackling NCDs entails the integration of a broad range of policies across the entire policy spectrum: from health, but also consumer, agricultural, food, trade, media, education, sport, employment and transport policies. Only a coordinated intervention from all relevant sectors may achieve the objectives of the NCD Action Plan. Similarly, only a multi-level approach, with mechanisms ensuring effective co-ordination between the different levels of intervention, may durably reverse the current surge of NCDs, as discussed below. Furthermore, the multifactorial nature of NCDs and the consequent need for a multi-sectoral, multi-level regulatory approach call for the involvement of a wide range of stakeholders in the NCD debate, including public authorities, civil society representatives and private actors from the relevant industries (subject to the need to avoid undue influence and conflicts of interest).

b. Towards an EU lifestyle risk regulation policy?

The momentum to address the burden of NCDs at EU level gathered in the 1990s resulted both from the pressing warnings of the international and the scientific communities and from the expressed acknowledgement that the EU had an important role to play in public health matters. More specifically, the introduction of a chapter on public health marked a turning point in the EU's approach to public health issues, not least as a result of the obligation which Article 168 TFEU imposes on the EU to ensure a high level of public health in all its policy areas.[18] This, in turn, led to the adoption of two EU programmes in the field of public health

[18] This obligation was further reinforced with the introduction, by the Lisbon Treaty, of Article 9 TFEU: 'in defining and implementing its policies and activities, the Union shall take into account requirements linked to the promotion of a high level of employment, the guarantee of adequate social protection, the fight against social exclusion, and a high level of education, training and protection of human health'.

for the periods of 2003–2008[19] and 2008–2013.[20] These programmes share the objective

> to promote health and prevent disease through addressing health determinants across all policies and activities',[21] not least 'by preparing and implementing strategies and measures, including those related to public awareness, on lifestyle related health determinants, such as nutrition, physical activity, tobacco, alcohol, drugs and other substances and on mental health'[22] and 'by tackling health determinants … , creating supportive environments for healthy lifestyles and preventing disease'.[23]

After several calls from the Council for EU action on NCDs,[24] the EU adopted three strategies intended to tackle the major NCD risk factors more comprehensively and support its citizens in improving their lifestyles: the EU Alcohol Strategy (2006),[25] the Obesity Prevention White Paper (2007)[26] and a Council Recommendation on smoke-free environments (2009)[27] which complements the adoption of the 2001 Tobacco Products Directive[28] and 2003 Tobacco Advertising Directive.[29] These three areas of EU intervention share several common features: they are intended to promote enabling environments more conducive to healthy lifestyles, and they recognize the need for a multi-sectoral, multi-level,

---

[19] Decision 1786/2002 of the European Parliament and the Council [2002] OJ L271/1.

[20] Decision 1350/2007 of the European Parliament and the Council [2007] OJ L301/3.

[21] Article 2(2)(c) of Decision 1786/2002 [2002] OJ L271/1.

[22] Para. 3(1) of the Annex of Decision 1786/2002 [2002] OJ L271/1.

[23] Article 2(2) and point 2.2 of the Annex of Decision 1350/2007 [2007] OJ L301/3. See also the *White Paper Together for Health: A Strategic Approach for the EU 2008–2013*, COM(2007) 630 final.

[24] Some of these calls have focused on one specific risk factor, whilst others have tended to be more horizontal in nature, targeting all risk factors. Examples of the latter type include: the Council Conclusions of December 2003 on Healthy Lifestyles; the Council Conclusions of June 2004 on Promoting Heart Health; and the Council Conclusions of June 2006 on the Promotion of Healthy Lifestyles and the Prevention of Type II Diabetes.

[25] COM(2006) 625 final.

[26] COM(2007) 279 final. For an assessment of the EU's obesity prevention strategy, see Amandine Garde, *EU Law and Obesity Prevention* (Kluwer Law International 2010).

[27] [2009] OJ C296/4.

[28] Directive 2001/37 [2001] OJ L194/26.

[29] Directive 2003/33 [2003] OJ L152/16.

multi-stakeholder approach. However, EU intervention has varied significantly in nature, scope and intensity, depending on the risk factor under consideration. If it has adopted a strong command-and-control approach in relation to tobacco control, it has proven extremely reluctant to intervene in relation to the excessive use of alcoholic beverages, with its nutrition and obesity prevention policy falling somewhere between these two extremes.

EU tobacco control efforts are marked by a strong regulatory involvement from the EU, coupled with recommendations to Member States and EU-wide anti-smoking campaigns. In this field, the EU has not hesitated to invoke its duty to mainstream public health into all EU policies to push the EU agenda, as illustrated by debates that accompanied the revision of the Tobacco Products Directive. The EU has also become a party to the FCTC, thus becoming an actor alongside its 28 Member States on the public health scene at global level.[30]

Even though the EU Alcohol Strategy entrusts Member States with the adoption of comprehensive multi-sectoral strategies, very few EU harmonizing rules have been adopted to date to combat alcohol-related harm. The Audiovisual Media Services Directive constitutes an exception, in that it lays down rules on the content of alcohol promotions in audiovisual media services.[31] These provisions are nonetheless extremely weak, and most Member States have relied on the minimum harmonization clause contained in the Directive to adopt stricter measures to better protect the health of their citizens – leading in turn to a high degree of fragmentation of the internal market.[32] Notwithstanding the fact that an effective multi-sectoral, multi-level strategy calls for EU intervention when policies have clear cross-border implications, the Union has responded to the calls for more robust EU intervention by reiterating that the primary responsibility for health matters lies with Member States – a response very much at odds with the approach the Commission has adopted in the field of tobacco control.[33] The EU has

---

[30] The EU has recently undertaken to sign, ratify and implement the FCTC Protocol at EU level. The FCTC Protocol to Eliminate Illicit Trade in Tobacco Products was opened for signature on 10 January 2013 and is available at: <http://www.who.int/fctc/protocol/about/en/>.

[31] Articles 9(1)(e) and 22 of Directive 2010/13 [2010] OJ L95/17.

[32] Oliver Bartlett and Amandine Garde, 'Time to Seize the (Red) Bull by the Horns: The EU's Failure to Protect Children from Alcohol and Unhealthy Food Marketing' (2013) 4 *European Law Review* 498.

[33] In its First Implementation Report, published in September 2009, the Commission praised the EU Alcohol and Health Forum: <http://ec.europa.eu/

been much more enthusiastic about facilitating the exchange of best practice and the adoption of self-regulatory standards. In 2007, it set up the European Alcohol and Health Forum that gathers a broad range of members, from industry operators to consumer, youth and public health organizations. The innovative characteristic of the Forum is to require that every one of its now 70 members commits to the adoption of at least one specific, concrete commitment to help fight alcohol-related harm, which are then made publicly available on a dedicated database.[34] The EU has also set up the Committee on National Alcohol Policy and Action for the coordination and further development of alcohol policies across the EU. Its work places particular emphasis on the identification and dissemination of good practice to support national policies. It is composed of delegates of Member State governments, together with observers from EFTA countries and the WHO.[35]

The approach the EU has adopted in the field of nutrition lies between the approaches it has adopted in relation to tobacco control and the fight against the harmful use of alcohol. For years, EU food law was characterized by an emphasis on food safety rather than nutrition issues.[36] Over the last eight years, however, the growing burden of NCDs has contributed to a significant re-evaluation of the EU's initial position, and the EU has developed a nutrition strategy, culminating in the publication in 2007 of the Obesity Prevention White Paper.[37] This strategy sets out an integrated EU approach to reduce ill health resulting from poor nutrition, overweight and obesity, which is characterized by a combination of both regulation and self-regulation. It is much more forthcoming than the EU Alcohol Strategy in identifying the policies in which the EU has a clear role to play, including through the adoption of binding rules if necessary. This difference suggests that the Commission envisages a stronger EU involvement in relation to nutrition and physical activity than in relation to alcoholic beverages, as demonstrated by the

health/archive/ph_determinants/life_style/alcohol/documents/alcohol_progress.pdf>. The second report, which was due in 2012, has still not been published, though the EU published, on 9 August 2013, a study whose purpose was to assess the added value of an EU strategy to support Member States in reducing alcohol-related harm: <http://ec.europa.eu/health/alcohol/docs/report_assessment_eu_alcohol_strategy_2012_en.pdf>.

34 <http://ec.europa.eu/health/alcohol/forum/index_en.htm>.

35 <http://ec.europa.eu/health/alcohol/events/index_en.htm#anchor1>.

36 Caoimhin MacMaolain, *EU Food Law; Protecting Consumers and Health in a Common Market* (Hart Publishing 2007) 223–224.

37 COM(2007) 279 final.

range of food information rules it has adopted over the years and which are discussed below.[38] Nevertheless, a significant part of EU activity in the field of nutrition has occurred via the EU Platform on Nutrition, Health and Physical Activity. The Platform, set up in 2005, served as a model for the EU Forum on Alcohol and Health. Its functioning is therefore identical: it is a multi-stakeholder forum that requires that each of its 33 members adopts at least one commitment to participate in the Platform's activities.[39] To facilitate the exchange of best practice between the EU and Member States, the Commission also coordinates a High Level group on nutrition, gathering representatives of the 28 EU Member States as well as Norway and Switzerland.[40] The High Level group and the Platform meet together regularly to improve the coordination of their activities.

This brief overview shows that the EU has become increasingly aware of the mounting pressure of NCDs on the EU's economy and the well-being of its citizens, even though the approaches which it has developed to address the four main NCD risk factors have varied significantly in relation to their scope and their intensity, as well as the means of intervention on which the EU has relied.

2. The Nature of EU Regulatory Intervention and its Interaction between EU and National Lifestyle Policy Interventions

This section focuses more specifically on the regulatory instruments the EU has relied upon to promote healthier lifestyles in the EU and how EU regulatory intervention has interacted with regulatory intervention at national level. This question is all the more important as a clear consensus has emerged that effective NCD prevention and control strategies must be 'multi-level': the global operation of the major players of the food, tobacco and alcohol industries calls for a response at global and regional levels, whilst local cultures, circumstances and consumption patterns call for a response at national and local levels. It is therefore necessary to inquire not only about which regulatory intervention should be adopted to reverse current NCD trends (a), but also about the most appropriate level for such intervention (b).

---

[38] See in particular Regulation 1169/2011 on the provision of food information to consumers, [2011] OJ L304/18, and Regulation 1924/2006 on nutrition and health claims made on foods, [2006] OJ L404/9, as amended.

[39] <http://ec.europa.eu/health/nutrition_physical_activity/platform/index_en>.

[40] <http://ec.europa.eu/health/nutrition_physical_activity/high_level_group/index_en.htm>.

a. The nature of EU regulatory intervention

Providing consumers with information is necessary to empower them to make healthy choices and take responsibility for their consumption choices. Labelling rules have therefore been at the heart of the EU lifestyle policy. However, the 'information paradigm' has some limits, and the EU has developed other forms of lifestyle intervention to complement its information rules, including marketing bans, measures affecting product availability and fiscal measures.[41]

Information requirements and labelling rules Requiring that consumers be provided with specific information about a product or a service is a regulatory technique that has enjoyed considerable popularity in the development of EU measures affecting the protection of consumers' interests. The 'information paradigm', which is at the heart of the EU Consumer Strategies for 2007–2013[42] and 2012–2014,[43] places the onus on consumers to decide what is good for them and their families, expecting them to read the information and process it whilst taking their personal circumstances into account. The provision of information is seen as a compromise: protection is provided as a result of the introduction of duties on traders to inform consumers of the qualities of their goods and services, whilst avoiding intrusive controls, such as bans on particular types of contract, which may unduly diminish consumer choice.[44] Rather than banning the marketing of a given product because of its nicotine, alcohol or high sugar, fat or salt content, consumers are informed about this content, so that they can decide whether and, if so, how often they should consume this product. Interference with personal freedom is therefore limited: in a society where individuals are autonomous and

---

[41] Due to space constraints, our purpose here is to highlight the main areas of EU regulatory intervention rather than provide an exhaustive discussion of what the EU could be doing to promote healthier lifestyles. For a more systematic categorization of EU measures, see Alberto Alemanno and Amandine Garde, *Regulating Lifestyles in Europe: How to Prevent and Control Non-Communicable Disease Associated with Tobacco, Alcohol and Unhealthy Diets?* (2013:7 SIEPS 2013).

[42] COM(2007) 99 final.

[43] COM(2012) 225 final.

[44] Stephen Weatherill, *EU Consumer Law and Policy* (Edward Elgar 2005) 84. On consumer information, see also Geraint Howells, 'The Potential and Limit of Consumer Empowerment by Information' (2005) 32:3 *Journal of Law and Society* 349–370.

dislike limitations, it is expected that they take primary responsibility for the lifestyle choices they make on their own and their children's behalf.[45]

However, the information paradigm promoted at EU level may only be effective if the information made available to consumers is of sufficient quality to guide their choices and effectively allows them to 'protect' themselves. The responsibility for healthy choices is therefore shared between, on the one hand, consumers, who are expected to process the information made available to them when purchasing goods and services, and, on the other, regulatory authorities, which must ensure that enough information is made available to consumers and that such information is neither false nor misleading.[46]

In particular, the EU has adopted a broad range of labelling and information rules to ensure that consumers have enough information at their disposal to make healthy consumption choices. Thus, Directive 2001/37/EC obliges tobacco manufacturers not only to disclose the ingredients used in the manufacturing of cigarettes and other tobacco products, but also to affix health warnings to their products.[47] As far as food is concerned, Regulation 1169/2011 on consumer food information[48] requires that consumers are sufficiently informed of the nutritional content of the food they buy.

If consumer information must be sufficient, it must also be loyal and trustworthy. This general principle of EU law is at the very heart of Directive 2005/29 on unfair business-to-consumer commercial practices.[49] The provisions of this framework directive, which applies in the absence of more specific provisions, have been tailored to tobacco control and food law. Thus, Directive 2001/37 on tobacco products prohibits the use of certain texts, such as 'low tar', 'light', 'ultra-light' and 'mild', names, pictures and figurative or other signs, likely to mislead the consumer into the belief that such products are less harmful

---

[45] Marine Friant-Perrot and Amandine Garde, 'From BSE to Obesity – EFSA's Growing Role in the EU's Nutrition Policy' in Alberto Alemanno and Simone Gabbi (eds), *New Perspectives in EU Food Law – Ten Years of European Food Safety Authority* (Ashgate 2013).

[46] Amandine Garde, 'Freedom of Commercial Expression and the Protection of Public Health in Europe' (2010) 12 *Cambridge Yearbook of European Legal Studies* 225.

[47] Directive 2001/37/EC, Art. 5.

[48] [2011] OJ L304/18.

[49] [2005] OJ L149/22. It was also underlying the provisions of its predecessor, Directive 84/450 on misleading advertising, [1984] OJ L250/17.

or give rise to changes in consumption.[50] Similarly, Regulation 178/2002 on food safety provides as a general principle of EU food law that food information shall not be misleading.[51] The scope of the notion of misleading food information has been further defined in Regulation 1924/2006 on nutrition and health claims made on foods[52] and in Regulation 1169/2011 on the provision of food information to consumers.[53]

Many criticize information requirements as ineffective in achieving their declared goal of making consumers capable of protecting themselves when making individual choices. To support their claim, they rely on mounting evidence suggesting that few individuals read the information provided to them and even fewer actually process this information.[54] Others suggest that, even assuming that information schemes reach their addressees, there may be several factors explaining why they cannot effectively achieve their intended objective of promoting healthier lifestyles. First, as the public is made up of a heterogeneous group of individuals, there might be differences in understanding.[55] Secondly, the assumption that individuals are able to base their decisions on the information provided to them is increasingly being questioned today, due to cognitive limitations.[56] To address these two phenomena, which are often generically, yet inaccurately, referred to as 'information overload', the EU has started to reflect on the adoption of simplified information schemes, such as affixing pictorial warnings on tobacco products or

---

[50] Article 7 and Recital 27 of the Preamble of Directive 2001/37 [2001] OJ L194/26.

[51] Articles 8 and 16 of Regulation 178/2002 [2002] OJ L31/1.

[52] [2007] OJ L12/3. In particular, nutrition and health claims may only be made on food if they have been authorized and provided that the conditions for their use are duly respected. The Court recently interpreted this Regulation in relation to claims made on alcoholic beverages: Case C-544/10 *Deutsches Weintor eG v Land Rheinland-Pfalz* (nyr).

[53] [2011] OJ L304/18.

[54] See, for example, Steven L. Schwarcz, 'Rethinking the Disclosure Paradigm in a World of Complexity' (2004) 2004 *University of Illinois Law Review* 1–38.

[55] William M. Sage, 'Regulating Through Information: Disclosure Laws and American Health Care' (1999) 99:7 *Columbia Law Rev* 1701–1829.

[56] See, for example, Christine Jolls and Cass R. Sunstein, 'Debiasing through Law' (2006) 35:1 *The Journal of Legal Studies* 199–242; and, for a more popular treatment of behavioural sciences, see, for example, Dan Ariely, *Predictably Irrational* (Harper Perennial 2009).

front-of-pack labelling on foodstuffs.[57] In particular, the newly adopted tobacco products directive replacing the previous one[58] combines a textual warning with a corresponding coloured photograph, thus making pictorial warnings on tobacco products compulsory (as opposed to optional as they have been since 2001) and the health message conveyed to consumers more effective.[59] Similarly, the Commission, in its proposal for the Food Information Regulation, suggested that the front-of-pack labelling of packaged food should become mandatory to facilitate healthier choices 'at a glance', that is, without requiring that consumers engage in a thorough reading of the nutrition table on the back of the pack. However, this proposal did not make its way through the legislative process, and Regulation 1169/2011 as adopted merely allows Member States to recommend a front-of-pack labelling scheme on a voluntary basis, as the UK has recently done with the agreement struck between the public health ministry and major retailers that food labels should combine traffic-light labels with Reference Intakes.[60]

Marketing bans The EU has also restricted the possibility for industry operators to promote certain goods and services. In effect, growing evidence that advertising and other forms of promotion do impact on lifestyle choices supports the argument that public authorities have an interest in regulating marketing practices beyond the regulation of misleading claims.

---

[57] See Article 34 of Regulation 1169/2011 on the provision of food information to consumers, [2011] OJ L304/18.

[58] The Commission published a proposal for a revised Tobacco Products Directive in December 2012: *Proposal for a Directive of the European Parliament and of the Council on the approximation of the laws, regulations and administrative provisions of the Member States concerning the manufacture, presentation and sale of tobacco and related products*, COM(2012) 788 final. This was adopted in March 2014 as Directive 2014/40 and entered into force on 19 May 2014.

[59] Article 9 of the Commission's Proposal, COM(2012) 788 final. For more information on the revision of Directive 2001/37, including the impact assessment and relevant independent studies carried out for the Commission, see <http://ec.europa.eu/health/tobacco/products/revision/index_en.htm>. See also Alberto Alemanno, 'Out of Sight, Out of Mind – Towards a New EU Tobacco Products Directive' (2012) 18:2 *Columbia Journal of European Law* 197.

[60] On the UK scheme, see <http://www.nhs.uk/Livewell/Goodfood/Pages/food-labelling.aspx>. On 19 June 2013, the Department of Public Health published guidance on front-of-pack labelling: <https://www.gov.uk/government/publications/front-of-pack-nutrition-labelling-guidance>.

Marketing restrictions generally consist of limitations to the advertising and other forms of promotion (including sponsorship, merchandizing and product placement) of certain products. These restrictions generally translate into restrictions on the ability of economic operators to promote and market their products either to the general public or to particularly vulnerable segments of the population, not least children.[61] Directive 89/552 on the free movement of broadcasting services banned the advertising of tobacco products on television.[62] Directive 2033/33 subsequently extended this ban to all forms of tobacco advertising and sponsorship affecting the internal market – a measure that proved highly controversial and is discussed in more detail below.[63] Directive 2010/13 on audiovisual media services completed the picture by banning all forms of audiovisual commercial communications for tobacco products falling within its scope (including product placement).[64] This latter Directive also lays down conditions on the marketing to children of alcoholic beverages and nutrition-poor food. If these provisions are largely insufficient, they still allow Member States – by virtue of the clause of minimum harmonization characterizing this Directive – to adopt stricter, more protective standards, and a wide range of them have done so, subject to the State of Establishment principle at the heart of the Directive and the general free movement Treaty provisions.[65]

Given the prominent role played by the appearance, imagery and more generally the packaging of products, marketing restrictions now also extend to product packaging and labelling. Whilst regulations aimed at prohibiting misleading packaging practices have existed for decades in order to limit unfair competition, the focus of the regulatory interventions on packaging practices is now shifting to another policy goal: that of limiting the consumption of those products which – due to their

---

[61] Amandine Garde, 'Advertising Regulation and the Protection of Children-Consumers in the European Union: In the Best Interest of … Commercial Operators?' (2011) 19:3 *The International Journal of Children's Rights* 523–545.

[62] [1989] OJ L298/23. See Article 13.

[63] [2003] OJ L152/16.

[64] [2010] OJ L95/1. See in particular Article 9(1)(d) on audiovisual commercial communications in general; Article 10(2) on sponsorship; and Article 11(4)(a) on product placement.

[65] Audiovisual commercial communications for alcoholic beverages are covered in Articles 9(1)(e) and 22; audiovisual commercial communications for unhealthy food are covered in Article 9(2). The Directive also contains more general, non-product-specific provisions relating to the content and the amount of marketing allowed in the Audiovisual Media Service Directive. These provisions are discussed in detail in Bartlett and Garde, *supra* note 32.

constituents – are increasingly perceived as unhealthy. By banning the use of trademarks, logos, colours or graphics, the debates surrounding the plain packaging of cigarettes epitomize such a trend. Yet plain packaging must be interpreted within a broader trend aimed at reducing the visual appeal of products (or their packaging).[66] As regulators have become suddenly aware of the power of marketing in inducing consumer choices, they seem ready to offset those marketing techniques which have been used since the 1960s and which are increasingly used to market products perceived as unhealthy. As a result, besides the most extreme form (generally called plain packaging), other less intrusive forms of standardized packaging are emerging and are often described as space appropriation schemes, as illustrated by the debates surrounding the revision of the Tobacco Products Directive.[67]

Measures affecting product availability Measures affecting product availability are probably the oldest form of regulatory intervention used to tackle lifestyle-related problems. Their rationale is to reduce the availability of a given product in order to reduce its overall consumption. The classic example of regulatory intervention aimed at controlling product availability is the creation of a (retail) monopoly, entrusted with the importation of, and trade in, tobacco, alcohol or food, or the licensing and the operation of specific activities, such as gambling services.[68] Another more recent example of measures affecting product availability is offered by product reformulation, which consists of changing the formula of a given product in order to reduce the presence of one or more of its constituents. The EU has trodden rather carefully and has not

[66] Alberto Alemanno, 'The Legality, Rationale and Science of Tobacco Display Bans after the Philip Morris Judgment' (2011) 4:2 *European Journal of Risk Regulation* 591–599; *id.*, 'The HOB-Vín Judgment: A Failed Attempt to Standardise the Visual Imagery, Packaging and Appeal of Alcohol Products' (2013) 4:1 *European Journal of Risk Regulation* 101–112.

[67] For more information on the revision of Directive 2001/37, see <http://ec.europa.eu/health/tobacco/products/revision/index_en.htm>.

[68] Several cases have involved the compatibility with the general provisions of the EU Treaties of national monopolies in the area of tobacco, alcohol and gambling: on tobacco, see Case 59-75 *Manghera* [1976] ECR 91 and Case C-387/93 *Banchero* [1995] ECR I-4663; on alcohol, see Case C-189/95 *Franzen* [1997] ECR I-5909 and Case C-170/04 *Rosengren* [2007] ECR I-4071, as well as the decision of the EFTA Court in Case E-6/96 *Tore Wilhelmsen* [1997] EFTA Court Report 53; and on gambling, see for example, Joined Cases C-338/04, C-359/04 and C-360/04 *Placanica* [2005] ECR; and Case C-243/01 *Gambelli* [2003] ECR I-13031.

legislated much in this field. Nevertheless, it has promoted the exchange of best practice.[69] It remains that in the absence of an EU regulatory intervention in this field, some Member States have imposed regulatory restrictions on the use of certain nutrients. For example, in March 2003, Denmark became the first country in the world to strictly regulate the sale of many foods containing trans fats.[70]

Fiscal measures Finally, in light of the fact that price remains one of the major drivers of consumption,[71] a range of fiscal measures may be envisaged as part of the NCD prevention and control agenda.[72] A variety of economic instruments allows public authorities either to promote healthy lifestyles by lowering the price of healthy goods and services, for example fruit and vegetables, or to discourage unhealthy eating by increasing the price of goods and services such as cigarettes, alcoholic beverages or food high in fat, sugar or salt. In particular, taxation rates may be lowered and subsidies introduced on healthy goods and services to increase their consumption, whereas taxation rates may be increased on unhealthy goods and services to decrease their consumption.

The Common Agricultural Policy (CAP) can play a potentially powerful role in increasing the availability and the affordability of healthy food.

---

[69] For example, the EU has adopted the EU Salt Reduction Framework which sets a benchmark of a minimum of 16 per cent salt reduction over four years for all food products across the full range of food products from premium to economy items, so that all population groups could benefit, and also encompassing salt consumed in restaurants and catering. For information on the EU Salt Campaign, see: <http://ec.europa.eu/health/nutrition_physical_activity/high_level_group/nutrition_salt_en.htm>. On 7 December 2012, the Commission published a survey on the actions taken by Member States to reduce the excessive salt intake across the EU: <http://ec.europa.eu/health/nutrition_physical_activity/docs/salt_report1_en.pdf>.

[70] For an overview of restrictive measures adopted vis-à-vis trans fat, see <http://www.news-medical.net/health/Trans-Fat-Regulation.aspx>.

[71] In a pan-European study of determinants of food choice, the four most important factors were 'quality or freshness', 'price', 'taste' and 'trying to eat healthily': M. Lennernäs et al., 'Influences on Food Choice Perceived to Be Important by Nationally-Representative Samples of Adults in the European Union' (1997) 51:2 *European Journal of Clinical Nutrition* 8.

[72] The theoretical prediction underpinning excise duties according to which the induced relative price effect actually works by decreasing consumption is supported by empirical evidence: see Bruno S. Frey, 'Excise Taxes: Economics, Politics, and Psychology' in Sijbren Cnossen (ed.), *Theory and Practice of Excise Taxation: Smoking, Drinking, Gambling, Polluting, and Driving* (OUP 2005) 230–241.

This is all the more so as the EU has extensive competence in this field. It is therefore not surprising that the Obesity Prevention White Paper has identified the CAP as an area of EU intervention.[73] Suffice it to note, in this chapter, that the reform of the raw-tobacco sector has reduced EU subsidies on tobacco.

Fiscal measures used in lifestyle policy may be defined as taxes that are placed upon given substances (such as tobacco, alcohol and unhealthy food or beverages) or services in order to dissuade from their consumption ('excise duties').[74] The EU has adopted minimum rates of excise duties on cigarettes, alcoholic beverages and environmental emissions. However, these measures were not necessarily adopted with public health protection in mind but rather to raise revenues.[75] Moreover, they have tended to be measures of minimum harmonization only: hence the continuing diversity of prices across the EU – though the scope of variation has been somewhat reduced by the amendment of the tobacco taxation directive.[76] More recently, the idea has emerged to extend fiscal

---

[73] However, it is not discussed in any detail here. For more information on the contribution of the CAP to healthier diets, see Lisselotte S. Elinder et al., *Public Health Aspects of the EU Common Agricultural Policy: Developments and Recommendations for Change in Four Sectors: Fruit and Vegetables, Dairy, Wine and Tobacco* (Finland, National Institute of Public Health 2005); Christopher Birt et al., *A CAP on Health? The Impact of the EU Common Agricultural Policy on Public Health* (London, Faculty of Public Health 2007); Josef Schmidhuber, *The EU Diet: Evolution, Evaluation and Impacts of the CAP* (Rome, FAO 2008); and Amandine Garde, *supra* note 26, chapter 7.

[74] Franco Sassi and Alberto Alemanno, 'Taxation and Economic Incentives in NCD Prevention' in Alberto Alemanno and Amandine Garde (eds), *Emergence of an EU Lifestyle Policy – The Case of Alcohol, Tobacco and Unhealthy Diets* (CUP 2014).

[75] The rates and structures of the minimum excise duties applicable are set in sectoral directives. For alcoholic beverages, see Directive 92/83 [1992] OJ L316/21 and Directive 92/84 [1992] OJ L316/29. For manufactured tobacco products, see Directive 92/79 [1992] OJ L316/8, Directive 92/80 [1992] OJ L316/10 and Directive 95/59 [1995] OJ L291/40 – these three Directives have been more recently amended by Directive 2010/12 [2010] OJ L50/1; in the interest of clarity and rationality, these Directives on tobacco excise duties have been codified by Directive 2011/64 [2011] OJ L176/24. For carbon emissions, see Council Directive 2003/96 [2003] OJ L283/51. Common provisions have also been adopted on the control, holding and movement of duty-suspended products in Directive 92/12 [1992] OJ L76/1 and Directive 2008/118 [2009] OJ L9/12.

[76] Council Directive 2011/64/EU of 21 June 2011 on the structure and rates of excise duty applied to manufactured tobacco.

measures to food whose consumption is linked to obesity and other health-related risks.[77] Here again, the stated aim of a 'fat tax' or a 'soda tax' is not only to offset the price imbalance between healthier and unhealthier food – the latter tending to be much cheaper – but also to raise revenue, either general revenue or resources to be invested more specifically in nutrition or physical activity programmes.[78] If the EU has not adopted any harmonizing legislation on food taxes, some Member States have started to experiment with them.[79] In the absence of common EU rules on indirect taxation, they retain the freedom to adopt such taxes, provided that they are not discriminatory and do not protect the home market to the detriment of the markets of other Member States.[80]

b. The relationship between EU and national lifestyle regulatory intervention

As this short survey has shown, the EU has adopted a range of measures intended to promote healthier lifestyles. However, EU intervention is constrained not only by the existence of sufficient political will but also by the key constitutional principles of competence, subsidiarity, proportionality and respect for fundamental rights.[81]

If the EU does not have the required powers to take certain lifestyles measures or if the EU does not exercise its powers either because of subsidiarity concerns or because it lacks political will, then Member States can adopt national rules intended to promote the health and

---

[77] See, for example, Hanna Rosin, 'The Fat Tax: Is it Really Such a Crazy Idea?' (1998) *The New Republic*, 18 May.

[78] See, for example, Kelly D. Brownell et al., 'The Public Health and Economic Benefits of Taxing Sugar-Sweetened Beverages' (2009) 361 *The New England Journal of Medicine* 1599–1605; Andrew Leicester and Frank Windmeijer, 'The "Fat Taxes": Economic Incentives to Reduce Obesity' (2005) *Institute for Fiscal Studies*, Briefing Note 49.

[79] See, for example, in Denmark, *Lov om afgift af mættet fedt i visse fødevarer* (Act on a tax on saturated fat in specific food) *LOV nr 247 af 30/03/2011 Gældende (Fedtafgiftsloven)*, adopted 31 March 2011 and withdrawn November 2012; in Hungary, 2011, *évi CIII. Törvény a népegészségügyi termékadóról*, Date of publication: 19 July 2011. *Magyarközlöny* (*Hungarian Gazette*) 2011, *évi 85. Szám*, 25125.

[80] Alberto Alemanno and Ignacio Carreno, 'Fat Taxes in the European Union between Fiscal Austerity and the Fight Against Obesity' (2011) 4 *European Journal of Risk Regulation* 571; Amandine Garde, *supra* note 26, chapter 7.

[81] The relationship between the EU's developing lifestyle policy and the key constitutional principles laid down in the EU Treaties is discussed more thoroughly in Alemanno and Garde, *supra* note 3.

well-being of their citizens, subject to their compliance with the general free movement Treaty provisions, and Articles 34 and 56 TFEU more specifically.

As a result of the limits placed on the EU by the principle of conferral, the EU cannot adopt all the measures which are necessary to prevent NCDs: some measures will originate from the EU, whereas some others will have to be adopted by the Member States, at national or at local level. Relevant legal bases allowing for the adoption of binding EU measures include: Article 38 (agriculture), Article 91 (transport), Article 113 (taxation), Articles 114 and 59 (internal market), Article 153 (workers' protection), Article 169 (consumer protection) and Article 207 (commercial policy) TFEU. Yet, most lifestyle-inspired legislation adopted by the EU to date has been based on Article 114 TFEU (internal market).

In the absence of common rules, Member States can regulate areas of shared competence where the EU has not (yet) 'occupied the field'. For example, and as mentioned above, Denmark has strictly regulated the content of trans fat in food, whilst some Member States are considering the adoption of plain packaging for tobacco products.

Similarly, if the EU approximates the laws of the Member States through minimum harmonization, Member States can exceed the minimum standards laid down at EU level. It is on this basis that several Member States have exceeded the requirements of the Audiovisual Media Services regarding the marketing of alcoholic beverages and unhealthy food to children. However, if Member States decide to exercise their margin of discretion, they are constrained by the general Treaty provisions, and Articles 34 and 56 TFEU more specifically.[82]

The fact remains that drawing the boundaries between legitimate and illegitimate EU intervention under Article 114 is far from straightforward, as the Court's case law illustrates. In particular, the question arises as to the extent to which the EU could adopt harmonizing rules relating to 'selling arrangements', to use the language developed by the Court's case law on Article 34 TFEU. In particular, vivid debates have arisen during the revision of the Tobacco Products Directive: could the EU approximate the laws of the Member States on tobacco display and tobacco vending machines? If the EU has decided not to press ahead with these measures, hard questions nonetheless remain unanswered regarding

---

[82] For an illustration of the relationship between the Audiovisual Media Services Directive and stricter national rules, see Case C-34/95 *Konsumentombudsmannen (KO) v De Agostini (Svenska) Forlag AB* [1997] ECR I-3875.

the extent to which selling arrangements could validly be harmonized at EU level.[83] In any event, until the EU adopts harmonizing rules, Member States retain their freedom to adopt national measures in these fields. Thus, several of them have adopted *inter alia* bans on vending machines as part of their national tobacco strategies.

Any national measures falling within the scope of any of these categories are likely to be challenged before the Court of Justice of the European Union (CJEU) (or the EFTA Court) and to be found in breach of the free movement of goods or services. In these circumstances, Member States will have to establish that they introduced these measures to protect public health and that they complied with the principle of proportionality.

Whilst a certain degree of fragmentation of lifestyle policies in Europe is unavoidable, it is paramount to ensure as much coherence as possible within the parameters laid down by the EU Treaties. It is therefore all the more important to ensure that the emerging EU lifestyle policy is based on evidence rather than mere assumptions.

III. THE ROLE OF EVIDENCE IN LIFESTYLE INTERVENTION AND ITS IMPACT ON THE PROPORTIONALITY ANALYSIS

This section focuses on how the EU and Member States should frame their lifestyle intervention to comply with the principle of proportionality. In so doing, it distinguishes the evidence burden imposed on the EU and its Member States in both an *ex ante* (standard-setting) and an *ex post* (judicial review) scenario.

Like any other risk regulatory intervention,[84] lifestyle risk regulation – be it adopted at EU or Member State level – must also be backed up by evidence. When discussing evidence in the policy process, it is crucial to distinguish between evidence on causes (in other words, the causal link between a suggested risk factor and an illness or otherwise undesirable

[83] These questions are discussed in Gareth Davies, 'Can Selling Arrangements be Harmonised?' (2005) 30:3 *EL Rev* 370–385. In relation to lifestyle risk regulation more specifically, see Frederic Geber, 'Lifestyle Risks and Harmonization of National Law' in Alberto Alemanno and Amandine Garde (eds), *Emergence of an EU Lifestyle Policy – The Case of Alcohol, Tobacco and Unhealthy Diets* (CUP 2014).

[84] Alemanno, *supra* note 1

health outcome) and evidence on policy interventions (in other words, the potential of different paths of action to promote health or reduce harm).

Due to a multitude of reasons, it is extremely difficult to gather both sorts of evidence to support action aimed at regulating lifestyles. First, regarding the evidence on causes, the phenomena that public authorities strive to regulate under this form of intervention are, by nature, multifactorial. The main lifestyle risk factors result from the combination of several dynamics – be it excessive consumption, genetic make-up, brain-reward mechanisms and socio-economic factors – which all present different explanatory factors. Moreover, as many factors may contribute to some health conditions, the causal link between a risk factor and the harm may be impossible to estimate with any degree of accuracy. For example, how many car accidents are directly 'caused by' alcohol, and how much obesity is 'caused by' advertising of foods high in fat, sugar or salt? Any form of regulatory intervention has to acknowledge the complexity stemming from the multifactorial nature of NCDs.

Secondly, once the 'right evidence' has been collected to substantiate and identify the policy problem at stake, it remains necessary to translate research into policy and effective action. That is where there is a need to show that the policies chosen by the legislator are backed up by the evidence required to prove their effectiveness. Yet, as many interventions lead to both potential harm and benefits, and the potential for both benefits and harm may be unevenly distributed in the population, it is often necessary to assess the overall balance between risks and benefits, and how these are distributed among different members of the population. A further issue related to translating research into policy is whether an intervention that is effective in a research setting may be as effective in a particular real-world context. This may lead to complex mathematical and statistical modelling, and, in the case of behavioural-informed intervention,[85] of randomized controlled trials (RCTs).[86] Thus, in the famous Cafeteria example, the school's management may try to

---

[85] For an overview of behavioural-informed regulation, see Alberto Alemanno and Alessandro Spina, 'Nudging Legally – On Checks and Balances of Behavioral Regulation' (2014) 12:2 *International Journal of Constitutional Law* 429–456.

[86] RCTs are specific experiments, widely used in the medical field, in which the efficacy of an intervention is studied by comparing the effects of the intervention on a study population which is randomly allocated in different subgroups. The subgroups are exposed to a differential course of treatment: one of them – the control group – is not treated (or receives a 'placebo'), whilst the other subgroup – the intervention group – is exposed to the treatment. The

influence students' diet by rearranging the display of food so as to make it more likely that the healthy option is chosen. To determine the effectiveness of this behavioural-informed policy, these are increasingly tested in controlled trials, prior to any large-scale and general implementation.[87]

Thirdly, given the comprehensive nature of lifestyle intervention, it is often difficult to pinpoint the effect of a given policy option when it belongs to a larger set of measures. How to distinguish the effect, in terms of tobacco prevalence, to be ascribed to plain packaging when at the same time excise duties on tobacco products have been raised? It can be anticipated that this point renders any proportionality assessment problematic, especially in relation to the evaluation of the 'necessity' of the measure, as this requires not only the identification of other policy options but also their individual contribution to the declared goal.

In sum, the multifactorial nature of its underlying phenomena, the interdisciplinary character of the evidence at stake, the measurement of the effectiveness of the different policy options as well as the identification of the individual contribution of each one of them to the policy objective represent some of the major challenges for the emerging EU lifestyle regulatory policy.

Whilst EU law has thus far been unsuccessful in determining the applicable standard of proof that the EU and the Member States have to meet in order to substantiate their proposed policy measures,[88] EU Courts have provided – through the proportionality scrutiny of those measures – some guidelines on the issue.

As all the methodological issues identified above could possibly emerge as part of the proportionality assessment of EU or Member States' lifestyle action, it is necessary to examine the role played by evidence in the proportionality scrutiny exercised by the EU Courts on both EU and national measures. In so doing, it is important to bear in mind that, in addition to the difficulties inherent in scientifically substantiating lifestyle measures, there are also other common challenges in integrating evidence into policymaking, such as the selective use of

---

impact of the intervention is then measured by comparing the results in both subgroups.

[87] On the rationale for the use of RCTs in policymaking, see Michael Abramowicz, Ian Ayres and Yair Listokin, 'Randomizing Law' (2011) 159:4 *University of Pennsylvania Law Review* 929–1005.

[88] Shuibhne and Maci, *supra* note 10

evidence,[89] the misrepresentation or misunderstanding of evidence[90] and the handling of minority opinions,[91] that are not discussed here.

1. Proportionality of Lifestyle Risk Regulation

Any EU measure must comply with the principle of proportionality that requires that the content and form of Union action shall not exceed what is necessary to achieve the objectives of the Treaties.[92] According to established case law, an EU act is proportionate when it is suitable and necessary to achieve its declared goal.[93] This principle also applies to Member States' action. Yet, given the potentially disruptive effect that national measures may have on the EU internal market, the CJEU tends to engage in a more intensive review of national than EU measures.[94]

In relation to both categories of measure, the principle of proportionality requires:

- that measures adopted by EU institutions should not exceed the limits of what is suitable or appropriate in order to attain the legitimate objective pursued by the legislation in question (suitability);
- that where there is a choice between several appropriate measures, recourse must be had to the least onerous method (necessity); and
- that the disadvantages caused must not be disproportionate to the aims pursued (*stricto sensu* proportionality).[95]

---

[89] One further important aspect of evidence-gathering is the selective use of evidence. Perhaps only some of the literature will be cited, or explanations rely on a particular strand of scientific evidence, ignoring or excluding other evidence.

[90] Thus, for instance, media stories often turn out to be based on anecdotes, unpublished reports or preliminary results, or they overstate, misrepresent or misunderstand the claims of the researcher.

[91] In reality, when scientists 'disagree with one another', this merely reflects the normal process of scientific inquiry, which consists of continuously questioning the results obtained.

[92] Art. 5(4) TFEU.

[93] Case 11/70 *Internationale Handeslgesellschaft mbH v Einfhur- und Vorratsstelle für Getreide und Futtermittel* [1970] ECR 1125.

[94] See Paul Craig, *EU Administrative Law* (OUP 2006) 688–689, 704–706.

[95] See, to that effect, Joined Cases C-96/03 and C-97/03 *Tempelman and van Schaijk* [2005] ECR I-1895, para. 48; Case C-86/03 *Greece v Commission* [2005] ECR I-10979, para. 96; Case C-504/04 *Agrarproduktion Staebelow GmbH v Landrat des Landkreises Bad Doberan* (*Agrarproduktion Staebelow*)

a. Suitability of EU lifestyle measures

Under the first limb of the proportionality test, the question is whether a given lifestyle intervention is suited to attain its declared objectives. Given the EU limited competences in public health, virtually all EU lifestyle policies tend to pursue both a harmonization and a public health objective.[96] Whilst most EU-wide schemes approximating domestic rules may be capable of overcoming the emerging disparities between national schemes, it is generally more difficult to determine the extent to which the chosen EU policy option is appropriate to contribute to the attainment of the other declared objective: a high level of public health protection. This inquiry, by shifting the focus of the suitability analysis from the harmonization objective to the public health goal, inevitably leads the Court to open the Pandora's box of a given measure's effectiveness in achieving a high level of human health protection via a reduction of morbidity and mortality induced by smoking, the harmful use of alcohol and unhealthy diets. One may first wonder the extent to which the Court is well placed and epistemically capable of conducting such an assessment.

As anticipated, there exist several difficulties in scrutinizing the suitability of a lifestyle measure in attaining its declared objective. These range from some broader issues such as the multifactorial nature of the phenomena that are regulated, to more specific ones such as the difficulty in pinpointing the exact contribution of every individual policy intervention. In particular, within a suitability analysis of any lifestyle intervention, the interpreter faces three major difficulties in determining the ability of a given measure to attain its declared purpose. The first is due to the inherent scientific uncertainty surrounding these forms of intervention. This encompasses the uncertainty related to the dynamics associated with the phenomenon (for example, obesity) that the regulation aims to regulate as well as the uncertainty related to the ability of a given policy option to tackle one or more of those dynamics. The second, which derives from the first, relates to the difficulty in establishing a causal link, or at least a correlation, between these measures and their expected outcome. These difficulties are further compounded by a third: the fact

---

[2006] ECR I-6779, para. 37; Case T-13/99 *Pfizer Animal Health v Council* [2002] ECR II-3305, para. 411; and the parallel Case T-70/99 *Alpharma v Council* [2002] ECR II-3495. See also, more recently, Case C-58/08 *Vodafone* [2010] ECR I-4999, para. 53.

[96] Alberto Alemanno, 'Out of Sight Out of Mind: Towards a New European Tobacco Products Directive' (2012) 18:2 *Columbia Journal of European Law* 197; Amandine Garde, *supra* note 26, chapter 3.

that lifestyles cannot be improved by individual measures taken in isolation. In lifestyle intervention there is indeed no 'silver bullet'. Rather, consensus has emerged that only a multi-sectoral policy may help facilitate healthier lifestyles, which makes the effectiveness of a specific intervention all the more difficult – if not impossible – to quantify.[97] As a result of this multi-sectoral, multi-level approach, the EU's emerging lifestyle policy is the result of a combination of both regulatory and self-regulatory measures adopted at both EU and national levels. Given the resulting complexity of the regulatory landscape, all efforts to determine the suitability of any particular lifestyle policy intervention appear particularly arduous and call for a more holistic analysis. Nevertheless, an approach that favours an overall assessment of the suitability of an individual measure to achieve its declared objective within its broader policy framework is not yet well established in the case law of the CJEU. There are, however, some encouraging signs in a few cases in which the Court examined the proportionality, and in particular the suitability, of a given measure by referring to the broader policy context within which the contested measure was adopted and called upon to operate.[98] It is predicted that the examination of lifestyle measures will require that the courts systematically embrace such an approach.

Suitability of a national lifestyle policy In the absence of harmonization, Member States remain competent to enact lifestyle-inspired measures within the limits set by the Treaty. This default framework is quite permissive in nature as it allows each country to determine the level of health protection it intends to pursue. As virtually all forms of lifestyle intervention aim to reduce the consumption of products that are freely traded across the EU, their implementation inevitably encroaches, at least potentially, upon the EU free movement provisions. Given the historically broad interpretation of these provisions, what determines the survival of Member State regulatory intervention is their 'justification', that is, whether they are proportionate to their objective of protecting public

---

[97] Amandine Garde, 'Freedom of Commercial Expression and Public Health Protection: The Principle of Proportionality as a Tool to Strike the Balance' in Lawrence W. Gormley and Niamh Nic Shuibhne (eds), *From Single Market to Economic Union – Essays in Honour of John A. Usher* (OUP 2012) 117.

[98] See, for example, *Franzen* [1997], para. 64; Opinion of AG Jacobs, *Gourmet*, para. 25: 'In general, I consider, advertising restrictions cannot but contribute to the effect to a non-negligible degree, alongside high excise duties and State control of retail sales for home consumption.'

health.[99] As the Court has held, the Member States 'enjoy a margin of discretion in determining, according to particular social circumstances and to the importance attached by those States to a legitimate objective under Community Law … the measures which are *likely to achieve concrete results*'.[100] The evidence adduced by the parties generally conditions whether a national measure is suitable to achieve its declared public health policy objective.

Yet the question remains what kind of, and how much, evidence can realistically be provided by a Member State to support the suitability of a given measure to achieve its declared policy objective.

The EFTA Court, when called upon to assess the suitability of the ban on the visual display of tobacco products at points of sale adopted by Norway, held in *Philip Morris* that

> where the EEA State concerned legitimately aims for a very high level of protection, it must be sufficient for the authorities to demonstrate that, even though there may be *some scientific uncertainty as regards the suitability and necessity of the disputed measure*, it was reasonable to assume that the measure would be able to contribute to the protection of human health.[101]

The Court continued: 'in the absence of convincing proof to the contrary, a measure of this kind may be considered suitable for the protection of public health'.[102] This is an original and unorthodox way of applying the precautionary principle to the suitability analysis.[103] Indeed, until now the trigger for the use of this principle had always been a situation of scientific uncertainty regarding the existence of an underlying hazard, as opposed to the uncertainty surrounding the effectiveness of a policy option aimed at tackling that hazard.[104] However, in the present case, the Court extends the application of the principle to those circumstances, that

---

99 Peter J. Oliver (ed.), *Oliver on Free Movement of Goods in the European Union* (5th ed., Hart Publishing 2010) 225.

100 Judgment of the Court (Fifth Chamber) of 15 June 1999. Sami Heinonen. Case C-394/97, ECR 1999 I-3599 para. 43.

101 Case E-16/10 *Philip Morris Norway AS./.Staten v/Helse- og omsorgs-departementet* (*Philip Morris*), EFTA Court, judgment of 12 September 2011. Emphasis added.

102 Para. 84.

103 See, on this point, Alemanno, *supra* note 66 (2011).

104 See, for example, Case T-13/99 *Pfizer Animal Health v Council (Pfizer)* [2002] ECR II-3305.

is, when the hazard is well identified but the effects of the measures that prevent it from turning into a risk are scientifically uncertain.[105]

As a result of the application of a precautionary approach to the suitability analysis of the contested measure, any court may grant a rather wide margin of manoeuvre to States in selecting lifestyle measures whose effects cannot be proven either because they have never been applied (for example, plain packaging) or because their effectiveness in reducing consumption cannot easily be demonstrated (for example, visual display ban). Moreover, it is well known that the effect of any form of lifestyle intervention tends to appear gradually over time. More critically, the specific effects of lifestyle control policy are difficult to discern from those stemming from the overall policy. In these circumstances, the Court might recognize some general ability of a given policy tool to achieve its public health objective. Yet the question whether it may produce a partial effect on one or more target groups is likely to be left unanswered by the Court.[106]

In any event, it is important to highlight that this evidence (on both suitability and necessity) plays differently depending on the procedural rules applicable to the kind of legal action. Thus, as the role of the CJEU differs in direct and indirect actions, the burden falls on the Commission to establish an infringement procedure against a Member State for the enactment of a (disproportionate) lifestyle measure (which has to prove that the contested measure breaches free movement). By contrast, in a preliminary reference, it will be for the relevant Member State to justify any restriction imposed on free movement. In the latter scenario, the referring Court may also provide evidence, thus conditioning the proportionality analysis by the CJEU or by the EFTA Court.[107]

b. Necessity of an EU lifestyle policy measure

The second limb of the proportionality test requires an inquiry into the necessity of the lifestyle measure under review: the measure adopted through EU action must not go beyond what is necessary to achieve its declared objective.[108] In practical terms, the necessity limb requires

---

105 Alemanno, *supra* note 66 (2011).

106 See, by analogy, Opinion of AG Maduro in Case C-434/04 *Criminal Proceedings against Jan-Erik Ahokainen and Mati Leppik* [2006] ECR I-9171, para. 24.

107 Shuibhne and Maci, *supra* note 10.

108 See, for example, Case 137/85 *Maizena Gesellschaft mbH and others v Bundesanstalt für landwirtschaftliche Marktordnung (BALM)* (*Maizena*) [1987] ECR 4587, para. 15; Case C-339/92 *ADM Ölmühlen GmbH and Ölwerke Spyck*

verification of whether less restrictive measures could also achieve the declared goal. If alternative policy options are available, the legislator is bound to choose the least intrusive of all equally effective means. This examination inevitably requires a comparative analysis between the measure under examination and other policy options available. As anticipated, in a sector such as lifestyle risk, this analysis is extremely difficult to carry out in light of the multi-sectoral and multi-level approaches required. In particular, the different nature and origin of the proposed measures render the evaluation of their 'necessity' problematic, as this requirement entails not only the identification of other policy options but also of their individual contribution to the declared goal. In other words, which policy options should be considered? How should they be measured and compared, and with reference to what benchmark? How to pinpoint the effect of a given policy option when it is part of a set of measures? Thus, for instance, how to distinguish the effect, in terms of health gains deriving from a drop in tobacco prevalence, to be ascribed to the introduction of plain packaging when at the same time excise duties on tobacco products have been increased?

In addressing these questions the EU Courts have historically been influenced mainly by what the parties involved in the dispute submit. However, the current practice of carrying out an impact assessment (IA) for all major Commission initiatives seems to lead the Courts – under the pressure of the parties and/or *sua sponte* – to rely on such *ex ante* evaluations before reaching their conclusions.[109] Thus, as the IA guidelines require the Commission to establish 'which policy options and delivery mechanisms are most likely to achieve' the objectives pursued by the underlying initiative,[110] the Court might take this assessment into account when determining whether the final measure is necessary and, as a result, complies with the principle of proportionality.[111]

---

v Bundesanstalt für landwirtschaftliche Marktordnung (*ADM Ölmühlen*) [1993] ECR I-6473, para. 15; and Case C-210/00 *Käserei Champignon Hofmeister GmbH & Co. KG v Hauptzollamt Hamburg-Jonas* (*Käserei Champignon Hofmeister*) [2002] ECR I-6453, para. 59.

[109] Case C-310/04 *Spain v Council* [2006] ECR I-7285; C-58/08 *The Queen, on the application of Vodafone Ltd and Others v Secretary of State for Business, Enterprise and Regulatory Reform* [2010] ECR 4999; C-343/09 *Afton Chemical Limited v Secretary of State for Transport* [2010] ECR 7023; T-252/07, T-271/07 and T-272/07 *Sungro, SA, Eurosemillas, SA, Surcotton, SA* [2010] ECR II-55.

[110] Impact Assessment Guidelines (2009) 28.

[111] Alberto Alemanno, 'The Better Regulation Initiative at the Judicial Gate: A Trojan Horse within the Commission's Walls or the Way Forward?' (2009) 15:3 *European Law Journal* 382–400; Alberto Alemanno, 'A Meeting of Minds

Necessity of a national lifestyle measure In order to prove the proportionality of national measures pursuing legitimate interests, Member States are expected, 'where they adopt a measure derogating from a principle enshrined in EU law, to show in each individual case that that measure is appropriate for securing the attainment of the objective relied upon and does not go beyond what is necessary to attain it'.[112] Moreover, according to established case law, the reasons invoked by a Member State by way of justification must be accompanied by an analysis of the appropriateness and proportionality of the measure adopted by that State and specific evidence substantiating its arguments.[113] Accordingly, Member States are required 'not only to establish that … the measure at issue is proportionate but also to indicate the evidence capable of substantiating that conclusion'.[114]

Whilst this appears a significant burden placed on the relevant Member State, especially in the case of a direct action, the Court's review of that evidence varies. Thus, in the context of a national restriction on gambling, the Court stated:

> if a Member State wishes to rely on an objective capable of justifying an obstacle to the freedom to provide services arising from a national restrictive measure, it is under a duty to supply the court called upon to rule on that question with *all the evidence of such a kind* as to enable the latter to be satisfied that the said measure does indeed fulfil the requirements arising from the principle of proportionality.[115]

Moreover, whilst in direct actions the Court is expected to make this determination alone on the basis of the evidence submitted by the parties, in preliminary references it tends to defer to the referring Court.[116] This enables the national authorities to consider other pieces of evidence available at the national level and may potentially lead to a different assessment of the necessity of the measure.

In any event, the Court has ruled that the standard of proof cannot be so high as to require the Member State to prove, positively, that no other conceivable measure could enable the objective pursued to be attained

---

on Impact Assessment: When Ex Ante Evaluation Meets Ex Post Judicial Control' (2011) 17:3 *European Public Law* 485–505.

[112] Cases C-147/03 *Commission v Austria* [2005] ECR I-5969, para. 63, and C-73/08 *Bressol and Others* [2010] ECR I-2735, para. 71.

[113] See, for example, *ibid.*

[114] C-542/09 *Commission v The Netherlands*, nyr, para. 82.

[115] C-316/07 *Stob and others* [2007] ECR I-8069, para. 71 (emphasis added).

[116] *Bressol*, *supra* note 112, para. 77.

under the same conditions.[117] Given the uncertainties surrounding both the evidence about the causes and the evidence about policy interventions, this *obiter dictum* carries great value in the examination of lifestyle interventions as it grants some margin of discretion to national authorities.

c. *Stricto sensu* proportionality

As discussed so far, it is established case law that an EU act is proportionate when it is suitable (first limb) and necessary (second limb) to achieve its declared goal.[118] However, in some cases the applicant has been able to add a third limb to the proportionality assessment carried out by the Court and argue that the burden placed on him/her by the measure should be regarded as disproportionate to the benefits secured. Thus, in *Pfizer* the Court clearly stated: 'a cost/benefit analysis is a particular expression of the principle of proportionality'.[119] However, it emerges from the case law that the Court undertakes this cost–benefit scrutiny only when the applicants specifically invoke it.[120] The *onus* therefore is on them to raise arguments that place the matter before the Court – a highly burdensome task. Yet, given the increasing number of ready-made IA reports containing a quantification of both costs and benefits of each policy option considered within the proposed legislation (or looking into how costs are distributed within society),[121] it will become easier for the applicant to gather this information and use it in proceedings. As a result, this trend might lead the Court to address more frequently the third limb of the test so as to modify the nature of the proportionality scrutiny.[122] Nevertheless, in the recent *HOB-vin* case before the EFTA Court, the UK and Norway questioned the need to engage with a *stricto sensu* proportionality analysis requiring that the benefits stemming from lifestyle

---

117 See Case C-110/05 *Commission v Italy* [2009] ECR I-519, para. 66.

118 Case 11/70 *Internationale Handeslgesellschaft mbH v Einfhur- un Vorratsstelle für Getreide und Futtermittel* [1970] ECR 1125.

119 See T-13/99 *Pfizer Animal Health v Council* [2002] ECR II-3305, para. 410. See also Case C-343/09 *Afton Chemical Limited v Secretary of State for Transport* [2010] ECR I-7027, para. 56.

120 Craig, *supra* note 94, 656.

121 As illustrated above, both the IA report and the (final) opinion of the Impact Assessment Board are published after the Commission has adopted the corresponding proposal and are publicly available on the Commission webpage. For two examples of recent IAs preceding the adoption of EU lifestyle regulation, see the IA Report on Nutrition Labelling Issues, SEC(2008) 94, and the IA Report on the Revision of the TPD, SWD(2012) 452 final.

122 Alemanno, *supra* note 111 (2009).

measures should justify their costs.[123] Instead, they proposed that, in light of the 'difficult evaluations of political, social and economic consideration' inherent to such policy measures, a measure like the Icelandic requirement that visual imagery on alcoholic products be approved, should be subject only to a 'manifest inappropriateness' test and, as such, should be justified on public health grounds.[124] Ultimately, the Court decided not to examine the *stricto sensu* proportionality of the contested measures.[125] In any event, lifestyle regulatory interventions are characterized by methodological difficulties in determining the individual benefits that derive from each intervention and, as such, require that a refined, not purely mathematical proportionality assessment be carried out.

2. The Standard of Review Applied to Lifestyle Measures

Traditionally EU Courts have adopted a relatively light degree of scrutiny on those social and economic measures involving complex policy assessments. The approach seems particularly deferential when called upon to review evidence-based measures such as those involved in lifestyle risk regulation. Thus, according to established case law, 'where a Community authority is required to make complex assessments in the performance of its duties, its discretion also applies, to some extent, to the establishment of the factual basis of its action'.[126]

This deferential approach to judicial review of EU measures has been further elaborated in the *Upjohn* judgment, dealing with medicinal products, where the Court of Justice of the EU has declared:

> where a Community authority is called upon, in the performance of its duties, to make complex assessments, it enjoys a wide measure of discretion, the exercise of which is subject to a limited judicial review in the course of which *the EC judicature may not substitute its assessment of the facts for the assessment made by the authority concerned*. Thus, in such cases, the EC

---

[123] Case E-2/12 *HOB-vín ehf. ./. The State Alcohol and Tobacco Company of Iceland (ÁTVR) (HOB-vin)*, EFTA Court, judgment of 11 December 2012, nyr.

[124] Report for the Hearing, paras 103 and 105.

[125] For a review of this judgment, see Alemanno, *supra* note 66 (2013).

[126] Case 138/79 *Roquette Frères v Council* [1980] ECR 3333, para. 25; Joined Cases 197/80 to 200/80, 243/80, 245/80 and 247/80 *Ludwigshafener Walzmühle v Council and Commission* [1981] ECR 3211, para. 37; Case C-27/95 *Bakers of Nailsea* [1997] ECR I-1847, para. 32; Case C-4/96 *Nifpo and Northern Ireland Fishermen's Federation* [1998] ECR I-681, paras 41 and 42; Case C-120/97 *Upjohn* [1999] ECR I-223, para. 34; and Case T-13/99 *Pfizer Animal Health v Council* [2002] ECR II-3305, para. 168.

> judicature must restrict itself *to examining the accuracy of the findings of fact and law* made by the authority concerned and to verifying, in particular, that the action taken by that authority is not vitiated by a manifest error or a misuse of powers and that it did not clearly exceed the bounds of its discretion.[127]

Over time, the General Court of the EU has expressly extended this deferential standard of review to those situations where EU institutions are 'required to undertake a scientific risk assessment and to evaluate highly complex scientific and technical facts'.[128]

However, this 'reductionist approach' following the traditional limited court control in complex technical matters such as the control of '*erreur manifeste d'appréciation*' has progressively been criticized for failing to satisfy the demand for effective scrutiny.[129] Given the growing quantity of data required to justify regulatory action, Courts are somehow expected – in order to satisfactorily discharge their duty – to merge procedural judicial review with substantive judicial review. As a result, EU Courts now often recall that, whilst the Commission must be allowed a wide discretion whilst exercising 'complex scientific assessments', that discretion is not excluded from review.[130] We might therefore expect, as the EU policy process becomes more 'evidence-based', that the Courts

---

[127] See Case C-120/97 *Upjohn Ltd* [1999] ECR 223, para. 34 (emphasis added). See also Case C-405/92 *Mondiet* [1993] ECR 6133. See, for a similar statement, in the competition law field, Joined Cases 56/64 and 58/64 *Consten and Grundig v Commission* [1966] ECR 299, 347. See, in particular, the most recent interpretation of this judgment in Case C-168/01 *GlaxoSmithKline Services Unlimited v Commission* [2006] ECR 9291, para. 241, where it is said that: 'the Court dealing with an application for annulment of a decision applying Article 81(3) EC carries out, in so far as it is faced with complex economic assessments, a review confined, as regards the merits, to verifying whether the facts have been accurately stated, whether there has been any manifest error of appraisal and whether the legal consequences deduced from those facts were accurate'.

[128] See Case T-13/99 *Pfizer Animal Health v Council* [2002] ECR II-3305, paras 168–169 and 323.

[129] Karl-Heinz Ladeur, 'The Introduction of the Precautionary Principle into EU Law. A Pyrrhic Victory for Environmental and Public Health Law? Decision-Making Under Conditions of Complexity in Multi-Level Political Systems' (2003) 40:6 *CMLR* 1465; Garde, *supra* note 46, 225–256; Alemanno, *supra* note 10 (2011).

[130] See, for example, Case C-79/09 *Gowan Comércio Internacional e Serviços Lda v Ministero Della Salute* [2010] ECR I-13533, para. 55.

will engage more thoroughly with the evidence underpinning those measures, be it of a scientific or socio-economic nature.

In particular, as previously illustrated, the current practice of carrying out an IA for all major Commission initiatives[131] might lead the EU Courts to refer to such previous evaluations before reaching their conclusions. As IAs contain a pre-legality check of the proposed legislation *vis-à-vis* general principles of law, such as the proportionality principle, it is likely that Courts, when called upon to review the legality of adopted legislation, will refer to the IA analysis.

Such judicial review 'is often seen by critics as an interference with the internal workings of the legislature and as an intrusion into the most holy-holies of the legislature's prerogatives'.[132] In particular, given the non-legally binding nature of most of the 'procedural rationality' requirements, such as IAs, there is a risk that Courts, when engaging in their review, 'make value judgements about which procedural rules merit protection themselves'.[133] However, this concern must be mitigated. It appears inevitable, and somehow necessary, that, as the EU policy process becomes more evidence-based, when EU Courts are called upon to verify the legality of its 'outcome', they also consider its 'input' into that process.[134] Contrary to what has recently been argued,[135] this judicial trend does not necessarily translate into the emergence of a 'new, distinct model of judicial review', often called 'semi-procedural', capable of questioning the legislature's prerogative. Rather, this judicial trend, which aims to inject more 'procedural rationality' into judicial review, must be interpreted as a sign of the development of a more nuanced 'evidence based review reflex'.[136]

3. Towards Evidence-Based Judicial Review

Today EU Courts, when called upon to establish the legality of an act, supplement their *substantive* scrutiny with references to some of the procedural features that have progressively found their way into the decision-making process. Studies, consultation procedures outcomes and

---

131 Impact Assessment Guidelines (2009) 28.

132 Bar-Siman-Tov, *supra* note 10, 1915, 1918.

133 *Ibid.*, 289.

134 Werner Vandenbruwaene, 'Multi-tiered Political Questions: The ECJ's Mandate in Enforcing Subsidiarity' (2012) 6:3 *Legisprudence* 321–346, 335.

135 *Ibid.*

136 For a first discussion of this phenomenon, see Alemanno, *supra* note 10 (2013).

parliamentary debates all provide useful 'raw material' orienting the Court when making determination about the legality of a given act. Whilst not all these documents are the products of new procedural requirements, there has been an increasing trend towards anchoring policymaking into more evidence and deliberation.

There are at least two positive consequences that we are likely to witness along the emergence of EU lifestyle regulation, stemming from this enhanced 'rationality review'.

First, by leading courts to play with evidence drawn from different disciplines, the 'evidence-based judicial reflex' forces judges to leave their 'comfort zone' and engage with bodies of knowledge stemming from different disciplines from the law, including statistics, economic analysis, epidemiology and toxicology, public surveys, psychology, and so on.[137] Secondly, whilst there is a risk that due to their epistemic unease courts may misinterpret or misuse the evidence available (or – what is worse – even delegate their responsibility to other non-majoritarian actors, such as experts or scientific advisory bodies),[138] there is also an opportunity that judges will incorporate new sources of knowledge into their reasoning so as to improve their understanding of a given phenomenon. Too often judges refer to common-sense assumptions and general knowledge whilst exercising judicial review, rather than rationalizing their evaluations on empirically sound arguments.[139] It is argued that the emergence of the 'evidence-based judicial reflex' may counter the natural tendency of judges to apply a predominantly intuitive rationale in judicial review and promote a more rational approach to adjudication. This may promote a powerful incentive for judges to enhance their epistemic capacity and promote a more interdisciplinary understanding of the law. As Dawson recently put it: 'The "catalytic" court, even if it can and should not substitute its judgment for that of political actors of new governance itself, may at least provoke a process of dialogue and reflection able to make regulatory decisions more cognisant of broader "public interests"'.[140]

---

137 Alemanno, *supra* note 10 (2013).

138 See, for example, David L. Featherman and Maris A. Vinovskis (eds), *Social Sciences and Policy-Making: A Search for Relevance in the Twentieth Century* (University of Michigan Press 2001); Elaine Mak, 'Judicial Review of Regulatory Instruments: The Least Imperfect Alternative?' (2012) 6:3 *Legisprudence* 301, 314–319.

139 For some examples, see Shuibhne and Maci, *supra* note 10.

140 Mark Dawson, *New Governance and the Transformation of European Law* (Cambridge University Press 2011) 264.

IV. CONCLUSIONS

Our analysis demonstrates that the emerging policy of lifestyle risk regulation, by prompting a new dialectic between positive and negative integration instruments, is likely to lead EU Courts to further delineate the boundaries of EU legitimate action in the risk arena.

Besides the inherent complexity of this emerging and contested policy, as epitomized by the multifactorial character of its underlying risk factors, the very nature of the EU itself gives rise to additional complex issues around roles, obligations and rights. In particular, the constitutional structure of the EU as a union of Member States with a diverse mix of cultural, social, political and economic structures presents both challenges and opportunities for the development of an EU-wide policy.

In this context, the proportionality principle is set to play a special role. This appears all the more true given the marked shift in recent case law towards more engagement with standards of proof, as opposed to the deference traditionally granted in the past to both EU and national policymakers. As AG Jacobs wrote extra-judicially: 'proportionality is a flexible tool of judicial review, which is applied differently in different context'.[141] Hence the interest in predicting how this principle will be applied to lifestyle regulation and what type of evidence may be required from the EU and the Member States. Our analysis predicts that a more evidence-based approach to judicial review may be capable of promoting a broader culture of proof, evidence and rationality in policymaking. Due to the nature of the disputes that are set to arise around both EU and national lifestyle measures, this development appears opportune, yet it raises new questions for the role that both policymakers and courts are expected to play.

---

[141] Francis G. Jacobs, 'Recent Developments in the Principle of Proportionality in European Community Law' in Evelyn Ellis (ed.), *The Principle of Proportionality in the Laws of Europe* (Hart Publishing 1999) 20.

8. Transnational risk regulation and contractual governance

Fabrizio Cafaggi

Risks spread across territories regardless of the jurisdictional boundaries. They correlate with the scope of markets, of economic activities, including production and consumption, and the geographic impact of natural events. These characteristics have made it ever more difficult to regulate risks at domestic level, calling for international regulatory coordination among national regulators in order to adapt to the transnational reach of regulated entities' activities.[1] In this perspective general principles concerning risk assessment and risk management have been developed by international organizations.[2] The globalization of production processes with the contribution of new information and transport technologies has expanded and fragmented the number of relevant actors liable to create risks while increasing the volume and intensity of trade. Both the characteristics of the risks and their assessment and management presuppose coordination to detect, to manage and to mitigate the consequences once risks occur.[3] The transnational dimension brings changes along several dimensions: actors, instruments, effects. After briefly surveying some of these changes we shall concentrate on *contractual risk regulation*. By contractual risk regulation we mean a form of

---

[1] See Jonathan B. Wiener, Michael D. Rogers, James K. Hammitt and Peter H. Sand, *The Reality of Precaution. Comparing Risk Regulation in the United States and Europe* (RFF Press 2011). See the OECD project on international regulatory cooperation whose first results are available at <http://www.oecd.org/officialdocuments/publicdisplaydocumentpdf/?cote=GOV/RPC%282012%298/ANN6&docLanguage=En > last visited 15 May 2015.

[2] See OECD Recommendation of the Council on the governance of critical risks adopted by Ministers 6 May 2014, available at <http://www.oecd.org/mcm/C-MIN%282014%298-ENG.pdf > last visited 15 May 2015.

[3] See Julia Black, 'The Role of Risk in Regulatory Processes' in Martin Cave, Robert Baldwin and Martin Lodge (eds), *The Oxford Handbook of Regulation* (OUP 2010) 302.

regulation translating into agreements between regulators and regulated. Such form is compatible with different degrees of overlap from those where regulators and regulated differ entirely to those where there is partial coincidence between the two categories. After describing the general features of contractual risk regulation we shall examine different forms and instruments, including transnational commercial contracts, certification contracts and their interaction.

I. CONTRACTUAL GOVERNANCE AND TRANSNATIONAL RISK REGULATION IN GLOBAL SUPPLY CHAINS: AN ASSESSMENT

Risks can be process-related and materialize in the course of production or be incorporated in the product or service and emerge at the time of use/consumption. Such time and space span requires an integrated approach, capturing the causal chain between sources of the risks and their effects, which may be spatially and temporally separate. Since processes can include multiple firms located in different parts of the world they may be subject to different, and potentially conflicting, domestic regulations. Hence domestic legal systems, including public and private actors, have to grapple with the double challenge of coordinating both regulators' and regulatees' actions in risk regulation across jurisdictional boundaries. These challenges require a new institutional design influencing both rules and institutions. The move to transnational risk regulation (TRR) calls for a reconceptualization of both actors and instruments. It does not necessarily translate into harmonization but it certainly requires strong coordination.

As to actors, changes concern both the public and private spheres. In the public domain one of the most common institutional responses to regulatory differentiation at domestic level has been the creation of transnational regulatory networks operating via guidelines and soft instruments to be implemented at the national level according to the individual administrative toolboxes of each state.[4] These networks often combine standard setting and monitoring and very rarely directly engage in enforcement that remains highly decentralized. Examples range from financial markets (International Organization of Securities Commissions, International Association of Insurance Supervisors, Basel) to health and

---

[4] See Anne-Marie Slaughter, *The New World Order* (Princeton University Press 2004).

drugs, from food safety to data protection. Within the public domain, private actors including both regulated entities (firms) and non-governmental organizations (NGOs) have increased their participation and involvement into standard setting and monitoring.

Who are the regulated entities in risk regulation orchestrated within the public sphere? The conventional view still looks at individual enterprises. According to a different emerging approach the unit of analysis in TRR should go beyond the individual enterprise, even when it represents the most powerful node along the chain, and encompass the entire chain, that is, the supply chain. Such an approach is spreading but it has not yet become the majoritarian view. Moving to the supply chain as regulated entity requires defining control systems over the emergence and management of the risk that encompass a multiplicity of actors. The level of control exercised by the chain leader over risk assessment and management is limited (capability wise) and expensive, making necessary the involvement of the relevant chain's participants in order to achieve monitoring and management at a cost-effective level.

Furthermore, supply chain regulation is not limited to the direct chain's participants; new intermediaries have gained influence in coordinating the regulator (chain leader) and the regulated (suppliers, importers, distributors) when assessing and managing the risks. They include trade associations and certification and assurance quality schemes. Within contractual risk regulation the analysis will first focus on the supply chain approach and then introduce the intermediaries to show their relevance in governing risks by agreements.

Within the private sphere changes have been brought by market transformations and by the growing power of NGOs, often supported by national governments against the spread of industry standards.[5] Within industry the increasing market power of retailers has shifted the locus of regulation but also transformed regulatory instruments. In certain areas like environment and food safety, private regulation has used primarily certification and other forms of market-based regulation. Sustainability standards represent today one of the most popular forms of risk regulation. Risk assessment and management schemes have developed increasingly, allowing the tailoring of regulation to the evolution of

[5] In the field of environmental risk see Christine Overdevest, 'Comparing Forest Certification Schemes: the Case of Ratcheting Standards in the Forest Sector' (2010) 8:1 *Socio-economic Review* 47–76; Christine Overdevest and Jonathan Zeitlin, 'Assembling an Experimentalist Regime: Transnational Governance Interactions in the Forest Sector' (2012) 8:1 *Regulation and Governance* 22–48.

business and organizational models. But the causal connection is a two-way road. Regulatory standards depend on the evolution of organizations but contribute to shaping their structure as well. Often it is very hard to detect the cause and the consequences of a scheme. The relationship between regulators and regulated in the private sphere may take different forms depending on the degree of coincidence between the two. As we shall see, contractual models of risk regulation range from those where standard setters differ entirely from regulated entities to those where regulatory standards are defined exclusively by the regulated entities acting at the same time as regulators and regulated.

Hence the relationship between regulators and regulated differs in the private and public domains.

The distinction between public and private is ever more overcome by the emergence of hybrids. Many hybrid forms of collaboration between public and private actors have been set forth in risk regulation. These forms do not usually reflect national boundaries; rather, they include organizations whose composition is transnational. In the private domain enterprises located in different jurisdictions increasingly engage in collective standard setting and promote the birth and consolidation of new regulatory intermediaries.

In relation to instruments, TRR calls for transnational responses that do not necessarily require full standards' harmonization but strong and adequate coordination both in risk assessment and management among rule makers and regulated entities. Public and private regulators collaborate with enterprises to regulate risks in different ways.

The analysis will show the inadequacy of a conceptual framework that juxtaposes public regulation, associated with administrative instruments and hierarchy, and private regulation, based instead on contract and consent. Within contractual risk regulation we observe different forms of regulation from hierarchical to collaborative, depending on the distribution of power between regulators and regulated and among regulated.

Within the private sphere, among the most relevant developments is certainly that of certification and assurance schemes. Initially developed as a market instrument to promote product differentiation, certification has been more recently incorporated in public regulatory schemes to complement monitoring and enforcement. It has acquired a more generalized objective and has spread across industries. Certifiers and auditors have developed transnational organizations able to inspect and certify enterprises operating with their supply chain across multiple jurisdictions, overcoming coordination problems related to public domestic regulators. Certification scheme owners, more than auditing, directly participate in risk assessment and risk management, often being the first to detect hazards and promote action plans. This is not to say that they are always effective. Major failures of private schemes have caused accidents in the area of environmental protection, product safety and, more recently, fundamental rights (privacy and data protection). One of the most significant fallacies is related to the conflicts of interest embedded in the contract between enterprises (potentially certified) and monitors (the certifiers).[6]

As mentioned, collaborative risk management occurs not only between private actors but also between public and private. The role of direct collaboration between international organizations and private actors has been growing.[7] These forms translate into formal and informal agreements between public and private organizations (industry and/or NGOs) related to standard setting, monitoring and enforcement concerning sustainability.

Recent examples of TRR based on collaborative endeavours include, for example, the Sustainability Assessment of Food and Agriculture (SAFA) guidelines issued by the Food and Agriculture Organization (FAO).[8] These guidelines, similarly to the OECD guidelines on multinational enterprises, are not directed to states but are directly addressed to enterprises. Enterprises that voluntarily adopt SAFA guidelines self-assess their sustainability performance on the basis of criteria and indicators defined in the guidelines.[9] In order to comply with those guidelines not only performance but also corporate governance of the regulated entity might have to be redefined.[10] Formally the voluntary adoption by individual enterprises locates this scheme outside contractual governance given that the FAO is the standard maker and the corporation the standard taker without, for the time being, any direct relationship

---

6 See on this problem Timothy D. Lytton and Lesley K. McAllister, 'Oversight in Private Food Safety Auditing Addressing Auditor Conflict of Interest' (2014) 2014 *Wisconsin Law Review* 289.

7 See OECD project on international regulatory cooperation, the first results of which are available at <http://www.oecd.org/officialdocuments/publicdisplaydocumentpdf/?cote=GOV/RPC(2012)8/ANN6&docLanguage=En> last visited 15 May 2015.

8 See SAFA guidelines, available at <http://www.fao.org/fileadmin/templates/nr/sustainability_pathways/docs/SAFA_Guidelines_Final_122013.pdf> last visited 15 May 2015.

9 *Ibid.*

10 In SAFA, however, the unit of analysis in risk regulation remains the individual enterprise or the group when it constitutes an autonomous legal entity. Due diligence remains the primary organizational tool through which multinational enterprises assess and manage risks.

between the two. There is no contract between the regulator and the firm. In fact the informal interaction between enterprises that use SAFA and the SAFA management infrastructure will qualify as a powerful form of collaborative transnational governance even without a formal agreement. Firms are free to adopt the guidelines, their performance does not have immediate consequences and in particular low scoring does not oblige them in any formal way vis-à-vis SAFA.

A further development, in part a response to the weaknesses of the conventional strategies and in part to keep or regain effective control over TRR by large enterprises, is the use of global supply chains (GSC) as regulatory instruments for risk regulation within a more general trend related to the development of transnational private regulation (TPR).[11] Standards are defined and implemented contractually by using transnational commercial contracts between participants in supply chains. This is one example of the much broader phenomenon on which we want to focus: contractual governance of risk regulation.[12]

II. CONTRACTUAL RISK REGULATION

Contractual governance of risk regulation, as in general other forms of TPR, is characterized by the stricter nature of the standards that go beyond those defined by international institutions and correspond or rise above the highest domestic level of the jurisdictions affected by the risk-related activity. But stringency is not the only dominant regulatory feature. Being based on voluntary standards TPR has to provide regulatees with the right incentives to join and to participate actively in the regulatory process and avoid exit strategies from the regime. Regulated entities when deciding to join a private scheme have to improve their position in the market, seek access to new opportunities and manage their risks more cost-effectively. Only if the benefits are higher than the costs will they decide to join the scheme.

Contractualizing risk regulation modifies the relationship between regulators and regulated. It emphasizes at least three important dimensions: (1) the necessity to cooperate in risk assessment and management between regulators and regulated; (2) the idea of risk regulation as a process rather than a product based on the assumption of incomplete

---

[11] See Fabrizio Cafaggi, 'New Foundations of Transnational Private Regulation' (2011) 38:1 *Journal of Law and Society* 20–49.

[12] See for the US experience Jody Freeman and Martha Minow (eds), *Government by Contract – Outsourcing and American Democracy* (HUP 2009).

information on both sides; and (3) the use of contracts as instruments to allocate liabilities for regulatory failures when risks are not detected in time or materialize because of failure to take prompt action.

In theory contractual risk regulation is based on consent. Standards are voluntary and regulated entities are free to join and exit. Voluntariness may however be limited; yet this would not undermine the contractual nature of risk regulation. As we shall see, contracts may be signed even when consent is limited. Voluntariness may be quite limited in the area of contractual governance when joining regulatory schemes is a precondition to access global supply chains. *De jure* voluntary standards in these instances may become *de facto* economically mandatory standards with which participants to the chain have to comply. It is often the case that the chain leader makes the decision to join a risk management scheme and then imposes on its suppliers to join or simply comply with the standards even without formally becoming part of the scheme. Hence the cost–benefit analysis in the latter case is related to the risk of losing the current benefits rather than gaining new ones. Even when some of the participants are forced to join a scheme the cooperative nature of the regulatory relationship between regulators and regulated remains. Parties can choose to cooperate or be forced to cooperate in risk assessment and management.

The assumption of *de jure* standards' voluntary nature is relevant to identify the pillars of private contractual governance but it should not lead to the mistaken conclusion that consent is the basis of the contractual regulatory regime. As we shall see, contractual governance exhibits a wide variety of relationships between regulators and regulated, ranging from highly hierarchical to much less so.

The use of contractual governance in TRR is not an alternative to domestic public regulation; rather, it operates as a complement. Within contractual risk regulation, supply chain management plays an increasingly important role. Supply chain management constitutes an innovative tool to achieve regulatory coordination of enterprises belonging to the same chain yet formally regulated by institutions located in different jurisdictions. Within supply chains multiple parties conclude contracts that are functionally linked but likely to be subject to different regimes depending on the applicable law. Risks associated with product safety may be regulated by the law of contract of country 1 between retailer and producer, country 2 between producer and first tier supplier, country 3 between first and second tier suppliers, and country 4 between second and third tier suppliers. However, given parties' autonomy often provisions concerning risk regulation reflect codes of conduct or standards common to all the parties within the chain. Hence contractual governance may reduce costs related to divergent standards and increase effectiveness in monitoring compliance that would otherwise require coordination of inspection authorities of several states.

In this chapter the role of transnational contracts as regulatory instruments for risk regulation will be analysed to identify strengths and weaknesses of this tool compared with other forms within the domain of TPR and with the use of contractual governance by public entities.[13] The main purpose is to show how TRR by contract operates in some fields and why it has emerged as an alternative or as a complement to global administrative regulation. The approach is descriptive rather than normative.

III. TRANSNATIONAL COMMERCIAL CONTRACTS AS REGULATORY INSTRUMENTS: THE MOBILE DIVIDE OF RULE MAKING AND RULE TAKING

Contracts as regulatory tools reflect a transformation in regulatory thinking: the need to provide incentives rather than command and punishment and the necessity to collaborate in order to achieve better and more cost-effective compliance. But contracts have primarily developed as instruments for market exchanges. Their regulatory function calls for important changes that private autonomy can only partially achieve.

The use of transnational commercial contracts as regulatory instruments for risk regulation is certainly on the rise, standing out among the various instruments of TPR. Ever more regulatory provisions concerning safety, environmental and social standards are integrated in commercial contracts. But the new regulatory objectives incorporated into contracts are in turn transforming contractual design and implementation.[14] While at first sight the expansion of commercial contracts' scope might appear relatively smooth, more radical transformations are 'hidden' by the pursuit of regulatory objectives. These transformations concern the content of obligations, their enforcement and the remedies in case of

---

[13] We refer to forms of public regulation where the regulated entity commits to adopt and manage a regulatory programme under the supervision or oversight of an agency or a public regulator. Performance by the regulatory entity may, for example, require the adoption of a compliance programme where the enterprise defines a plan to regulate risk within its supply chain.

[14] See Margaret M. Blair, Cynthia A. Williams and Li-Wen Lin, 'The New Role for Assurance Services in Global Commerce' (2008) 33 *Journal of Corporate Law* 325; Lytton and McAllister, *supra* note 6, 290.

non-compliance. Depending on the contractual technologies changes may take different forms and require local adaptations. Even within the model of standard contract forms the inclusion of regulatory provisions applicable to a very high number of suppliers located in different jurisdictions requires the definition of common terms and conditions to be 'adapted' both formally and substantively to local contexts and legal environments. TRR poses daunting challenges to both traditional functions of transnational commercial contracts and their structure, forcing redefinition of hierarchy and cooperation.[15]

Supply chains are composed of a large number of enterprises, among which one or two leading firms may dictate the standards, operating as regulators, and the upstream suppliers and, when the leader is the final producer, the downstream retailers, act as regulated entities.

The regulatory process can follow different patterns depending on the relationship between the leaders and the different tiers of the chain. The degree of hierarchy or cooperation when implementing regulation partly depends on exogenous factors related to market and contract power of each enterprise and partly on the regulatory choices made by the empowered decision-maker when selecting the risk management standard and its governance. Hence there is a bilateral causal relationship between the economic determinants of the chain's structure and the regulatory pillars upon which supply chains define regulatory instruments: the structure of the chain influences the regulatory strategy, which in turn may require the adoption of new corporate governance models.

Multinational enterprises may engage in standard setting through the enactment of codes of conduct or guidelines produced by them individually or by incorporating into their contracts principles and rules issued by collective private bodies like trade associations, technical standard setters (International Organization for Standardization (ISO), International Electrotechnical Commission) or multi-stakeholder organizations.[16] When the latter occurs they have to implement those rules taking into account the specific chain's features, determined among other things by their internal sourcing and procurement policies.

---

[15] See Fabrizio Cafaggi, 'The Regulatory Functions of Transnational Commercial Contracts: New Architectures' (2013) 36:6 *Fordham International Law Journal* 1557.

[16] See for different approaches Roundtables on sustainable biofuels (<www.rsb.org>), Roundtables on sustainable palm oil (<www.rspo.org>) and Roundtable on sustainable soy (<www.responsiblesoy.org>).

Contractual risk regulation related to product safety usually requires (a) that the entire production process is subject to a single and integrated safety management scheme; and (b) the emergence and occurrence of risk are traceable via the use of a common software and single electronic platforms among the participants, warranting simultaneous access to information about the activities of each enterprise that can help detect hazards and manage risks. Collective action by supply chain participants requires a shared understanding of risk regulation. Parties involved in a risk management scheme should act on the basis of a common definition and understanding of (1) what constitutes a risk, (2) how the risk ought to be assessed and detected, (3) how it can be managed, and (4) what action plans can be adopted when risk materializes in order to mitigate adverse consequences. Lacking this common understanding, cooperation in risk management can hardly occur even if there is a single coordinator.

A comprehensive analysis of contractual governance and risk regulation is beyond the scope of this chapter. Within risk regulation the focus of the analysis will be on product safety.

IV. TRR IN PRODUCT SAFETY AND CONTRACTUAL GOVERNANCE: RECOMBINING COMMERCIAL AND REGULATORY LOGICS?

As we shall see, the regulatory function in transnational contracts introduces some elements of differentiation compared to the commercial part both in relation to the content and the scope of the obligations, to monitoring contractual performance and to the function of remedies when compliance is lacking. Regulatory functions call for structural changes in contractual architectures. Unlike the commercial dimension of product non-conformity, which focuses on the divergence between what was promised and what has been delivered, for example the protection of the individual expectation interest, the regulatory dimension is collective rather than individual, and concentrates on the risks of harm associated with the marketing of a dangerous and unsafe product.

Regulatory obligations concerning risk assessment and management related to safety make their way into commercial contracts via clauses that incorporate by reference the relevant provisions of individual or collective codes of conduct, and impose compliance with its requirements to the regulated entities. These obligations can become part of the conventional product conformity standard and/or express and implied warranty. Alternatively, they can be separated and subject to specific liability and remedial regimes.[17] If standards are predefined and incorporated into contracts as a result of the exercise of authority, cooperation among regulated suppliers only occurs at the implementation stage since the standard setting is characterized by the exercise of the chain leader's hierarchical power. When the choice of regulatory standards is negotiated with suppliers, cooperation between regulators and regulated characterizes the entire regulatory process from drafting to implementation including, at times, even enforcement.

As it has been said, the GSC is predominantly organized through bilateral sequential contracts that follow the pathway of production and distribution processes. The regulatory content of these bilateral contracts reflects suppliers' guidelines produced by the chain leaders, usually referred to or incorporated by reference into the bilateral contract. The content of these obligations may concern process and/or product requirements related to social, environmental or safety standards that have to be met in order to comply with technical standards and codes. Within this framework the regulatory chain often ends up mirroring the shape of the contractual chain; each contract introduces obligations upon the producer and a right to monitor compliance on the buyer's side. The latter acts as an agent of its buyer and becomes responsible for monitoring compliance of the upstream chain's participants and subcontractors.[18] Use of bilateral contracts does not exclude the possibility to impose obligations related to other participants in the chain. Transnational commercial contracts often include producers' obligations to assure that subcontractors will comply with quality and safety requirements and other regulatory provisions.[19]

Even taking into account the foregoing forms of responsibility for collective behaviour, tensions between the commercial and the regulatory logics may occur. While the legal infrastructure of commercial exchanges within the chain may reflect bilateral contracting with some degree of content coordination defined in the guidelines, the managerial framework may demand the creation of a closer coordination organized around a

---

[17] See Fabrizio Cafaggi and Paola Iamiceli, 'Supply Chains, Contractual Governance and Certification Regimes' (2013) 37 *European Journal of Law and Economics* 131–173.

[18] Both General Terms and Conditions (GTC) of multinational corporations (MNCs) and Suppliers' guidelines make reference to producers' obligations to ensure compliance by their suppliers beyond privity requirements. See for example, UNILEVER, GTC Art. 6-6 available at <http://www.unilever.com/Images/GTCs-Purchase-of-Goods.14.05.08 tcm244-409248.pdf> last visited 15 May 2015.

[19] See UNILEVER GTC, *ibid.*

collective electronic platform where parties simultaneously have access to provide or use available information in order to ensure traceability of both product and process. *The safety management scheme may follow a different logic from the commercial one made of reciprocal obligations among all participants and the recognition of an authority that can take organizational responsibility.*

Symmetrically monitoring compliance can be segmented in bilateral sequential relationships following the contractual infrastructure or result in collective monitoring via multiparty contracts as when 'peer monitoring' of regulatory compliance becomes the core feature of contractual governance.[20] In the former instance the buyer's contractual right to monitor regulatory compliance by the seller in contract 1 becomes an obligation towards the buyer downstream in contract 2 when the buyer becomes the seller, and so on moving down the chain. Rights to monitor are instrumental to the achievement of a collective objective: compliance with regulatory standards. This mechanism ensures continuity and consistency when bilateral sequential contracts rather than multiparty contracts are deployed. The interdependence of conducts related to risk management might be at odds with bilateral contracting when collective monitoring is required. As we shall see, even if the dominant pattern assumes a regulatory shape that reflects the chain's commercial structure, risk regulation may promote or require changes towards multiparty contracts or agreements among parties involved in different production stages. This happens in relation to risk management operations that necessitate information sharing related to the emergence of hazards to be promptly traced or in relation to product recalls that impose taking unsafe products away from the market. Most of the information sharing occurs via electronic shared platforms that have to be fed by each participant according to 'technical requirements' defined by the platform's owner.[21] The use of these platforms is more fine-tuned with multiparty agreement than with sequential contracting but it is ordinarily applied to supply chains governed via bilateral contracts.[22]

---

[20] Peer monitoring of regulatory provisions can combine simultaneous with sequential monitoring depending on how the information about each participant is shared and how the response to hazards is organized.

[21] See for example the Core Code of Conduct Version 1.0 adopted by UTZ, available at <http://www.scsglobalservices.com/files/en_utz_core_code_for_group_certification_2014.pdf> last visited 15 May 2015, where it is stated that each certified entity has to provide data concerning the process and the product.

[22] As we shall see, these platforms can be managed by the chain leader or by the certification body.

V. POWER IN GSC AND THE BOUNDARIES OF CONTRACTUAL RISK REGULATION: HIERARCHICAL VERSUS COLLABORATIVE CONTRACTUAL GOVERNANCE

GSCs can include a large number of regulated entities (over 100,000 across the globe per chain); the quantitative and qualitative impact of their risk policies may certainly be greater than that of some individual states' domestic regulation. Risk regulation operates through a wide range of tools depending on the chain's structure. Leading firms coordinate supply chains by issuing suppliers' guidelines, terms and general conditions, and defining sourcing policies which set common obligations with which the entire chain has to comply.[23] These instruments encompass both the commercial and regulatory dimensions, including risk regulation. They are incorporated into the contracts along the chain. Supply chain coordination is also achieved through compliance programmes based on due diligence that increasingly requires control over the chain regardless of whether it is organized as a group or as a chain of contracts.[24]

This description, useful for analytical purposes, presupposes the persistence of a clear-cut distinction between regulators and regulated: the multinational is the regulator; the supply chain participants are the regulated entities. However, such account does not always correspond to reality, especially when contractual governance is deployed to ensure compliance in transnational settings. In fact there is no predefined scheme and the identification of regulators and regulated can become a dependent variable of both the supply chain's structure and the distribution of contractual power: hence the distinction between rule makers and

---

[23] See for example UNILEVER GTC, sourcing policies available at <http://www.unilever.com/Images/GTCs-Purchase-of-Goods.14.05.08_tcm244-409248.pdf> last visited 15 May 2015, or Wal-Mart, available at <http://corporate.walmart.com/global-responsibility/ethical-sourcing/standards-for-suppliers> last visited 15 May 2015.

[24] See the Report of the Special Representative of the Secretary General on the issue of human rights and transnational corporations and other business enterprises, John Ruggie, 'Guiding Principles on Business and Human Rights: Implementing the United Nations "Protect, Respect and Remedy" Framework', A/HRC/17/31, March 2011 (endorsed unanimously by the United Nations Human Rights Council on 16 June 2011), Principle 15 on due diligence. Available at <http://business-humanrights.org/en/un-guiding-principles> last visited 15 May 2015.

rule takers depends upon the structure and internal power allocation of the chain. When power distribution is uneven it is easy to discern between regulators and regulated, rule makers and rule takers. The power wielder is the regulator; those who do not have contractual power are the rule takers, forced to join the regulatory scheme and to comply with its rules. When power is distributed or dispersed along the chain the hierarchical model is replaced by a cooperative framework coming close to the coincidence between regulators and regulated, blurring the distinction between rule making and rule taking.[25] To (over)simplify: *the higher the level of hierarchy, the sharper the distinction between rule makers and takers; the lower the level of hierarchy, the less clear-cut the distinction between regulators and regulated becomes, albeit without disappearing*. Active participation in standard setting by the suppliers does not imply that regulators and regulated completely overlap and the distinction shades away. We can therefore distinguish between hierarchical and collaborative contractual risk regulation.

Power structures in supply chains determine contractual technologies as well. In hierarchical chains one regulator chooses the standard and the implementation's instruments. The most common technology is based on standard contract forms, usually drafted by one enterprise, the chain leader that predefines guidelines for suppliers whose consent is based on a take-it-or-leave-it basis. The relationship between different tiers is imposed on suppliers whose regulatory obligations are defined in the guidelines issued by the leader rather than being negotiated. The lead enterprise is effectively acting as the regulator by determining general regulatory terms and conditions that participants to the supply chain, that is, the regulated, have to abide by.[26]

A different contractual technology emerges when contractual and regulatory power is diffused and, to some extent, shared; the definition of regulatory obligations is the product of bargaining rather than the outcome of hierarchy. Here regulatory contracts are relational; the

---

[25] For a wider taxonomy of supply chain structure see Gary Gereffi, John Humphrey and Timothy Sturgeon, 'The Governance of Global Value Chains' (2005) 12:1 *Review of International Political Economy* 78–104. For the purpose of this analysis a simplified picture with two polar models indicates the causal relationship between power allocation and the distinction between rule makers and rule takers.

[26] The model is rather diffused. Most of the main MNCs have supplied general terms and conditions or guidelines that define common rules parties have to abide by. These include, for example, Unilever, Wal-Mart, Cargill, Nestlé and Danone.

content and the modes of implementation of regulatory obligations are the result of collaborative contractual governance. Collaboration emerges not only in relation to the standard's definition but also and even more when non-compliance arises and parties have to devise joint solutions. The collaborative model assumes that implementation may require adjustments and adaptations often negotiated by the parties, sometimes integrated by intermediaries. In the latter model the use of bilateral contracts becomes more problematic.[27] In 'supply chain regulation' the identification of regulators and regulated occurs by looking not only at the rule-making process but also at how contracts allocate tasks, risks and costs among the chain's participants. This process is highly sector and market specific. Risk regulation within product safety may in fact be specific to individual commodities.

The foregoing analysis shows that within contractual governance it is not useful to assume a clear-cut distinction between rule makers and rule takers.[28] Depending on the degree of power concentration and on the need for collaboration in joint problem solving when standard non-compliance materializes, the distinction may blur. The lack of a clear distinction between regulators and regulated imposes a more sophisticated account of the different types of contractual technologies chosen by the parties along the chain and the increasing role of third party intermediaries in determining how the effects of regulatory non-compliance should be remedied along the chain. From this conclusion we can draw implications about the necessity to investigate more deeply the different contractual technologies adopted in supply chains in order to evaluate the role of chain participants at both contract drafting and implementation stage, including that on monitoring regulatory performances.

---

[27] See below on the distinction between bilateral and multiparty contracts.

[28] See on these issues David Levi Faur and Shana M. Starobin, 'Transnational Politics and Policy: From Two-Way to Three-Way Interactions' (2014) Working Paper No. 62 *Jerusalem Papers in Regulation & Governance*; on file with the author; and Tim Buthe, 'Distributional Consequences of Transnational Private Regulation: Institutional Complementarity as a Structural Source of Power in Global Product and Financial Markets' (2013) Duke University *Rethinking Regulation Working Paper* No. 6.

VI. TRR BY CONTRACT: GOVERNING RISK INTERDEPENDENCIES

From a functional perspective, risk regulation, at both domestic and transnational level, is characterized by a high level of interdependency of regulated entities' conduct, which reflects the nature of risk. These interdependencies occur in relation to the same risk when conduct of the chain participants may affect the probability and magnitude of risks or may concern different risks, for example those related to product safety and to environmental risks. With the increasing relevance of process standards, risk management has moved towards the upstream part of the supply chain. Standard setting, instead, has moved downwards towards distribution and retailers.[29] These changes pose daunting challenges to the design of contractual governance to be addressed in the following sections.

The magnitude of risk, its occurrence and the management of its consequences strongly depend upon the interaction between regulated entities, both within individual chains and between chains. Risks may involve multiple enterprises with their supply chains or be limited to a single enterprise and its chain. Whether and how suppliers comply with safety requirements, and what happens when a health-related risk emerges but its origins are unknown and hard to detect, are key factors in designing reciprocal obligations among participants and the role of a coordinating private authority within and between chains. This is clear when risks related to foodstuffs materialize and generate, for example, pandemics. But it is also clear when environmental risks generated during production processes occur. Contractual governance permits governing the interdependencies both in relation to emergence of risk and its management.

The distinction between risks that occur within chains and risks that may include multiple chains is very significant for contractual governance. The analysis of the remaining part focuses upon single chain risk assessment and management but the necessity to coordinate with other supply chains calls for an even broader approach when hazards emerge over time, concern the entire market and product withdrawal or recalls are necessary.

---

[29] This is particularly true in relation to agrifood businesses and less so for areas like civil aviation or extractive industries.

The relevance of interdependencies partly depends upon the consolidation of a regulatory approach based on prevention.[30] A preventive approach tries to define *ex ante* where hazards can emerge, how they should be detected and handled; it presupposes the involvement of those actors in the chain best positioned to detect harms and to act upon the information related to the hazard.[31] Such information can exist *ex ante* or, more often, it becomes available after risks materialize, calling for flexibility in allocating responsibilities along the chain, depending on the nature of the risk, and its magnitude and effects. Since the assumption of full information about the role of interdependencies is unrealistic at best, the preventive approach has to be combined with contractual flexibility in designing a management system that will adapt as information becomes available.

Risks related to hazardous products, the primary example in this chapter, may depend on the concurrent mishandling of production/distribution by many enterprises over the course of production and distribution. For example, in product safety the structure of the production process requires coordination to detect hazards not only during the process but also *ex post*, when harms only become apparent to the end-user in the final product. Even in the latter instance it is necessary to identify at which point of the production process things went wrong in order to manage the risks and eventually correct regulatory failures related to process design.

Product traceability is a powerful illustration of regulatory interdependencies and their effects on the contractual infrastructure. In order to address safety hazards and mitigate potential harms coming from outbreaks and pandemics, traceability of the product during the production process has become necessary. Traceability is often a precondition for risk management which requires allocation of tasks and identification of a coordinator that can ensure effective information flows, prompt reactions and remediation when hazards materialize. The regulatory dimension concerns risks not only for the individual end-user of the

---

[30] Within the broad category of prevention the precautionary principle constitutes one possible expression. The preventive regulatory approach cuts across the public/private divide which becomes relevant when instruments and costs of implementation have to be allocated.

[31] The preventive approach is often associated with the endorsement of the precautionary principle that has developed differently in Europe and the US. See on the comparative perspective the research by Wiener, Rogers, Hammitt and Sand, *supra* note 1.

unsafe product but also for the whole community where those products will be used.

The example of the Hazard Analysis for Critical Control Point (HACCP) in food safety further illustrates the issue of interdependency of participants' conduct in the supply chain and the necessity to adapt existing contractual architectures to coordinate multiple actors while assessing and managing safety-related risks. The establishment of HACCP and compliance with the requirements have become mandatory in many legal systems.[32] ISO 22000 on food safety requires the adoption of an HACCP plan.[33] An HACCP plan identifies several critical control points to detect and manage hazard. Each control point may coincide with a single enterprise or with a group. An HACCP plan has to identify responsibility and authority within each control point. The HACCP, initially applied to the processing stage, was later extended to the production stage, with some adaptations dependent on the difficulty of identifying hazards at an earlier stage.

The HACCP has a relatively uniform structure but individual schemes may implement it differently. Transnational commercial contracts may simply incorporate the relevant obligations by reference to the standard or adapt their contractual structure with different tiers of suppliers, ensuring that effective management coordination can take place. In both instances, changes to the conventional infrastructure are needed. Compliance with HACCP calls for cooperation among regulated entities to a higher extent than ordinary contractual liability regimes for breach of safety requirements in bilateral contracting. The incorporation of codes implies that each party accepts to subject itself to the governing body of the standard and its decisions. Technically, the contractual obligation related to risk management is enforceable only by the party in 'privity' but in practice the incorporation produces commitments towards all the participants in the management scheme. The contractual incorporation constitutes the legal basis for exercising regulatory authority over the scheme's participants. This is a typical tension between the dominant commercial logic and the regulatory logic.

---

[32] EU legislation, Regulation 853/2004; in the US the Consumer Product Safety Act, Consumer Product Safety Improvement Act and in relation to food the Food and Safety Modernization Act (FSMA 2010).

[33] See ISO Standard 22000 7.6 establishing the HACCP plan, on file with the author.

Interdependencies among conduct of regulated entities call for multiple actors' coordination that may differ depending on the contractual technology. Such coordination is easy to accommodate in multiparty contracts, for example when there is coincidence between the scope of the series of economic exchanges and the scope of regulation. When, for example, the chain is organized via horizontal networks of enterprises, each contributing to the production process, there is some symmetry between the commercial and regulatory dimension. This is the case where the production process requires simultaneous rather than sequential performances by each participant in the chain. It becomes more difficult when the exchanges are segmented into bilateral sequential contracts along the chain. In that framework there might be a structural dissonance between the commercial dimension, organized around bilateral exchanges, and the regulatory function, based on multiparty coordination along the chain. Performance of regulatory obligations in bilateral contracts has to be monitored and coordinated since the effects of non-compliance inevitably spill over the contracts downstream and require corrective actions and joint problem sharing among parties that may not be in contractual 'privity'. The primary goal of the transnational regulatory provisions is not allocation of liability for the occurrence of harms but the prevention and remediation of the effects of the non-compliance in order to restore the functioning of regulatory process and to mitigate potential adverse consequences stemming from the risk's occurrence.

The logic of commercial contracts is risk allocation in order to define the boundaries of liability for non-performance, identifying also who should bear the cost of such non-performance. The logic of regulatory provisions is to foster cooperation in order to activate joint problem-solving mechanisms in cost-effective ways. The challenge to contractual governance of TRR is therefore related to the search for the best compromise between these two often conflicting logics.

VII. MONITORING COMPLIANCE AND CONTRACTUAL GOVERNANCE

Monitoring compliance with transnational regulatory requirements has changed dramatically in the last two decades in relation to both actors and instruments.[34] There has been a strategic move from inspection by

[34] See Christine Parker and Vibeke Lehman Nielsen, *Explaining Compliance: Business Responses to Regulation* (Edward Elgar 2011).

public authorities to safety management systems by private actors.[35] Contractual governance of risk regulation cannot ignore the requirements of domestic legislation. It often provides additional monitoring devices that save costs and, in principle, may increase effectiveness. TPR via transnational commercial contracts focuses on monitoring compliance with safety requirements, modifying the allocation of tasks between transnational private players and domestic administrative authorities.[36] In earlier times public entities were asked to inspect regulated entities to verify compliance with standards. In cross-border trade, inspections could take place both at the production site and at the stage of import.[37] These inspections focused on the compliance with public regulation but disregarded the organizational framework within which inspections would occur. Symmetrically the remedies would concentrate on violations without investigating either their causes or their deep consequences. The role of private monitoring of regulatory provisions was limited and buyers would focus more on quality and conformity, being involved in regulatory matters only if breaches of safety requirements could engender contractual or tortious liability.

The move towards safety risk management along supply chains has changed both the regulatory approach and the role of contracts, underlining the importance of the regulatory infrastructure. Third party verification regimes, including certification and quality assurance schemes, operate as primary monitors often on the basis of explicit legislative/administrative recognition. This change, promoted also in domestic legislation, has brought about new contractual infrastructures that need to reflect the organizational approach to safety rather than the obligations of

[35] See Cary Coglianese and David Lazer, 'Management-Based Regulation: Prescribing Private Management to Achieve Public Goals' (2003) 37:4 *Law and Society Review* 691–730. This change is demonstrated by contractual practices. See for example Art. 7.2 of Unilever GTC, where it is stated that quality assurance schemes replace direct inspections by the buyer.

[36] As mentioned, the role of public domestic authorities has not been replaced by third party intermediaries but has changed. There are instances of formal delegation and instances of informal delegation to private intermediaries but domestic authorities maintain the final responsibility. For an illustration of the relationship between public agencies and private intermediaries in the US see Lesley K. McAllister, 'Regulation by Third Party Verification' (2012) 53:1 *Boston College Law Review*; and Lytton and McAllister, *supra* note 6.

[37] Cary Coglianese, Adam M. Finkel and David Zaring, 'Consumer Protection in an Era of Globalization' in Cary Coglianese, Adam M. Finkel and David Zaring (eds), *Import Safety: Regulatory Governance in the Global Economy* (University of Pennsylvania Press 2009).

individual actors in bilateral contracts. Not only safety management systems require higher coordination among parties, calling for multiparty agreements that imply mutually enforceable obligations; but also, and more importantly, change the monitoring approach by shifting the responsibility and the costs on private parties. Administrative authorities in the new framework operate more as meta-regulators that oversee private regulation and monitoring rather than direct monitors of regulated entities.[38] The drivers of contractual governance as an instrument of TRR are multiple, varying depending on the sector and the specific regulatory objectives. In this chapter we shall focus mainly on two drivers: (1) the necessity to coordinate monitoring of regulated entities located in different jurisdictions in order to govern risk interdependencies; and (2) the need to delegate private actor effective monitoring that national authorities are unable to perform for lack of legal power, resources or expertise.

Increasing use of contractual technologies characterizes both dimensions: in the first instance contracts are instruments that simultaneously link regulators and regulatees and coordinate the latter to detect and manage risks across jurisdictions; in the second instance 'implicit' contracts delegate to transnational private actors monitoring compliance and, to some degree, enforcement of risk-related violations. There is a clear functional correlation between the 'delegation contract' among transnational public and private actors and the 'regulatory contract' between private regulators and regulatees. The scope and form of delegation influence the relationship between regulators and regulated entities. Within this conceptual framework, contractual governance permeates transnational risk management. Whether this development meets the minimum legitimacy and effectiveness thresholds is a complex empirical question whose answer is beyond the scope of this chapter.

VIII. THE ROLE OF PRIVATE INTERMEDIARIES IN TRANSNATIONAL CONTRACTUAL GOVERNANCE: RISK ASSESSMENT AND RISK MANAGEMENT

Within this framework, especially in relation to environmental, social and safety risks, supply chains have been integrated by 'new' intermediaries:

---

[38] Cary Coglianese and Evan Mendelson, 'Metaregulation and Self-Regulation' in Martin Cave, Robert Baldwin and Martin Lodge (eds), *The Oxford Handbook of Regulation* (OUP 2010) 146.

those governing certification and quality assurance bodies.[39] This process has enhanced the effectiveness and, to some extent, the legitimacy of the regulatory process via contractual governance, but it is not costless.

Process and products certification and quality assurances have become necessary requirements to access global supply chains. They have developed for different reasons: partly to address the failures of public domestic authorities that could not adequately and cost-effectively monitor regulatory compliance by global supply chains; and partly to provide downstream chain leaders closer control over the upstream part of the supply chain located too far away from MNC headquarters.

The number of suppliers and their location make it hardly possible for the chain leader to have direct control. Certification is therefore modifying delegation related to compliance monitoring. While absent certification MNCs would delegate to first tier monitoring compliance both with commercial and regulatory provisions, with the use of certification the oversight is moving from within the supply chain to third parties that may not even have direct contractual relationships with the chain leader; however, they clearly act on its behalf and that of the final beneficiaries. The chain leader, via quality assurance, certification and auditing, is able to gain closer control over the process through certification than it could with direct control; in addition it shifts monitoring costs of regulatory performances and compliance on the supply chain. Often it gains control while shifting costs and responsibilities.

Certification's content has also changed over time. While in the past safety was addressed separately from environmental and social issues, nowadays there is a consistent trend towards integration of these three aspects within the sustainability framework.[40] The role of intermediaries in safety regulation through the supply chain should therefore be analysed in the light of such an integrated approach.

---

[39] Certification and quality assurance are not new. What is relevant is their expansion at transnational level and the role they play in ensuring coordination among firms with common regulatory requirements. See Tim Bartley, 'Certification as a Mode of Social Regulation' in David Levi-Faur (ed.), *Handbook on the Politics of Regulation* (Edward Elgar 2011) 441–452.

[40] See for example SAFA guidelines issued by the FAO, available at <http://www.fao.org/fileadmin/templates/nr/sustainability_pathways/docs/SAFA_Guidelines_Final_122013.pdf> last visited 15 May 2015; ISEAL Alliance standard-setting and impact codes, available at <http://www.isealalliance.org/our-work/defining-credibility/codes-of-good-practice/standard-setting-code> last visited 15 May 2015.

In this domain TRR is governed primarily by contracts between private parties, the certifier and the certified, the assurer and the assured, whose regulatory functions can cover both risk assessment and management. Certification contracts are linked to commercial contracts implicitly or expressly.[41] The certification contract incorporates by reference the standard and the evaluation scheme provided by the scheme owner.[42] Contractual governance of risk regulation requires considering the links between the different contracts and the integration between risk assessment and risk management.

Certification or quality assurances are technically 'independent' services remunerated by the producer on the basis of a contract but the certifier's real role is that of a compliance monitoring 'agent' for the chain leader and possibly for the regulatory beneficiaries (consumers, environmental organizations). The modes through which the link between contracts is established define the nature of delegation to the certifier and its effectiveness as a regulatory tool.

Interdependencies require coordination between logics that might not be entirely consistent. From the perspective of duration, for example, there might not be full alignment between the commercial and the certification contract. Certification contracts often have longer duration and may reflect a performance improvement scheme where the certified commits to increase the degree compliance over the course of the years.[43] Differences in contractual duration may pose additional coordination problems as it might be the case that the certification contract failure to comply with standard is detected at the time of inspection during the production process, whereas non-compliance with conformity requirements in transnational commercial contracts emerges at the time of delivery. As a result, what constitutes a breach in the certification contract may qualify as an anticipatory breach in the commercial contract

---

41 The references to certification schemes for individual commodities are made on suppliers' guides and procurement policies that are incorporated in contracts. See for example Nestlé responsible sourcing guidelines available at <http://www.nestle.com/asset-library/documents/library/documents/corporate_social_responsibility/nestle-responsible-sourcing-guidelines.pdf> last visited 15 May 2015.

42 See for example GLOBALGAP sub-licence and certification agreement available at <http://www1.globalgap.org/north-america/upload/CBs/130111_GGNA_CB_Sublicense_and_Certification_Agreement_v1.2.pdf> last visited 15 May 2015.

43 See for example the UTZ code, where those certified are supposed to improve their safety compliance over four years according to a predetermined scoring system.

and pose coordination problems in assessing liability consequences and coordination among remedies relevant for contractual governance.

Certification scheme owners are not only engaged in monitoring compliance with international standards but directly contribute to assess risks and design management systems along the chain. Each certified entity, being an individual or a group producer, is asked to run a risk assessment and adopt a risk management plan.[44] Such design often forces rethinking some of the pillars of the chain organizational structure and that of the chain leader. For example, the sourcing policies through private procurement of MNCs have changed rather significantly since the consolidation of certification and quality assurance schemes. There has been an integration of procurement and sustainability officers at the global level which interface with suppliers.

As a result, scheme certification owners interplay with chain leaders, especially their procurement officers, in monitoring and solving problems arising from non-compliance, complementing domestic public actors and sometimes replacing them on the basis of legislative delegation, as happens in food safety.[45]

Third party certifiers, auditors and quality assurers modify quite significantly the contractual governance of TRR. They influence standard setting by introducing safety criteria that implement principles of their codes of conduct. Codes of conduct may include a long and detailed list of obligations to assess risks and establish a management plan at individual or group level within the supply chain. These obligations, the standard of performance, the tolerance for non-compliance, the identification of the breaching area, are all within the scope of the codes and the certification contract, with a strong impact on the transnational commercial contract defining the economic terms of the exchange. They define in concrete terms the content of each party's obligation when complying with an HACCP; they determine remedial actions to be undertaken in case of non-compliance.[46] Eventually they sanction the non-compliant and may significantly influence their participation in the chain and the

---

[44] See for example UTZ Coffee Code of Conduct, section 2 management system, version 1.2, November 2010 currently under revision, available at <www.utz.org>, last visited 31 January 2014.

[45] See in the US the FSMA 2010.

[46] For example UTZ certified Coffee Code cit. 9. A 1 'The certificate holder conducts a hygiene and food safety risk analysis concerning post harvest handling facilities … Based on the risk analysis the certificate holder makes and implements an action plan on how to assure hygiene and food safety in post harvest handling facilities.'

related regulatory process.[47] But codes define additional elements related to duration and improvement that have a direct impact on the commercial contracts between suppliers and buyers and overall chain architecture.

The influence of certifiers' choice of instrument on supply chain governance is quite significant. One noticeable illustration is the development of group certification among smallholders in farming contracts. In the agrifood supply chain, group certification is promoting aggregation of smallholders to comply with regulatory requirements with significant spillovers on the commercial side of the contractual relationship. Increasingly, certification schemes differentiate between stand alone and group certification and design different organizational structures and standards for the two types of producer. The degree of delegation tends to be higher for group certification. The creation of group certification results in delegation of monitoring responsibility to the group leader, who reports to the certifier or quality assurer and takes responsibility to devise an effective monitoring system according to the criteria set out in the certification guidelines.[48] Coordination occurs within the group, which is often a separate legal entity (a cooperative or an association) providing services to the participants.[49]

But how far is the use of contractual governance in TRR modifying the boundaries between commercial and regulatory management of supply chain relationships? Certification contracts complement commercial contracts in performing risk regulation along the supply chain. The intermediaries have control over the regulatory process but try to stay away from the commercial side of the relationship and refrain from intervening in contractual disputes concerning the consequences of price volatility. This divide is increasingly problematic and new forms of governance will emerge to coordinate the commercial and the regulatory dimensions.

---

[47] For example GLOBALGAP General Regulations version 4.0 (2013) Art 6.4 available at <www.globagap.org>.

[48] See in the agrifood group certification GLOBALGAP General Regulations, available at <www.globalgap.org> and UTZ certified Core Code of Conduct version 1.0 for group and multi-group certification.

[49] The definition of what constitutes a group varies from code to code: they can be informal networks, or corporate entities in the form of companies or cooperatives.

IX. CONCLUDING REMARKS

The use of contractual governance and in particular of transnational contracts as instruments of TRR is gaining importance but has not yet attracted sufficient attention in both theoretical and empirical research. It modifies the actors and the instruments of risk regulation and has had an impact on the design of regulatory strategies. Risk regulation through contractual governance permits achieving degrees of standard harmonization and more effective monitoring of regulatory performance by chain participants across different jurisdictions. In order to achieve harmonization, private standards used in contractual governance have to comply with all the domestic public standards where regulated entities operate. Hence they are stricter than public standards. In theory global private standards can achieve two objectives: a reduction in fragmentation and an increase in safety. But how effective is contractual governance in risk regulation? Systematic data are not yet available!

As we have seen, there is no single regulatory strategy within contractual governance: the relationship between regulators and regulated, the degree of cooperation among regulated entities and the distribution of tasks within the group of regulated entities are dependent upon the combination of exogenous variables concerning the economic determinants of the length, interconnectedness and modularity of the chain and the degree of market concentration or dispersion. We have assumed that allocation and distribution of regulatory power depend upon that of contractual power but have suggested that the choice of regulatory instruments, for example the specific contractual technology, also bears some consequences on the type of contractual risk regulation.

Contractual governance of risk management transforms the function of contracts by addressing and solving collective action problems. Interaction of regulated entities to coordinate risk management is the result of a governance process which depends on the choice of instrument within available contractual technologies. A wide range of instruments from standard contract forms to highly relational contracts can be deployed. Such choice is determined partly by exogenous factors related to the structure of the chain (and the distribution of power within) and that of the markets where participants operate; and partly by the regulatory approaches. Hence the analysis of the interaction among supply chain participants governed by commercial contracts to comply with regulatory objectives of risk regulation shows multiple patterns depending on the interplay between these two groups of determinants.

The increasing role of intermediaries in certification and quality assurance further suggests that contractual governance of risk regulation in supply chains is the result of the interaction between chain participants, private intermediaries and national governments. The transnational commercial contract may directly refer to the certification standard and implicitly establish a link between the two contracts (production and certification contracts). The link underlines the existence of interdependencies between the activity of the certifier and the buyer as far as monitoring regulatory compliance and sanctioning non-compliance is concerned.

Third party intermediaries play a major role in assessing and managing safety and environmental risks taking place along supply chains. They certainly contribute to implement the precautionary principle in many areas and foster prevention by setting up programmes incorporated in contractual arrangements with the chain participants. Framing these innovations within the alternative public/private governance does not illuminate the deep nature of the change that arises in the private sphere since it is strongly influenced by the strategic moves of public domestic and international actors. Contractual governance as an instrument of risk regulation demonstrates further how the public/private divide in TRR has to be dis-embedded from domestic grounded distinctions in order to capture the causal correlations between the increasing use of contractual technologies and the changes in risk regulation.

Who decides what and how regulatory provisions become part of contractual governance? To what extent does contractual governance permit regulatory beneficiaries to become part of these regulatory instruments? This decision is made not only within chains but is also driven by the market structure. Clearly, in the field of food safety the concentration of distributors at international level has given international big retailers the power to regulate private standards previously in the hands of food processors.[50] Retailers' dominance has not only reallocated power but

---

[50] On the shift of regulatory power in agrifood from producers to retailers see Linda Fulponi, 'Private Voluntary Standards in the Food System: The Perspective of Major Food Retailers in OECD Countries' (2006) 31:1 *Food Policy* 1–13 (February) 1; Spencer Henson and John Humphrey, 'The Impacts of Private Food Safety Standards on the Food Chain and on Public Standard-Setting Processes', Paper Prepared for FAO/WHO, May 2009, available at <http://ec.europa.eu/food/international/organisations/sps/docs/private_standards_codex_en.pdf>; Joint FAO/WHO Food Standards Programme, 'Codex Alimentarius Commission, 33rd Session, Consideration of the Impact of Private Standards', Geneva, Switzerland, 5–9 July 2010, available at <ftp://ftp.fao.org/codex../Meetings/CAC/cac33/

stimulated the emergence of new players: chain intermediaries. In global supply, chain intermediaries, local and international, including credit institutions, have always also played a role. Those who act within global chains are often new intermediaries whose mission and objectives contribute to reshape contractual governance of risk regulation. The claim is that new intermediaries are further changing contractual governance of risk regulation by integrating monitoring and standard setting. They contribute to the coordination of different nodes of the chain and often solve conflicts related to the allocation of compliance costs.[51]

The use of contractual governance for TRR poses broader questions concerning interest representations of those who are supposed to benefit from compliance and would be harmed by violations of regulatory requirements. The conventional contractual toolbox relies upon consumer protection via consumer contracts and administrative regulation but it divides rather clearly the commercial dimension of business to business and the regulatory dimension of business to consumer. Incorporating regulatory provisions coming from public and private standards reconfigures this divide and opens the space for a more integrated framework where consumer, investor and environmental regulation enter the domain of transnational commercial contracts and become active participants in contractual risk regulation.

---

cac33_13e.pdf>; The World Bank, *Agricultural Innovation Systems: An Investment Sourcebook*, Washington DC, 2012.

[51] Intermediaries both old and new play a major role as informal conflict resolution agents that make the use of courts and formalized dispute resolution mechanisms less relevant.

9. Systemic risk and macroprudential regulation

Franklin Allen and Elena Carletti

1. INTRODUCTION

During the recent financial crisis, microprudential regulation of the banking system turned out to be unable to maintain financial stability largely because it did not recognize the problem of systemic risk. This chapter discusses in detail the sources of systemic risk, their importance for financial stability and the macroprudential policies that are necessary to address them.[1]

Systemic risk arises from the following sources:

1. common exposure to asset price bubbles, particularly real estate bubbles;
2. liquidity provision and mispricing of assets;
3. multiple equilibria and panics;
4. contagion;
5. sovereign default;
6. currency mismatches in the banking system.

We discuss each of these in turn in Section 2. Section 3 then considers the macroprudential policies that can be used to counter these systemic risks.

[1] This contribution has also appeared in Franklin Allen and Elena Carletti, 'Systemic Risk and Macroprudential Regulation' in Franklin Allen, Masahiko Aoki, Jean-Paul Fitoussi, Noburino Kiyotaki, Roger Gordon and Joseph E. Stigliz (eds), *The Global Macro Economy and Finance*, IEA Conference Volume No. 150-III (Palgrave Macmillan 2012) 191–210.

2. SYSTEMIC RISK

1. Real Estate Bubbles

Herring and Wachter[2] and Reinhart and Rogoff[3] provide persuasive evidence that collapses in real estate prices, either residential or commercial or both, are one of the major causes of financial crises. In many cases these collapses occur after bubbles in real estate prices that are often created by loose monetary policy and excessive availability of credit. When the bubble bursts, the financial sector and the real economy are adversely affected.

The current crisis provides a good example of this. Allen and Carletti[4] argue that the main cause of the crisis was that there was a bubble in real estate in the US and in a number of other countries such as Spain and Ireland. When the bubble burst in the US, many financial institutions experienced severe problems because of the collapse in the securitized mortgage market. Problems then spread to the real economy. Figure 9.1 shows the movement in property prices in the US, Spain and Ireland. It can be seen that in all three countries house prices rose significantly and then dropped.

The real estate bubble in these countries was the result of loose monetary policy and global imbalances that led to excessive credit availability. Central banks, in particular in the US, set very low interest rates during the period 2003–2004 to avoid a recession after the tech bubble in 2000 and the 9/11 terrorist attacks in 2001 at a time when house prices were already rising quite quickly. As argued by Taylor,[5] these levels of interest rates were much lower than in previous US recessions relative to the economic indicators at the time captured by the 'Taylor rule'. In such an environment of low interest rates, people in the US started to borrow and buy houses to benefit from their growing prices. Unlike stock prices, where returns follow random walks, returns

---

2 Richard J. Herring and Susan Wachter, 'Real Estate Booms and Banking Busts: An International Perspective' (1999) 99–27 *Wharton Financial Institutions Center Working Paper*.

3 Carmen M. Reinhart and Kenneth S. Rogoff, *This Time is Different: Eight Centuries of Financial Folly* (Princeton University Press 2009).

4 Franklin Allen and Elena Carletti, 'An Overview of the Crisis: Causes, Consequences and Solutions' (2009) 10 *International Review of Finance* 1–26.

5 John B. Taylor, 'The Financial Crisis and the Policy Responses: An Empirical Analysis of What Went Wrong' (2008) *Stanford University Working Paper*.

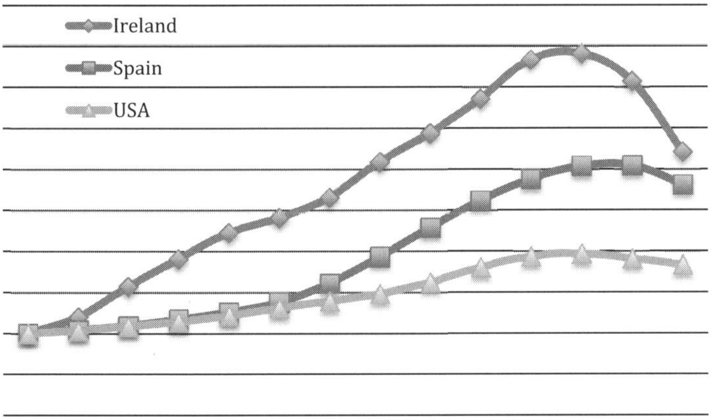

Source: IMF.

Figure 9.1 *Housing prices in Ireland, Spain and the US*

on housing are positively serially correlated, as found by Case and Shiller,[6] Englund, Quigley and Redfearn[7] and Glaeser and Gyourko.[8] This means that by lowering interest rates significantly below the current rate of house price appreciation, the Fed effectively created a profitable opportunity to buy property. Other public policies such as the tax deductibility of interest rates on mortgages contributed further to the housing boom.

As shown in Figure 9.1, Spain and Ireland also had very large run ups in property prices. According to Taylor,[9] these countries also had loose monetary policies relative to the Taylor rule. Spain, which had one of the largest deviations from the rule, also had the biggest housing boom as measured by the change in housing investment as a share of GDP. Other countries in the Eurozone such as Germany did not have a housing boom. Their inflation rates and other economic indicators were such that for them the European Central Bank's (ECB's) interest rates did not correspond to a loose monetary policy.

[6] Karl E. Case and Robert J. Shiller, 'The Efficiency of the Market for Single-Family Homes' (1989) 79:1 *American Economic Review* 125–137.

[7] Peter Englund, John M. Quigley and Christian L. Redfearn, 'Improved Price Indexes for Real Estate: Measuring the Course of Swedish Housing Prices' (1998) 44 *Journal of Urban Economics* 171–196.

[8] Edward L. Glaeser and Joseph Gyourko, 'Housing Dynamics' (2007) Paper No. 2137 *Harvard Institute of Economic Research.*

[9] Taylor, *supra* note 5.

As Allen and Gale[10] have argued, asset price bubbles are also caused by growth in credit. During the recent crisis, credit expanded rapidly in the countries with a loose monetary policy due to the presence of global imbalances. Several Asian countries have accumulated large amounts of foreign exchange reserves since the late 1990s. Figure 9.2 shows that much of this acquisition of reserves was by Asian countries. The reserves in Latin American and Central and Eastern European countries did not increase significantly. There are a number of reasons behind this accumulation. Allen and Carletti[11] argue that the Asian countries affected by the crisis of 1997 started accumulating reserves in response to the tough conditions that the International Monetary Fund (IMF) imposed on them in exchange for financial assistance. The motivations for the reserve accumulation of China, which is the largest holder, are probably more complex than this. Beside the precautionary reason, China started accumulating reserves to avoid allowing its currency to strengthen and damage its exports as well as to increase its political power. The accumulated reserves were mostly invested internationally. Much was invested in US dollars in debt securities such as Treasuries, and Fannie and Freddie mortgage-backed securities. The Federal National Mortgage Association (Fannie Mae) and the Federal Home Loan Mortgage Corporation (Freddie Mac) are government sponsored organizations. The large supply of debt in the US helped to drive down lending standards to ensure that there was enough demand for debt from house buyers and other borrowers. However, funds did not only flow to the US. Spain and Ireland also ran large current account deficits.

The burst of a bubble has a clear effect on the stability of the financial sector, as documented in Herring and Wachter[12] and Reinhart and Rogoff.[13] In the current crisis, for example, the sudden drop in asset prices starting in summer 2007, triggered by the fall in real estate prices and the large volatility that followed, worsened the balance sheets of financial institutions significantly and froze several financial markets including also the normally stable interbank market.

---

[10] Franklin Allen and Douglas Gale, 'Bubbles and Crises' (2000) 110:460 *The Economic Journal* 236–255; *id.*, *Understanding Financial Crises*, *Clarendon Lecture Series in Finance* (OUP 2007).

[11] Allen and Carletti, *supra* note 4.

[12] Herring and Wachter, *supra* note 2.

[13] *Supra* note 3.

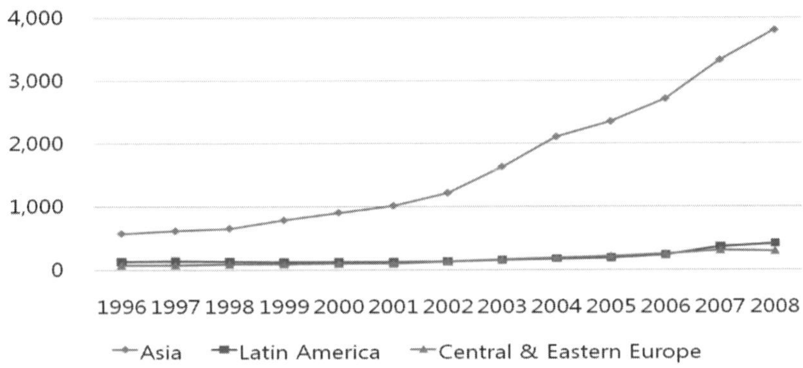

Source: IMF website, http://www.imf.org/. 'Asia' comprises the six East Asian countries: China, Hong Kong, Japan, Singapore, South Korea and Taiwan.

Figure 9.2 A comparison of foreign exchange reserves in different regions

The financial crisis then spread to the real sector. The burst of a bubble can, however, also create direct damaging effects on the real economy. In the current crisis, for example, the bursting of the property bubble in Spain led to a doubling of unemployment without the financial sector being much affected, at least initially. This was thanks to strict financial regulation and the use of some macroprudential instruments such as countercyclical loan loss reserve ratios. The fact that the burst of a bubble can affect both the financial and the real sector significantly underlines the importance of preventing bubbles.

2. Liquidity Provision and Mispricing of Assets

Another important source of systemic risk is inefficient liquidity provision and the mispricing of assets. Asset pricing theory in financial economics relies on the assumption of fully rational agents and perfect and complete markets. Under these assumptions, assets are always correctly priced at their fundamental values. Agents understand risks perfectly; financial institutions and liquidity do not play any role and crises should not occur. The recent crisis, however, has shown the flaws of these theories in practice. Financial markets, including money markets, can work badly, and financial institutions and their role as liquidity creators can be at centre stage.

The theories explaining the role of liquidity in creating systemic risk[14] combine the functioning of financial institutions and markets in a model of liquidity. Financial intermediaries provide liquidity insurance to consumers against their individual liquidity shocks. Markets allow financial intermediaries (and hence their depositors) to share aggregate risks. If financial markets are *complete*, the financial system provides liquidity efficiently in that it ensures that banks' liquidity shocks are hedged. By contrast, in the plausible case where markets are *incomplete*, banks cannot hedge completely against shocks and the financial system stops providing an efficient level of liquidity. This can generate mispricing of assets and even the prices of safe assets can fall below their fundamental values. The reason is that, with incomplete markets, liquidity provision is achieved by selling assets when liquidity is required. If liquidity is scarce, asset prices are determined by the available liquidity or, in other words, by the 'cash-in-the-market'. Some financial institutions must hold extra liquidity that allows them to buy up low price assets when liquidity is scarce. However, holding liquidity is costly as it prevents investment in the more profitable long asset. With incomplete markets, the suppliers of liquidity must be compensated for the cost of holding liquidity across states rather than state by state as with complete markets. To do this, asset prices must be low in the states where banks need more liquidity. This is inefficient as banks in need of liquidity have to sell at a low price to the providers of liquidity. There is negative insurance and suboptimal risk sharing. If asset prices are sufficiently low the banks in need of liquidity will go bankrupt and this can lead to large deadweight costs. The asset price volatility is costly because depositors are risk averse and their consumption varies across banks with high and low idiosyncratic liquidity risk. This leaves scope for central bank intervention to improve welfare.

To summarize, liquidity is costly to hold and asset price volatility is necessary to provide incentives to agents to hold it. But price volatility can cause crises. When prices fall to low enough levels, financial

---

[14] See, for example, Allen and Gale, *supra* note 10 (2007) and Franklin Allen and Douglas Gale, 'Asset Price Bubbles and Monetary Policy' in Meghnad Desai and Yahia Said (eds), *Global Governance and Financial Crises* (Routledge 2004) Chapter 3, 19–42; Franklin Allen and Elena Carletti, 'Credit Risk Transfer and Contagion' (2006) 53:1 *Journal of Monetary Economics* 89–111; *id.*, 'Mark-to-Market Accounting and Liquidity Pricing' (2008) 45 *Journal of Accounting and Economics* 358–378; Franklin Allen, Elena Carletti and Douglas Gale, 'Interbank Market Liquidity and Central Bank Intervention' (2009) 56:5 *Journal of Monetary Economics* 639–652.

institutions can go into bankruptcy. There is a market failure that provides the justification for central bank operations and other kinds of intervention to improve the allocation of resources and to avoid crises.[15]

3. Multiple Equilibria and Panics

The importance of panics in the current crisis is unclear. However, they remain an important source of systemic risk and thus deserve some attention as one of the macroeconomic aspects of systemic risk. Two distinct theories for the origins of banking panics have been proposed in the academic literature.[16] One line of argument maintains that panics are undesirable events caused by random deposit withdrawals unrelated to changes in the real economy. In the seminal work by Bryant[17] and Diamond and Dybvig,[18] for example, panics are self-fulfilling events. Agents have uncertain needs for consumption and long term investments are costly to liquidate. They deposit their endowment in a bank in exchange for a demand deposit contract which insures them against their liquidity needs. If all depositors believe that the other depositors withdraw their funds only according to their consumption needs, then the good equilibrium arises in which the bank can satisfy all depositors' demands without liquidating any of the long term assets. If, however, depositors believe that other depositors will withdraw prematurely, then all agents find it rational to redeem their claims and a panic occurs.

The second set of theories suggests that banking crises are not random events but a natural outgrowth of the business cycle. The idea is that an economic downturn will reduce the value of bank assets, raising the possibility that banks are unable to meet their commitments. If depositors receive information about the impending downturn in the cycle, they will anticipate financial difficulties in the banking sector and try to withdraw their funds prematurely, as in Gorton.[19] This attempt will precipitate the

---

15 Allen, Carletti and Gale, *supra* note 14.

16 For a survey, see Franklin Allen, Ana Babus and Elena Carletti, 'Financial Crises: Theory and Evidence' (2009) 1 *Annual Review of Financial Economics* 97 116.

17 John Bryant, 'A Model of Reserves, Bank Runs, and Deposit Insurance' (1980) 4:4 *Journal of Banking and Finance* 335–344.

18 Douglas W. Diamond and Philip H. Dybvig, 'Bank Runs, Deposit Insurance, and Liquidity' (1983) 91:3 *Journal of Political Economy* 401–419.

19 Gary Gorton, 'Banking Panics and Business Cycles' (1988) 40:4 *Oxford Economic Papers* 751–781.

crisis. In this case crises are a response of depositors to the arrival of sufficiently negative information on the unfolding economic circumstances.

The empirical evidence is mixed. Friedman and Schwartz[20] argue that the systemic risk and financial instability in the US in the late eighteenth and early nineteenth centuries were panic based, as evidenced by the absence of downturns in the relevant macroeconomic time series prior to the crises. In contrast, Gorton,[21] Calomiris and Gorton[22] and Calomiris and Mason[23] provide a wide range of evidence that many of the crises that occurred in the US in that period were fundamental based.

We have here only touched on some highlights of the literature on banking crises and panics. More complete surveys are provided by Gorton and Winton,[24] Allen and Gale[25] and Freixas and Rochet.[26]

4. Contagion

One source of systemic risk that does appear to have been important during the recent financial crisis is contagion. This refers to the possibility that the distress of one financial institution propagates to others in the financial system, thus leading ultimately to a systemic crisis. Central banks often use the risk of contagion to justify intervention, especially when the financial institution in distress is big or occupies a key position in particular markets. This is the origin of the term 'too big to fail'. The

---

20 Milton Friedman and Anna Jacobson Schwartz, *A Monetary History of the United States, 1867–1960* (Princeton University Press 1963).

21 *Supra* note 19.

22 Charles W. Calomiris and Gary Gorton, 'The Origins of Banking Panics, Models, Facts, and Bank Regulation' in R. Glenn Hubbard (ed.), *Financial Markets and Financial Crises* (University of Chicago Press 1991) 109–174.

23 Charles W. Calomiris and Joseph R. Mason, 'Fundamentals, Panics, and Bank Distress during the Depression' (2003) 93:5 *American Economic Review* 1615–1647.

24 Gary Gorton and Andrew Winton, 'Financial Intermediation' in George M. Constantinides, Milton Harris and Renè M. Stulz (eds), *Handbook of the Economics of Finance: Corporate Finance Volume 1A* (North Holland 2003) Chapter 8, 431–552.

25 *Supra* note 10.

26 Xavier Freixas and Jean Charles Rochet, *Microeconomics of Banking* (2nd edition, MIT Press 2008).

recent crisis abounds with examples of this. For example, Bernanke[27] argues that the takeover of Bear Stearns by JP Morgan arranged by the Federal Reserve Bank in March 2008 was justified by the likelihood that its failure would lead to a whole chain reaction where many other financial institutions would have gone bankrupt. There would have been contagion through the network of derivative contracts of which Bear Stearns was part.

When Lehman Brothers failed in September 2008, it was presumably expected by the Federal Reserve that its failure would not generate contagion. In fact there was contagion but it was quite complex. The problem spread first to the money market funds and the government had to intervene rapidly by providing a guarantee of all money market mutual funds. In addition, the failure of Lehman led to a loss of confidence in many financial firms as investors feared that other financial institutions might also be allowed to fail. The volumes in many important financial markets fell significantly and there was a large spillover into the real economy. World trade collapsed and in trade-based economies such as Germany and Japan GDP fell significantly in the fourth quarter of 2008 and the first quarter of 2010, respectively. This dramatic fall in GDP in many countries underlines the importance of the process of contagion.

Despite its importance, our understanding of the effects of contagion risk is still limited. The academic literature has provided a few explanations of the mechanisms at play, but much work is still needed. The literature on contagion takes a number of approaches.[28] In looking for contagious effects via direct linkages, early research by Allen and Gale[29] studied how the banking system responds to contagion when banks are connected under different network structures. It is shown that incomplete networks are more prone to contagion than complete structures. Subsequent research focused on network externalities created from individual bank risk. The main result in this theoretical literature is that greater connectivity reduces the likelihood of widespread default. However, shocks may have a significantly larger impact on the financial system when they occur.

---

27 Ben S. Bernanke, 'Opening Remarks' in *Maintaining Stability in a Changing Financial System* (2008) Federal Reserve Bank of Kansas City, Jackson Hole Symposium 1–12.

28 For a survey, see Allen, Babus and Carletti, *supra* note 16.

29 Franklin Allen and Douglas Gale, 'Financial Contagion' (2000) 108:1 *Journal of Political Economy* 1–33.

Wagner,[30] Ibragimov, Jaffee and Walden[31] and Allen, Babus and Carletti[32] consider a second type of contagion where systemic risk arises from common asset exposures. Diversification is privately beneficial but increases the likelihood of systemic risk as portfolios become more similar. The use of short term debt can lead to a further significant increase in systemic risk.

The recent crisis has shown that asset price volatility can also be an important form of contagion. Prices drop when banks have to sell their assets in response to a negative shock. These sales depress asset prices and may have negative spillovers on other banks in various ways. For example, low asset prices may affect the solvency of other financial institutions that need to raise liquidity in the market by selling assets.[33] Because of the low prices, banks in need of liquidity raise little money from the asset sale. This forces banks to sell larger quantities of assets with the consequence of further deterioration in asset prices. A similar mechanism holds when mark-to-market accounting is in use.[34] In an integrated financial system this form of contagion can easily transmit shocks internationally, in particular through large institutions operating cross border or on global financial markets.

The key issue is how likely contagion is in practice. A substantial strand of empirical literature is based on the first type of approach where financial institutions have direct linkages resulting from the mutual claims they have on one another. Most of these papers use balance sheet information to estimate bilateral credit relationships for different banking systems and estimate the stability of the interbank market by simulating the breakdown of a single bank. This literature is surveyed in Upper.[35] Overall the main finding in the empirical literature is that contagion is unlikely. However, there are a number of reasons for caution in accepting this result and concluding that policymakers need not worry about contagion between banks. The first is that they do not model price effects

---

[30] Wolf B. Wagner, 'Diversification at Financial Institutions and Systemic Crises' (2010) 19:3 *Journal of Financial Intermediation* 373–386.

[31] Rustam Ibragimov, Dwight Jaffee and Johan Walden, 'Diversification Disasters' (2011) 99:2 *Journal of Financial Economics* 333–348.

[32] Franklin Allen, Ana Babus and Elena Carletti, 'Asset Commonality, Debt Maturity and Systemic Risk' (2012) 104:3 *Journal of Financial Economics* 519–534.

[33] For example, Allen and Carletti (2006), *supra* note 14.

[34] Allen and Carletti (2008), *supra* note 14.

[35] Christian Upper, 'Simulation Methods to Assess the Danger of Contagion in Interbank Markets' (2011) 7:3 *Journal of Financial Stability* 111–125.

of bankruptcy. Cifuentes, Ferrucci and Shin[36] have argued that these price effects are the main transmission mechanism for contagion. As Upper[37] points out, they also rely on the initial shock being confined to a single bank. If there is an initial shock that affects several banks simultaneously, then this also makes contagion more likely.

5. Sovereign Default

The problems of Greece, Ireland and Portugal have underlined the problem of sovereign default. Until recently, there had been no credit risk for sovereign debt in developed countries for many years. The introduction of the euro led to a significant integration in the European bond market. The spread on the sovereign debt of the different euro countries had decreased significantly over the last decade. This reflected the idea that the monetary union across countries together with the fiscal rules of the Stability Pact would suffice to guarantee a greater fiscal harmonization across Europe and thus the solvency of all euro countries. During 2010 and the first part of 2011 it became clear that the architecture embedded in the Maastricht Treaty is not sufficient to achieve the predefined goals and that there can be credit risk in sovereign debt. This is a serious problem in its own right but also a critical problem because of its effect on the stability of the banking system.

The problems that started in Europe in the spring of 2010 show clearly that a sovereign debt crisis and the stability of the financial system are closely interlinked. The relation works both ways: the euro crisis puts pressure on the financial system and the financial crisis in Europe puts pressure on the euro. Moreover, the financial system and the Eurozone share important features like the lack of resolution procedures and burden sharing, the reliance on voluntary cooperation among Member States and the presence of imbalances. There is no resolution procedure in Europe for a sovereign default.

Cooperation and collaboration among European countries to bail out a government in distress are voluntary in that there are neither clear rules nor guidelines on how this should be pursued. Allen, Carletti and

---

[36] Rodrigo Cifuentes, Gianluigi Ferrucci and Hyun Song Shin, 'Liquidity Risk and Contagion' (2005) 3:2 *Journal of the European Economic Association* 556–566.

[37] *Supra*, note 35.

Corsetti[38] focus on sovereign default in the Eurozone from an economic and legal perspective.

The sovereign debt crisis has put pressure on banks' balance sheets through different channels. For example, it has increased the cost of funding for financial institutions since it has increased the risk of their assets. Being perceived as being riskier, financial institutions holding large proportions of sovereign debt issued by countries in distress may have to pay higher interest rates and have more difficulty in raising funds in the wholesale markets. There may be potential pressure on these financial institutions to raise capital and liquidity holdings. Finally, financial institutions operating in the country in distress may also suffer if the country experiences capital outflows and asset substitution and if the large amount of sovereign debt leads to a crowding out of private investments.

6. Currency Mismatches in the Banking System

One of the major problems in the 1997 Asian crisis was currency mismatch. Banks and firms in Korea, Thailand and the other countries had borrowed in foreign currencies, particularly dollars. When the crisis hit, the banks and firms found that they were unable to borrow. Central banks did not have enough foreign exchange reserves and were unable to borrow in the markets. As a result a number had to turn to the IMF. Despite being one of the most successful economies in the world in the preceding decades, the IMF forced South Korea to raise interest rates to maintain the exchange rate, and to cut government expenditure. Given that Korean firms used significant amounts of trade credit, the rise in interest rates was very damaging for them and many thousands of firms were driven into bankruptcy. Unemployment went from around 3 percent to 9 percent and there was a long recession. It was this experience that impressed upon the Koreans that they must accumulate sufficient reserves going forward. Allen and Hong[39] argue that this led to the large increase in reserves shown in Figure 9.2.

During the current crisis the major central banks agreed on foreign exchange swaps and this made a considerable difference in easing the

[38] Franklin Allen, Elena Carletti and Giancarlo Corsetti (eds), *Life in the Eurozone With or Without Sovereign Default?* (FIC Press 2011) <http://finance.wharton.upenn.edu/FIC/FICPress> last accessed 27 May 2015.

[39] Franklin Allen and Joo Yun Hong, 'Why Are There Large Foreign Exchange Reserves? The Case of South Korea' (2011) 38:2 *Korean Social Science Journal* 1–33.

international aspects of the crisis compared with 1997. Allen and Moessner[40] describe the problems raised by banks lending in a low interest rate foreign currency and funding these loans in various ways.

The foreign currencies that were typically used to make loans were the US dollar, the Japanese yen and the Swiss franc. These were funded in two ways. The first was the international wholesale deposit market. The second was to take deposits in domestic currency and then use the foreign exchange swap market to exchange these into the required foreign currency. The largest currency-specific liquidity shortage was 400 billion US dollars in the Eurozone. The second largest was $90 billion worth of yen shortfall in the UK, the next largest $70 billion worth of euros in the US, and after that $30 billion worth of Swiss francs in the Eurozone.

As the crisis progressed banks found it more and more difficult to fund these shortfalls. The international wholesale deposit market dried up for many banks and became difficult for many others. This forced funding of foreign denominated loans using domestic currency funding. Since longer maturities of domestic funding were also often unavailable, much of this funding was at short maturities so the foreign currency mismatch was exacerbated by a maturity mismatch. The volatility in the foreign exchange markets meant these mismatches created a large amount of systemic risk for many banks.

3. MACROPRUDENTIAL REGULATION

The discussion above has highlighted a number of sources of systemic risk in the financial sector. We next discuss macroprudential regulatory measures and policies that could be put in place to deal with the identified sources of systemic risk. What is most important is that the new macroprudential regulation deals with systemic risk and no longer only with the risk of failure of single financial institutions. The current crisis has clearly shown that the microprudential approach to financial regulation does not suffice to prevent systemic crisis

In this section we consider policies to deal with the six types of systemic risk identified above. The policies listed above are a useful start in trying to eliminate systemic risk. However, a more comprehensive

[40] William A. Allen and Richhild Moessner, 'Central Bank Co-operation and International Liquidity in the Financial Crisis of 2008–9' (2010) 310 *Bank for International Settlements Working Paper*.

approach is needed. Systemic risk is a complex and pervasive phenomenon that needs to be dealt with in many diverse ways.

1. Dealing with Asset Price Bubbles

As highlighted above, asset price bubbles seem to be one of the major causes of financial crises. In order to avoid future crises it is of the utmost importance to try to be able to predict them and prevent their emergence. In an important early paper, Borio and Lowe[41] argue that while it is difficult to predict asset price bubbles, and in particular property bubbles, it is not impossible. They provide evidence that rapid credit growth combined with large increases in real estate prices can lead to financial instability. In low inflation environments they suggest that inflationary pressures can first appear in asset prices rather than in the prices of goods and services. They argue that in such cases it may be appropriate to use monetary policy to prick asset bubbles and to preserve financial and monetary stability.

Bubbles, in particular real estate bubbles, seem to be caused by loose monetary policy and excessive credit supply. One way to prevent them is, then, through interest rate policy. In particular, very low interest rates at a time when property prices are surging should be avoided. Once they have started, the question is whether interest rates should be raised to prick them. It may be possible and desirable to do this in economies with a high degree of homogeneity, as in small countries like Sweden or possibly the UK. However, doing this may be difficult for political reasons. In particular, when such policies are first introduced, it may be difficult to explain why it is worth causing a recession to burst a property bubble.

The problem is more complicated in heterogeneous economies like the US, China and the Eurozone. Different regions within these economies differ in terms of economic fundamentals and the rate of property price increases. Using interest rates to prick bubbles will not be so desirable because this will adversely affect the areas that do not have bubbles. The recent events in the Eurozone constitute a clear example. The interest rate policy followed by the ECB was correct for countries like Germany where there was no bubble but it was inappropriate for Spain, where it contributed to the creation of the property bubble. A tighter policy may

---

[41] Claudio Borio and Philip Lowe, 'Asset Prices, Financial and Monetary Stability: Exploring the Nexus' (2002) 114 *Bank for International Settlements Working Paper*.

have been effective for preventing the bubble in Spain but at the cost of a recession or at least slower growth in some of the other countries.

When interest rates cannot be used, it may be better to use other forms of macroprudential regulation to prevent bubbles. One example would be limits on loan-to-value ratios that would be lowered as property prices increase at a faster pace. This can be effective for residential property but may be difficult to enforce for commercial property. The reason is that firms may be able to use pyramids of companies that effectively increase leverage. Another measure is to have property transfer taxes that are greater the higher is the rate of property price increase. Another, perhaps more direct, measure is to impose restrictions on real estate lending in certain regions.

Crowe, Dell'Ariccia, Igan and Rabanal[42] consider the effects of these types of macroprudential measure to eliminate real estate booms. They have been tried in several Asian countries, including Hong Kong, Korea and Singapore. They appear to be effective in the short term but not in the medium and long term.

Saying that monetary policy should not be used to prick bubbles in larger economies or in monetary unions where countries have different economic conditions does not imply that monetary policy should not be constrained. Loose monetary policy is arguably one of the main causes of the emergence of bubbles, as the recent crisis has shown. One of the most important macroprudential measures should be constraining monetary policy so that it does not trigger bubbles. Excessively low levels of interest rates should not be implemented, particularly when real estate prices are already rising. A possible way to do this is to set up a check and balance mechanism. The idea behind this is to introduce some form of accountability for central banks. Another, more drastic, way to do it is to give central banks the clear mandate to prevent asset bubbles.

As discussed in the previous section, the second major cause of bubbles is excessive credit. During the recent crisis, excessive credit emerged because of large global imbalances. To prevent bubbles in the future, it is important to solve this problem. While it is individually advantageous for countries to self-insure by accumulating reserves, this is an inefficient mechanism from a global perspective.

As argued above and in Allen and Hong,[43] the accumulation of reserves by the Asian countries was at least partly a response to the harsh

[42] Christopher Crowe, Giovanni Dell'Ariccia, Deniz Igan and Pau Rabanal, 'How to Deal with Real Estate Booms: Lessons from Country Experiences' (2011) 11/91 *IMF Working Paper*.

[43] *Supra* note 39.

policies that the IMF imposed on a number of countries during the Asian crisis in the late 1990s. Part of the problem was the fact that East Asian countries were not well represented in the senior staff of the IMF. It is therefore important to reform the governance structure of the IMF and of the other international organizations to ensure that the Asian countries receive equal treatment when they need financial help. This would reduce the need of these countries to accumulate reserves as a self-insurance mechanism.

To reduce the large accumulation of reserves by China, other measures are necessary, however. For example, senior Chinese officials have proposed having a global currency to replace the dollar. This has the advantage that reserves can be created initially without large transfers of resources and the attendant risk of a crisis. All countries could be allocated enough reserves in the event of a crisis so that they could survive shocks. The problem is that an international institution like the IMF would need to implement the currency. There would then be again the issue of whether all countries, and in particular the Asian ones, are properly represented in the governance process of this institution.

A more likely medium term scenario is that the Chinese Rmb becomes fully convertible and joins the US dollar and the euro as the third major reserve currency. With three reserve currencies there would be more scope for diversification of risk and China itself would have little need of reserves. This is perhaps one of the most practical solutions to the global imbalances problem. The Chinese have already taken some steps in this direction. They have started to allow the settlement of trade in Rmb. They have also allowed the issue of Rmb bonds by Western companies such as McDonald's in Hong Kong. Of course, the most important aspect of being a reserve currency is full convertibility of the Rmb. That is still some way off and this is the sense in which this solution to the global imbalances problem is a medium term one.

2. Policies with Regard to Mispricing of Assets

As discussed above, one of the major problems in the current crisis is that many securitized securities appear to have been mispriced. One explanation is that this is due to cash-in-the-market pricing and limits to arbitrage. Another is that it is due to asymmetric information and in particular to adverse selection. The problem is to design policies that allow this problem to be corrected. This was the origin of the Troubled Asset Relief Program in the US. The idea was that by buying large amounts of the toxic assets the Treasury could restore the functioning of the market. In practice they were unable to actually implement the program. This type of direct intervention seems problematic to say the least. Clearly there are significant political economy issues. There are also issues of whether such a scheme could actually restore the market to proper functioning. This is one of the most important areas of macroprudential policies. As yet no convincing solutions have been suggested.

Given the lack of an immediate solution to this problem, what should governments do? One of the major problems is that recent reforms have ensured that financial institutions mark their assets to market. In normal times this is undoubtedly the best system. Financial institutions have traditionally used historic cost accounting for many of their assets. This system has the disadvantage that it allows institutions to hide falls in asset values for significant periods of time. A good example is the S&L crisis in the US in the 1980s. This kind of episode encouraged the move to mark-to-market accounting by the International Accounting Standards Board and US Financial Accounting Standards Board (FASB).[44] The divergence between asset prices, particularly those of securitized products, and apparent fundamentals in the current crisis meant that mark-to-market accounting came under severe criticism by financial institutions and was relaxed by the FASB under political pressure from Congress.

How should the advantages and disadvantages of mark-to-market accounting be balanced? As long as markets are efficient, mark-to-market accounting dominates. However, if as during times of crisis they cease to be efficient, market prices do not provide a good guide for regulators and investors. The key issue then becomes how to identify whether financial markets are working properly or not. Allen and Carletti[45] suggest that when market prices and model-based prices diverge significantly (more than 2 percent, say), financial institutions should publish both. If regulators and investors see many financial institutions independently publishing different valuations they can deduce that financial markets may no longer be efficient and can act accordingly.

3. Panics

As argued previously, it is unclear whether panics have played an important role in the current crisis. In contrast, panics were thought to be the main cause for the occurrence of crises in the past. Starting with the

---

[44] See, for example, Allen and Carletti, *supra* note 14 (2008); Guillaume Plantin, Haresh Sapra and Huyn Shin, 'Marking-to-Market: Panacea or Pandora's Box?' (2008) 46.2 *Journal of Accounting Research* 435–460.

[45] Franklin Allen and Elena Carletti, 'Should Financial Institutions Mark to Market?' (2008) 12 *Bank of France Financial Stability Review* 1–6.

influential work of Friedman and Schwarz[46] it was widely believed that the crises that occurred in the US in the latter part of the nineteenth century up until the early 1930s were mostly caused by panics. The introduction of deposit insurance for retail depositors represented one simple way to stop them. The idea is that if people know that the government will cover any losses, it becomes rational for everybody to leave their money in the banking system. This eliminates runs stemming from panics.

This system was effective in eliminating runs until recently. However, deposit insurance is only for small depositors. It does not cover large deposits or wholesale funding that, as shown in the recent crisis, constitute the majority of funding for many financial institutions. As a result, deposit insurance alone is no longer adequate to solve the problem of panics.

A simple possibility is to extend deposit insurance and guarantee all forms of short term debt. While this solution can be effective in preventing panics, it has the clear drawback of generating moral hazard. If banks have access to low cost funds guaranteed by the government, they have an incentive to take significant risks. A better solution to prevent risk taking may be to remove deposit insurance and deal with the problem of panic runs through lender of last resort policies. If depositors know that the central bank will provide the needed liquidity if they attempt to withdraw early, they will not withdraw and there will not be a run.

The other significant problem with deposit insurance and short term guarantees is that, if there are other types of systemic risk in addition to panics, then they can be extremely costly to implement. An example is Ireland, where the blanket bank debt guarantees in September 2008 effectively bankrupted the country and drove the government to seek funds from the European Financial Stability Fund.

4. Contagion

As argued above, contagion is one of the most important problems of systemic risk. Despite its importance, it is not yet fully understood how contagion can occur and very little work has been done so far on how to stop it. The channels for contagion are multiple, ranging from direct linkages among banks on the interbank market or the payment system to common asset exposure.

---

46 *Supra* note 20.

There may be a need for several policies and regulations that address the different channels and types of contagion. Capital regulation has been the main tool for regulating banks in recent years. This has been coordinated internationally through the Basel agreements. It is the main tool for ensuring stability in the international financial system. The traditional justification in the academic literature for capital regulation has been that it is needed to offset moral hazard from deposit insurance.[47] Because banks have access to low cost funds guaranteed by the government, they have an incentive to take significant risks. If the risks pay off they receive the upside, while if they do not the losses are borne by the government. Capital regulation is needed to offset the incentives for banks to take risks as it ensures that shareholders will lose significantly. Moreover, capital acts as a buffer to absorb losses, thus making banks more resilient to shocks and losses and, perhaps most importantly, reducing the risk of contagion.

There is a long-standing debate on how much capital banks should hold. The recent crisis and the current discussions behind the proposal for a new regulatory framework have highlighted the difficulties embodied in these proposals. The starting point of the discussion is that capital is a more costly form of funding than debt so that, if unregulated, banks minimize the use of capital. Thus, there is the need for a regulation that forces banks to hold minimum levels. The same argument is typically assumed in the academic literature.[48]

Modelling the cost of equity finance for financial institutions is one of the major problems in designing capital regulation. The first issue is whether equity is in fact more costly than debt. If that is so, the second issue is whether equity is more costly only in the financial industry or also in all other industries. It is the case that financial institutions hold approximately 10 percent of capital while industrial companies operate with 30–40 percent equity. Understanding the reasons for this large difference in capital structures is of crucial importance to designing capital regulation appropriately.

One simple answer as to why capital is privately more costly is that in many countries debt interest is tax deductible at the corporate level but dividends are not. It is not clear why this is and whether this should be the case. There does not seem to be any good public policy rationale for

---

47 For examples of exceptions, see Thomas F. Hellman, Kevin C. Murdock and Joseph E. Stiglitz, 'Liberalization, Moral Hazard in Banking, and Prudential Regulation: Are Capital Requirements Enough?' (2000) 90:1 *American Economic Review, American Economic Association* 147–165.

48 See, for example, Gorton and Winton, *supra* note 24.

having this deductibility. It seems to have arisen as an historical accident. When the corporate income tax was introduced interest was regarded as a cost of doing business in the same way that paying wages to workers was a cost. However, from a modern corporate finance perspective, this is not the correct way to think about it. Equity and debt are just alternative ways of financing the firm. If tax deductibility is why there is a desire to use debt rather than equity, then the simple solution is to remove it. If without deductibility financial institutions are willing or can be induced through regulation to use more equity, then financial stability would be considerably enhanced.

Other possible rationales for the high cost of equity are agency problems within the firm. According to this rationale, the cost of equity is that it does not provide the correct incentives to shareholders or managers to provide the right monitoring. High leverage is needed to ensure this. There is little empirical evidence that this is in fact a severe problem in the banking sector. For example, leverage in private equity and venture capital firms where the agency problem seems much greater is typically less than in banks.

A final point concerns the reason why financial institutions hold so little capital relative to other industries. The tax deductibility argument cannot explain this difference, as it holds for all industries. A more plausible explanation is that debt in the financial industry is implicitly subsidized through government guarantees and bailouts. If this is why financial institutions rely so much on debt, then it is necessary to remove guarantees and create credible enforcement mechanisms, that is, proper resolution procedures. Without this, banks will continue minimizing the amount of capital they hold and the society will bear the costs of this through increased financial instability.

In the current debates on capital regulation two main proposals have been put forth. The first concerns countercyclical capital regulation. The second concerns the use of hybrid instruments in the form of contingent convertible debt (CoCos).

One of the most widely suggested macroprudential policies is countercyclical capital regulation. The idea is that during normal times banks and other financial institutions can accumulate capital reserves and buffers that will allow them to survive serious shocks to the financial system. These measures are related to countercyclical loan reserves that have been implemented by the Bank of Spain for some time. Spanish banks did accumulate loan reserves in the period before the crisis and this helped them to weather the crisis better than they otherwise would. This experience suggests that countercyclical capital ratios may be helpful. However, they did not prevent the credit boom in Spain and the bubble in property prices, so not too much reliance should be placed on them.

It has been widely suggested that banks should issue convertible debt that could be converted into equity in the event of a crisis. The issue of this kind of security by the Royal Bank of Scotland and Lloyds in the UK and Unicredit in Italy is an example. The idea is that CoCos have two main advantages. First, it is not necessary for banks to raise capital in difficult times as it would already be available. Secondly, contingent capital allows the sharing of losses with debtholders. This would also have a disciplinary role and would induce bank managers to behave more prudently.

Another way to stabilize markets and avoid contagion is to have a combination of public and private financial institutions. This is the case for example in Chile, where Banco Estado is a publicly owned commercial bank that competes with private sector banks. In times of crisis, such a bank can expand and help stabilize the market as all market participants know that it is backed by the state and will not fail. That is what many central banks have effectively been doing by buying large quantities of commercial paper. These central banks have become like large commercial banks. But the officials in charge of central banks do not usually have much expertise in running a commercial bank or know much about credit risk. It would be better to have expertise in the public sector which allows the state to perform commercial banking functions during times of crisis. These state institutions would act as firebreaks and limit the damage that can be caused by contagion.

5. Sovereign Default

The Greek sovereign debt crisis in 2010 underlined the problems with the design of the Eurozone. The Stability Pact contained rules on the amount of current public deficits. The possibility that a country would go into default was not even contemplated in the architecture of the Eurozone. When the Greek crisis emerged, there were no guidelines or regulation that could be used. In the end the way the EU and the Eurozone dealt with the problem of sovereign default was to set up a bailout fund. This obviously creates moral hazard in that it changes the incentives of governments to deal with fiscal excesses. In addition there is the question of how sustainable the bailout mechanism is in terms of political economy. If Greece and any other countries do default or restructure their debt, Germany will pay a large share of the cost. This opens the question of how much German voters are willing to subsidize defaulting countries.

Similarly in other countries that end up making large contributions. In such a scenario there may be strong demands to pull out of the Eurozone to avoid having to make large transfers. This political economy problem is a very serious one. As the perception that a country might default increases, investors will have to make a judgment as to how this political process will play out. This makes the effect of the guarantees quite uncertain.

The Greek crisis has led to calls for the reform of the Growth and Stability Pact. As discussed above, this is designed to prevent governments from running up large debts and then not fulfilling their obligations. One issue is how meaningful the Pact is anyway because of the fact that once France and Germany flouted the Pact and were not penalized, it became clear the rules were unenforceable except on the small countries. However, perhaps a more serious problem with the Pact is that two countries that were among those that came under the highest pressure, namely Ireland and Spain, were actually doing extremely well in terms of the Pact criteria as they were running surpluses and had low levels of public debt. The reason they had a problem is because they ran a large current account deficit and imported large amounts of capital that fueled the property bubble. This raises the question of whether the Pact needs to be reformed to include restrictions on capital inflows that are invested in real estate.

The real problem with sovereign default is the contagion that will follow such an event. For example, if Greece does default then there is likely to be a severe problem of instability among Greek banks and among many other countries' banks. Under the current arrangements there would be great uncertainty as to how any workout would proceed and this in itself would considerably exacerbate the problems in the markets. After Argentina's default in 2001 it took a great deal of time to determine how much creditors would receive.

A better solution to the problem of sovereign default is perhaps a bankruptcy mechanism of some kind that would avoid the need for a bailout. This would remove a great deal of the uncertainty and could be expedited. Also there could be the equivalent of corporate debtor-in-possession finance for governments. If Greece does default then the first thing the Greek government could then do is to issue senior bonds to save its banking system. One way that such a mechanism could work is for the country to declare default. A team from the ECB and Commission would do an assessment of what the best repayment structure would be. If the country did not agree with the team's assessment then its alternative would be to withdraw from the Eurozone.

Another issue raised by the question of sovereign default is what risk weights should be attached to sovereign debt. Banking regulation should recognize that the market apparently views the debt of many countries as a worse credit risk than the debt of many corporations. One way to do this is to assign risk weightings and diversification requirements on sovereign debt. This should be done in conjunction with the introduction of a bankruptcy mechanism.

One of the major problems in the Eurozone that has been highlighted by the problems of Greece, Ireland and Portugal is that it is very difficult for countries to adjust their economies after a severe shock. For example, in Greece wage levels seem to be at too high a level. Should there be some mechanism within the Eurozone to deal with this wage rigidity? One possibility would be to allow temporary exit from the Eurozone and then reentry. Such exit and reentry might considerably help the adjustment process in such countries.

6. Currency Mismatches

As discussed earlier, one of the major problems in the 1997 Asian crisis was that the banks could not obtain foreign currencies. The main reason that currency mismatches were not such a problem in the current crisis was the introduction of central bank currency swaps. Allen and Moessner document how the swap system worked.[49] There were four overlapping networks:

- the Fed network to supply US dollars
- the ECB network to supply euros
- the Swiss franc network
- the Latin American and Asian networks

These swap networks involved considerable overlap.[50] As they were organized between central banks, the credit risk borne was sovereign rather than commercial. The receiving central bank would then pass on the foreign currency to firms and financial institutions so that they bore the commercial credit risk. Some of the swaps between central banks were collateralized with the currency of the counterparty central bank. These swaps considerably eased foreign exchange problems during the crisis and are widely regarded as having been successful.

---

49 *Supra* note 40.

50 As shown in Graph 7.1 in Allen and Moessner, *supra* note 40.

10. Financial crises and global financial regulation

Christopher Kobrak and Donald Brean

> The worldwide financial crisis has proven once again – even if it occurred in a particularly drastic way – that the markets require a state-run structural framework to prevent them from getting out of control. Given the ever-increasing international interdependence of our economies, this applies no longer solely on a domestic level but increasingly on an international level as well.
>
> *Angela Merkel, German Chancellor, G20 Seoul Summit, 2010*

> All in all, the 'crisis version' of the G20 has done a fantastic, even unprecedented, job.
>
> *Nicolas Sarkozy, former President of France, G20 Seoul Summit, 2010*

I. INTRODUCTION

1. Scope

The purpose of this chapter is to assess the international regulatory response to the 2008 Financial Panic and to suggest some reasons for an apparent disconnect between rhetoric and reality. We conclude that considering the gravity of the crisis and the promises made by politicians, the regulatory response has been less robust than promised. Many of the key pre-2008 regulatory approaches and even gatekeepers remain unaltered. Continuity rather than discontinuity better describes our financial architecture since the crisis.

In our search for explanations, we observe that some of the most important financial individuals and institutions failed to see the crisis coming, believing that banks' managers were sufficiently well informed and the banks sufficiently well capitalized to grasp and cope with their risks.[1] We argue that major portions of our financial architecture – at least two that are considered major causes of the crisis – are still with us; indeed, may have gotten worse since the crisis. We suggest that the problems require a more serious, cross-border approach, but that this approach is still hindered by national political agendas and legal impediments.

At the time of writing, 70 years after the Bretton Woods Conference, which tried to correct the financial failures of the first half of the 20th century, the worst crisis since the Great Depression has not led to a new consensus and greater sense of urgency about macroeconomic and regulatory policy; one that recognizes the need to find a new synthesis of national and international aspirations, for which Bretton Woods is rightly famous.

2. Presuppositions

The chapter takes as its starting point a view shared by many economists that an interrelated mixture of unsustainable debt levels and financial complexity led to the crisis. Although economists may disagree about the degree of fault attributable to each and their remedies, those same economists recognize that the higher debt levels, both private and public, required new intermediation between users and providers of funds, often divided by regulatory and geographic borders, and that this intermediation could not have been achieved without a high degree of financial product and organizational innovation, for which gatekeepers seemed ill-prepared.[2] The issue has absorbed a lot of intellectual and political energy all over the world, and in Europe in particular. To be sure, some

---

[1] Even many of the most important regulators recognize that gaps in the regulatory structure and government-sponsored organizations, such as Fannie Mae and Freddie Mac, contributed to the crisis. Bernanke also concluded that banks themselves failed to adequately monitor their own risks. Ben S. Bernanke, *The Federal Reserve and the Financial Crisis* (Princeton University Press 2013).

[2] Raghuram G. Rajan, *Fault Lines: How Hidden Fractures Still Threaten the World Economy* (Princeton University Press 2010); Nouriel Roubini and Stephen Mihm, *Crisis Economics: A Crash Course in the Future of Finance* (Penguin Press 2010); Carmen M. Reinhart and Kenneth Rogoff, *This Time is Different: Eight Centuries of Financial Folly* (Princeton University Press 2009); Anat Admati and Martin Hellwig, *The Bankers' New Clothes: What's Wrong with Banking and What to Do about It* (Princeton University Press 2013); Bernanke, *supra* note 1; Atif Mian and Amir Sufi, *House of Debt: How They (and You) Caused the Great Recession, and How We Can Prevent It from Happening Again* (University of Chicago Press 2014); and many others.

reforms have been made, and G20 governments have agreed on some important measures in the face of powerful interest group and constituency opposition. But considering the degree of consensus among economists and politicians about the dangers of the debt and the financial architecture that supports it, as well as political commitments to find solutions, surprisingly little has changed in the amount of debt and control of bank internalization of complex financial transactions. Well into 2014, key players, many of whom paid insufficient attention to the warning signs before 2007, congratulate themselves for their heroic efforts to avoid the Armageddon of another 1930s-style banking crisis.[3] Although many of their immediate reactions to the crisis should be applauded, this chapter will emphasize the part of the glass that is half empty, that part of long-term financial reform that has been left undone.

3. Political Dilemmas

There can be little doubt that after 2008 most citizens demanded better control of our financial system from their political leaders. But managing expectations is tough, especially with angry voters and with potentially volatile markets. Perhaps to quell market anxieties, some political leaders contended early on that new rules had been agreed and nearly implemented. In 2010, shortly before Europe's financial wounds opened, Angela Merkel praised the G20's appropriate reaction to the crisis and expressed her confidence that 'The G20 leaders are committed to do everything in their power to prevent such a crisis from happening again internationally.'[4] The European controls that she promised were to be established as of 1 January 2011 and have not yet been implemented. In 2010, too, while recognizing that reform was easier at the peak of the crisis and that even the shaky recovery encourages complacency, Nicolas Sarkozy claimed that regulations to control speculative funds, rating agencies, tax havens and outrageous bonuses had been agreed and implemented. In his own words: 'Reforms that would have been unthinkable have been decided and implemented: … speculative funds are now regulated; rating agencies are now registered; … bonuses by banks defined by strict rules, and penalties are in place in the event of losses or poor performance. Tax havens are disappearing.'[5] After passage of their own domestic efforts at bank reform, Dodd–Frank, many American

[3] Timothy F. Geithner, *Stress Test: Reflections on Financial Crises* (Crown 2014).

[4] G20, Seoul Summit. Munk School of Global Affairs, November 2010.

[5] *Ibid.*

politicians and regulators boasted a similar kind of triumph, ignoring the global nature of modern finance. With seemingly little regard for the limited scope and jurisdiction of the Wall Street Reform Bill, the head of the U.S. Commodity Futures Trading Commission, Gary Gensler, confidently asserted in June of 2013 that 'Swap dealers will be subject to robust oversight', lowering risk and promoting transparency for 'the American public'.[6] In contrast to Gensler, most observers bemoaned the lack of clarity about new derivative trading rules and predicted that banks would keep and even increase the amounts of unstandardized, and more lucrative, instruments on their own trading platforms. Indeed, just a few months before Gensler's comment JP Morgan Chase reported $70 trillion (as measured by notional value) of derivative instruments on its books.[7]

Managing expectations is a necessary part of governance. But politicians and regulators stress how much they can and have achieved, perhaps with too little regard for how much they can really control given our financial architecture. Public discussions fail to highlight the dangers of navigating between electorates' demands for services and a complex multinational financial system spawned to satisfy them. At the very least, politicians' comments may engender in general a false sense of security about any government's ability to subdue human foibles, outright greed, and overcome the limits of national and international regulations. Politicians' own unwillingness to give up control of their bailiwicks may also serve to limit frankness.

Misinformation can encourage complacency, which eventually turns into bitter disappointment. Perhaps no financial regulation can ever strike an ideal balance between risk taking and security, between innovation and stability. As one of the foremost commentators on financial crises, Hyman Minsky, argued, crises were an inevitable part of the social-psyche. Perhaps he is right. The human condition is doomed to repeat cycles of booms and busts. Good times breed a desire for more and an exaggerated optimism that eventually leads to another breakdown. For Minsky, regulation is no match for Keynesian 'animal spirits'.[8] The rules laid out under Basel I and II gave the financial sector more reporting, opportunities to bend rules, and very 'well capitalized American banks'

---

6 Commodity Futures Trading Commission (2013) <http://www.cftc.gov/index.htm> retrieved 13 June 2013.

7 JP Morgan Chase, *2013 Annual Report* 14 <http://www.chase.com> retrieved 23 July 2014.

8 Hyman P. Minsky, *John Maynard Keynes* (Columbia University Press 1975).

in 2007.[9] No matter how good the rules are, they must be interpreted and enforced by regulators, who show an ever-increasing and dangerous 'cosy' relationship with their charges, regulatory capture, as it is often called.[10] Indeed, the regulatory efforts that followed the Bankers' Panic of 2008 have added complexity and paperwork to a system already overloaded with both. The question is whether these efforts at reform are a cost-effective method of providing financial stability in light of the speed, amount and complexity of global financial activity.

4. Other Approaches

To be fair, part of the failure can be explained by legitimate differences of opinion about complex issues. Despite the cross-border scope of the problems, some observers argue that sound national financial standards are what is really needed to insure against global system risk. As mentioned, a series of international measures – Basel I, Basel II and new international accounting standards – failed to foretell or prevent the 2008 crisis. The growth of international cooperation and 20 years of relative calm may have served more to lull regulators' critical faculties rather than to ward off a financial bust. America's housing crisis, over-leveraged banks and European fault lines have shown that international regulation has been a poor substitute for tight national controls.[11] More generally, financial regulatory reform is a reflection of politics and national

---

[9] Lara Cathcart, Lina El-Jahel and Ravel Jabbour, 'The Basel Requirement Puzzle: A Study of Changing Interconnectedness between Leverage and Capital Ratios' (2013) *The Financial Engineering and Banking Society* Working Paper (2013); Christopher Kobrak and Michael Troege, 'From Basel to Bailouts: Forty Years of International Attempts to Bolster Bank Safety' (2014) Working Paper, Presented at the *European Banking and Financial History Conference*, June 2014.

[10] George J. Stigler, 'The Theory of Economic Regulation' (1971) 2:1 *The Bell Journal of Economics and Management Science* 3–21; Peter Kobrak, *Cozy Politics: Political Parties, Campaign Finance, and Compromised Governance* (Lynne Rienner Publishers 2002). Much of the literature on regulatory capture focuses on national politics, campaign contributions and the revolving door between the public and private sectors. The international dimension today may also involve a form of 'group think', a common intellectual faith that undermines sufficient critical distance. Michael Troege and Christopher Kobrak, 'Nous pouvons simplifier la régulation financière!' (2013) 767 *Revue-Banque*.

[11] Marc Levinson, 'Faulty Basel: Why More Diplomacy Won't Keep the Financial System Safe' (2010) 89:3 *Foreign Affairs* 76–88.

preferences, and therefore can never be divorced from governments, which will in the end still have to implement international rules.[12]

5. Global Finance Requires High Degree of Global Regulation

Despite the failures of international regulation and the need for national involvement, we see no alternative to increased coordination of financial regulation. Although all bank rules and ground rules for bank governance need not be determined by international bodies, the issues most threatening to world financial stability require broad agreement of and enforcement by at least larger countries. With new technologies and management skills, large transnational financial institutions still service global clients by moving vast volumes of funds while trading in complex derivative instruments with little or no public scrutiny. Over the past 15 years, this capacity has helped draw funds from diverse sources, lessening our financial dependence on straightforward, transparent bank lending, while ballooning bank assets and liabilities to unprecedented levels.[13] Despite attempts to make banking activities transparent, valuations of many contractual liabilities of banks often seem too complex for the bankers themselves and their overmatched regulators to determine. Derivative trading as measured by the notional value of contracts, which had grown in the ten years before the crisis from $80 to $600 trillion, an amount equal to ten times world product, jumped again by 33 per cent in the next two years to $800 trillion, 80 per cent of which was *not* traded on public exchanges.[14] Subverting accounting rules like 'marked to market' with prices that are really 'marked to models' gives some a sense of security, but often hides the degree to which banks are still at risk to 'unmodelled' events.

But laying out a precise alternative to our current financial regulations is well beyond the scope of this chapter. We will, however, trace what the G20 and the European Union have done – or not done – since 2008 to achieve a new common set of rules. Although the initial crisis had its origins in the United States and might be called a G1 problem, the

---

[12] Mark J. Roe, 'Capital Markets and Financial Politics: Preferences and Institutions' (2012) 7:1 Article 3 *Capitalism and Society* 1–38.

[13] Christopher Kobrak, 'From Multinational to Transnational Banking' in Y. Cassis, R.S. Grossman and C. Schenk (eds), *The Oxford Handbook of the History of Finance and Banking* (OUP 2016).

[14] Bank of International Settlements (BIS), Statistical Release, February 2013 <www.bis.org> retrieved 21 July 2014.

upheaval very quickly exposed weaknesses in global financial coordination. Some commentators fear that opportunities to fix international financial problems will be squandered.[15]

The bulk of the chapter is divided into two sections. The first describes the G20 preparedness for and reaction to events. Using some anecdotal evidence and hard data, we show how limited the response has been to at least two significant causes of the 2008 crisis. The evidence suggests that the G20's financial deliberations before 2008 showed little foresight about the dangerous state of global financial regulation, merely the problem of financial imbalances. The crisis brought the group together for a short while for a series of measures that calmed agitated markets. But soon after the crisis subsided, countries returned to pursuing their own national agendas with too little regard for their co-dependencies and the need for dealing with many problems in concert. In the second section, we highlight some European-specific aspects of the crisis and some shared resistance to group remedies.

II. FINANCIAL SUMMITS AND THE MORNING AFTER

The G20 was founded in 1999, specifically to deal with international financial issues. It includes representatives from 19 national governments and central banks, as well as the European Union. Both cumbersome decision-making mechanisms and, more importantly, an inability to shake national priorities – two related general circumstances – seem to prevent, however, concerted efforts to prevent and then limit the spillover effects of financial crises. Neither the general nor the financial G20 meetings expressed much anxiety before the financial crisis. The communiqué of the financial ministers in November 2007, just four months before the collapse of Bear Stearns, mentions 'financial market disturbances' and 'slower economic growth'. Following that failure and despite others in the United Kingdom, the world's financial leaders scheduled no meetings that spring or summer to map out plans for future large bank bankruptcies. Both the 2006 and 2007 reports devote a great deal of attention to macroeconomic policies, high commodities prices, climate change and

---

[15] Jean Pisani-Ferry, *The Euro Crisis and Its Aftermath* (OUP 2014); Philippe Legrain, *European Spring: Why Our Economies and Politics are in a Mess – and How to Put Them Right* (Creative Books 2014)

reform of the long-moribund Bretton Woods system.[16] Privately traded derivatives, subprime mortgages, unbridled securitization, rating agency oversight and financial firm incentives are absent, even though several serious economists had warned of their dangers.[17] Perhaps the most cogent evidence of the failures of international regulation and national implementation to predict and deal with problems came after the crisis. The US Treasury Department Report, dated 31 July 2009, *Assessment of Compliance with the Basel Core Principles*, found that American banks had complied completely with all but four of 25 items; the remaining four had been 'largely compliant'.[18]

1. First Reactions

In the wake of the 2008 financial crisis, the governments of the major world economies seemed to have had an epiphany about the need to coordinate the future of the world's financial architecture. In addition to providing a rather cogent explanation of what precipitated the crisis, including references to unsustainable government economic policies and regulation, in November 2008 the G20 pledged to implement improvements in four policy areas: strengthening transparency and accountability, enhancing sound regulation, promoting integrity in financial markets, and reforming international financial institutions. The G20 delegated to finance ministers the task of creating a specific action plan, including tasks to be completed by 31 March 2009, for each of the four. Like the general policy guidelines, the short- and medium-term action plans were admirable although vague about outcome and timing, as normally associated with action plans.[19] Consider a few examples:

---

[16] US Department of the Treasury, Resources Center, G20 Communiqués (2006–2007) <http://www.treasury.gov/resource-center/international/g7-g20/Pages/g20.aspx> retrieved 21 July 2014.

[17] Raghuram G. Rajan, 'Has Financial Development Made the World Riskier?' (2005) 11728 Working Paper *National Bureau of Economic Research*; Nouriel Roubini, 'Why Central Banks Should Burst Bubbles' (2006) 9 *International Finance* 87–107.

[18] US Treasury Report, *Assessment of Compliance with the Basel Core Principles for Effective Banking Supervision* <http://www.treasury.gov/resource-center/international/standards-codes/Documents/Banking%20Self-Assessment%207-31-09.pdf> 31 July 2009 retrieved 21 July 2014.

[19] US Department of the Treasury, Resources Center, G20 Communiqués (2008–2009) <http://www.treasury.gov/resource-center/international/g7-g20/Pages/g20.aspx> retrieved 21 July 2014.

1. Strengthening Transparency and Accountability
   - *Immediate*: 'Regulators and accounting standard setters should enhance the required disclosures of complex financial instruments by firms and market participants.'
   - *Medium term*: 'The key global accounting standards bodies should work intensively toward the objective of creating a high-quality global standard.'
2. Regulatory Regimes
   - *Immediate*: 'The International organization of securities regulators should review credit rating agencies' adoption of the standards and mechanisms for monitoring compliance.'
3. Risk Management
   - *Medium term*: 'Authorities should monitor substantial changes in asset prices and their implications for the macroeconomy and the financial system.'
4. Promoting Integrity
   - *Immediate (by 31 March 2009)*: 'Our national and regional authorities should work together to enhance regulatory cooperation between jurisdictions on a regional and international level.'

2. Delayed Implementation

Not only did the G20 meeting before the crisis fail to see the financial crisis coming, but also, since the crisis, few of the G20's once ambitious reform goals have been implemented. Those goals included giving greater financial clout to the International Monetary Fund (IMF), limiting financial bonuses, shifting more derivatives trading to clearing houses, tightening bank liquidity and solvency requirements, increasing reporting for hedge funds and other new financial organizations, and reducing flows of hot money (also carry trade) and the use of tax havens. Indeed, most remain vague goals. By 2010, it was clear that the proposals contained no enforcement mechanism, neither organizations nor penalties. Perhaps naively, they rely on peer pressure, which in other époques might have been an effective form of informal regulation but in the 21st century seems out of touch with reality. Since their earlier unity in face of the crisis and optimism about reforming finance, the G20 has made little real progress, even by the standards it set. Much of the reform is stalled by national preferences and a desire to further national interests in the face of weak economies. As late as winter 2013, the G20 had failed to meet nearly every deadline that it had set for itself.

A fundamental problem comes from how the G20 makes decisions. As in the European Union, relying on unanimity for important financial decisions naturally leads to gridlock and too much compromise. Former Bank of England Governor Mervyn King's proposal to make the G20 the governing council of the IMF, for example, went to the heart of the issue. It was part of a decade-long debate about how to streamline global financial decision-making. Universal cooperation might be possible in times of crisis, but avoiding crises required new institutions and organizations capable of making and implementing decisions. The G20 needed to morph simultaneously into an integral part of global financial coordination while simplifying procedures for voting decisions. To date, neither King's proposal nor any similar one for smoothing decision-making and enforcement has been adopted.

But the decision-making process itself is not the only problem. For several important issues and proposals, building consensus seems nearly impossible. Creating a tax on short-term cross-border flows – one of the IMF's proposals to reduce hot money transfers while building reserves to bail out weak financial institutions – seems stillborn. Many G20 members rejected it but for a variety of reasons. Two of the G20's most important financial players, the United States and the United Kingdom, feared its impact on their banks. But resistance has not come just from those countries. Canada, Australia and Japan opposed the tax on banks designed to create a fund to save weak firms – a strategy employed nationally in Denmark – on the grounds that their banks had proven their solidity during the crisis. The Eurozone came close to adopting the tax, but agreement broke down at the very last stages, as several countries behind the proposal seemed to lose their enthusiasm for it.

Ironically, even zealous national efforts to reform domestic finance helped block international reform. As the IMF's former Managing Director Dominique Strauss-Kahn opined, 'The Obama administration's efforts to push through Congress a financial package could hinder the development of a global regulatory regime because it may not be consistent with other nations' efforts', even before its passage and even though it contained many elements of the IMF's own proposals. But proposals that make sense addressing one nation's situation may just conflict with others'.[20] Since passage, Dodd–Frank has illustrated just this problem.

[20] Bob Davies, 'IMF: Financial Revamp at Risk' *Wall Street Journal* (New York, 22 April 2010).

As early as spring 2012, efforts to create a new financial order had come to a watershed moment. Public meetings in the United States designed to discuss the implementation of the Dodd–Frank legislation emphasized the need for combined international efforts in the United States and Europe, especially to coordinate activities beyond their borders. Fulfilling the G20's 2009 promises required jumping this last hurdle. Only national rules that worked together to close gaps and avoid overlap had any hope. Relying on regulators in other countries involves a level of trust that may not yet have been achieved. U.S. claims that its rules had a global reach and had primacy over European law on trades between European and American counterparties, for example, inflamed European and other national sensibilities.[21] Other financial reforms are behind schedule. As of late 2012, fewer than a third of the big banks abide by the new Basel III rules and many national governments have not passed legislation consistent with the rules. Most banks, especially the healthy ones, resent drawing up their so-called 'living wills'.

In late spring 2012, of the many goals articulated by the G20 in September 2009, the IMF found that five were not on track. Derivatives trading, data collection and 'shadow banking', for example, were substantially behind schedule. An IMF scorecard published in April 2012 found that, of the six types of reform, only forcing banks to hold better reserves was well advanced. Even that relatively pessimistic judgement was later called into question by failures in Europe to implement agreed bank safety standards. The Basel Committee on banking supervision reported that only three of 27 Basel member countries had published final rules for the implementation of Basel III guidelines, due to take effect in January 2013. Eighteen had drafted rules; six had done nothing. Even some of the drafted rules fell short of Basel standards. Some policy makers in Brussels wanted to hold up further reform until the EU had a bank supervisor. Chinese fears of an economic slowdown contributed to a year-long postponement of its reforms. Increasingly, the G20's long-term agenda is held hostage to short-term events.[22]

In its latest report, the Basel Committee on Banking Supervision – a useful forum for member banks to formulate and evaluate bank regulation but not a regulator itself – gives most Member States high marks for adopting Basel 2.5, enhanced measures related to securitization and trading exposures, due by the end of 2011. Of the major financial trading

---

[21] Michael Barnier, 'The US Must Not Override EU Regulators' *Financial Times* (London, 22 June 2012).

[22] Brooke Masters, 'The Economic Slowdown has Put Brake on Global Reform' *Financial Times* (London, 18 June 2012).

centres, the United States, however, lagged behind the others. The rules have thus far made little mark on derivatives trading. But with Basel III, rules for higher capital and liquidity requirements, both the European Union and the United States were laggards, behind Canada, China, South Africa, and even Argentina and Russia. Committee members agreed to implement Basel III, which had been released in December 2010, 'from 1 January 2013, *subject to transitional and phase-in arrangements*' (authors' italics).[23] Thus far, too, the implementation of Basel III and other guidelines has not had much effect on European banks' purchase of shaky government debt or rating agency liability, or several other crucial areas of financial reform.

An area of reform that seemed nearly universally agreed, over-the-counter (OTC) derivative trading, still remains unresolved, a hostage to national competition laws and bank self-interest. In September 2009, the G20 resolved that more OTC derivatives should be standardized, and contracts should be traded on exchanges and processed through clearing houses, in part to insure that participants provide adequate collateral for their trades. This proposal was designed to increase transparency and to decrease default by increasing margin deposits for contracts. Despite three years of detailed talks among market infrastructure participants – exchanges and other trading venues, banks and clearing houses – promising to leave virtually no area of trading untouched, many important issues remain and little has been achieved. Although analysts and participants expect more public trading and clearing, laws regarding what will have to be traded and by whom have not been codified, leaving participants unable to make decisions. Despite European (European Market Infrastructure Regulation) and American (Dodd–Frank) legislation empowering regulators to create rules having been passed two years ago, the rules have not materialized, missing the G20's self-imposed 2012 deadline. Europe is supposed to institute its version of rules for mandatory derivative clearing by 2014. Some institutional investors fear too that the new controls will add cost to trading, which will undermine derivatives value as an insurance mechanism by adding unneeded costs.

While bankers believe that existing European and American measures have gone too far, other experts feel that they have not gone far enough. Somehow the global reach of derivatives trading has not yet been fully integrated in plans. Singapore and Hong Kong officials are insisting that

[23] Basel Committee on Banking Supervision, Progress Report on Implementation of the Basel Regulatory Framework, April 2013. See also Kobrak and Troege, *supra* note 9, for a discussion of the shortfalls of the Basel Framework.

their mandatory clearing of derivatives by parties based in their jurisdiction by the end of the year occurs in their areas, a policy in conflict with similar measures envisioned in Europe. If countries fail to recognize each other's clearing houses and coordinate controls, conflicts between centres will arise, blocking effective implementation of G20 objectives.[24]

Researchers and participants have two principal fears regarding future regulations. First, the new standards may add more complexity to derivatives trading by creating incentives for new, even more complicated instruments to be developed to avoid the new rules. Secondly, and perhaps more importantly, some fear that trading will just pass to other regions, particularly Asia, that have shown less enthusiasm for reform. In November 2012, the Financial Stability Board reported that most countries had not yet passed mandates to transfer OTC derivative trading to exchanges and clearing houses.

Many financial exchanges perceive a huge new opportunity in the transfer of OTC trading to public exchanges and clearing houses, but some European regulators have had problems with the transfer. European anti-trust authorities blocked the merger between Deutsche Börese and NYSE Euronext on the grounds that the combination would create a 'near monopoly' for trading and clearing derivatives. Brushing aside arguments that trading derivatives was a global activity and frequently conducted outside of exchanges, the regulators blocked what would have been the world's largest exchanges for trading equities and derivatives. Moreover, even though only 10 per cent of OTC derivative trading has been transferred to public clearing, European officials are growing concerned that big investment banks are using their powers to supply information about Credit Default Swaps (CDSs), for example, to manipulate markets for their own advantage.[25]

3. Some Results by the Numbers

Markets have clearly stabilized since 2008, but by many measures we are as much at risk today as before the crisis. Bank balance sheets in many countries are still at multiples of their host countries' GDP. Even in large countries, such as Germany and the United States, large banks maintain assets that are equal to substantial portions of their host country's GDP. Deutsche Bank's assets are roughly 80 per cent of Germany's GDP; JP

---

24 Brooke Masters, 'Conflicting Signals: Global Finance' *Financial Times* (London, 2 April 2012).

25 Philip Stafford, 'ICE Plans CDS Exchange Trading' *Financial Times* (London, 17 October 2012).

Morgan Chase's assets are nearly 15 per cent of US GDP.[26] Although financial activity as a percentage of GDP is down since 2008, it still accounts for nearly 9 per cent of America's GDP, for example. Banks get a lot of funds from central banks, in the form of asset buybacks or liberal open-window policies, but with balance sheets that are stuffed with purchased securities and deposits from private banks, central banks have begun cutting back. And commercial banks are still highly dependent on short-term financing from private sources that from time to time show troubling signs of fragility. Moreover, other destabilizing features of finance before 2008 are once again causes for concern – for example, the carry trade and asset price bubbles.

Although some progress has been made in reining in derivatives, that progress is somewhat fragmented. In June 2012, the figure for total nominal value of derivatives stood at $700 trillion, only 10 per cent of which was offered on organized exchanges. According to JP Morgan Chase's *Annual Report*, existing rules require only standardized contracts to move to organized exchanges, and those only for financial counterparties (hedge funds and asset managers, for example) and governments, not non-financial clients who can continue to trade standardized contracts with the banks.[27] Bank reliance on 'off-balance sheet' accounting has diminished, but some banks still have the ability to practise regulatory arbitrage through the use of thousands of off-shore entities. Nearly a trillion dollars' worth of bank assets and liabilities are held by entities not obliged to report to the BIS.[28] The trend has continued into 2014. Interest rate and foreign exchange derivatives, which are easier to clear on exchanges and offset, still account for the lion's share (over $600 trillion in notional value and $16 trillion in market value). But even these contracts can create system risk, as was proven in the 2008 bankers' crisis. More problematic are CDSs and other complex (less standardized) derivatives. They still account for a mere $50 trillion in notional value and $3 trillion in market value. And, as the BIS reports, only 26 per cent are cleared through central counterparties.[29]

---

[26] Deutsche Bank, *2013 Annual Report* <http://www.db.com> retrieved 23 July 2014 and JP Morgan Chase, *supra* note 7; percentages calculated based on German GDP of $3.4 and American of $16.8 trillion.

[27] JP Morgan Chase, *supra* note 7.

[28] BIS, *supra* note 14.

[29] BIS, Statistical Release, May 2014 <www.bis.org> retrieved 21 July 2014. Although financial activity as a percentage of gross domestic product is down in some important financial centres, such as the United States, financial complexity

Clearly, the 2008 crisis encouraged additional debt – with a real and sometimes perceived need for stimulus – but if high levels of private and state debt helped bring on the crisis and add system risk, we still have a lot to worry about. Although in some categories of debt we have made progress, the overall debt levels of many countries remains high, even higher than before the crisis. From 2007 to 2012, private debt as a percentage of disposable income went from 137 to 184 in Canada, 93 to 101 in France, and 106 to 108 per cent in the whole Euro area.[30] The advance of public debt has been even more dramatic. From 2006 to 2014, Eurozone public debt climbed from 69 to 93 per cent of GDP. From 2006 to 2013, net public debt in the United States increased from 45 to 81 per cent, in Canada from 26 to 39, in France from 60 to 88, and finally in Great Britain from 26 to 81 per cent.[31]

The authorities or the markets have made progress in one troubling area of leverage: bank debt. Bank leverage is notoriously tricky to calculate, but by most accounts with a combination of higher profits, lower dividends, central bank asset buybacks and new capital, banks have reduced their dependence on debt since 2008.[32] But even this should be an area of more concern. As the Chairman of the Basel Committee on Banking Supervision and Governor of Sveriges Riksbank said in a recent

as measured in some ways is not. JPMorgan Chase's 2013 *Annual Report* (*supra* note 7) is 350 pages long, a near doubling in ten years.

[30] Volume 2012, Issue 1, No. 91, *OECD Economic Outlook* <http://www.oecd-ilibrary.org/economics/oecd-economic-outlook-volume-2012-issue-1/debt-indicators-in-the-private-sector_eco_outlook-v2012-1-table8-en> retrieved 29 July 2013.

[31] IMF, World Economic Outlook Database, April 2014 <http://www.imf.org/external/pubs/ft/weo/2013/01/weodata/index.aspx> retrieved 21 July 2014. There are also larger questions about how the debt has been used. See Therese Wilson, 'Credit and Over-indebtedness: Current Context, Regulatory Responses and Future Possibilities' 3–15; Toni Williams, 'Continuity, not Rupture: The Persistence of Neoliberalism in the Internationalism of Consumer Finance' 15–45; and Hans-W. Micklitz, 'Access to, and Exclusion of, European Consumers from Financial Markets after the Global Financial Crisis' 47–75, in Therese Wilson (ed.), *International Responses to Issues of Credit and Over-indebtedness in the Wake of the Crisis* (Ashgate 2013); see also Christopher Kobrak, 'The Political Economy of the Great Recession, Global Macroeconomic and Microeconomic Governance (2000–Present)' in Robert Wright (ed.), *Contemporary Economic Issues: Goals, Objectives, and Solutions (1980–Today)* (DWJ 2014).

[32] There has been ample discussion about the calculation of bank reserves, certain types of preferred shares and risk-adjusted measures of capital adequacy, all of which is beyond the scope of this chapter. Admati and Hellwig, *supra* note 2.

speech, the largest non-financial institutions maintain equity ratios of 50 per cent; with banks, 5 per cent is still common. Even though Basel I and II had failed at their appointed tasks of creating robust risk-adjusted standards of capital levels to protect society against financial system risk, the absence of just plain equity as a safety net did not seem to trouble him because, 'The Basel III leverage ratio provides that safety net.'[33] Whether new Basel III standards, stepped up 'stress testing' by regulators since the crisis, and the implicit government guarantee for big banks, or some combination of all three, explain the current calm in financial markets is unclear and may never be known.[34]

But what does seem clear is that using many of the same techniques that are recommended today, national and international financial regulators failed to see the problem coming, and launched a response that has relied on very low cost central bank and wholesale market funding that has enabled a great deal of 'business as usual', as evidenced by the continued growth of two contributing causes of the crisis – vast, complex financial flows and high debt levels. As measured by perceptions of informed commentators and some troubling financial data, on a global level there is much to be done. Indeed, the track record of our regulatory approach before the crisis should itself serve as an antidote to complacency.

III. EUROPE – FIXING EUROZONE FINANCE

The 2008 crisis clearly had American origins, which required both American and international responses, but it also exposed some financial, regulatory and political weaknesses in other parts of the world. In 2011,

---

[33] Stefan Ingves, keynote address to the 10th *Asia-Pacific High-Level Meeting on Banking Supervision*, jointly organized by the Basel Committee on Banking Supervision, the Financial Stability Institute, and the Executives' Meeting of East Asia-Pacific Central Banks Working Group on Banking Supervision, Auckland, New Zealand, 25–27 February 2014, 2–3.

[34] Krugman's review of Geithner's account of the crisis is interesting in this regard. Although Krugman is very critical of much of Geithner's account, he does not question Geithner's view that the stress testing contributed greatly to strengthening faith in capital markets (2014), ignoring other possible explanations, such as that provided by Andrew G. Haldane and Piergiorgio Alessandri, 'Banking on the State' (2009), presentation delivered at the Federal Reserve Bank of Chicago 12th annual International Banking Conference on *The International Financial Crisis: Have the Rules of Finance Changed?*, 25 September 2009.

the financial crisis morphed into a Euro crisis. Europe, which had taken the lead in calling for renewed international cooperation for global banking and financial reform through the G20, found itself enmeshed in paralysing internal political strife involving the common currency, the Euro, and associated problems of sovereign debt of the EU Member States. Only in a state of crisis and with prodding and help from international organizations has Europe started to tackle the institutional and organizational reforms necessary for a common currency zone. The immediate policy focus is on the debt and currency challenges that beset the EU, whereas the longer-term aim is to create a secure yet flexible financial system that takes its proper role in promoting growth, employment and competitiveness.

1. The Importance of Banking Union

To give shape to our discussion, the following remarks address a crucial but contentious overarching initiative: to establish unitary banking in Europe. The focus on banking is especially relevant in Europe, where a disproportionate share of government and industrial finance is intermediated through banks as opposed to flowing through financial markets.[35] A banking union in Europe is necessary to redress EU internal inconsistencies with respect to the management and control of the common currency of the 17 Member States of the Eurozone. A banking union should have three major components: a single bank supervisor, a common bank crisis management and resolution system, and a uniform system for protecting depositors' savings. These structural features of the EU banking union would be complemented by changes in the rules on how banks operate, including those of the sort under development by the Bank for International Settlements and the Financial Stability Board.

---

[35] In each of the 17 Member States of the Eurozone, the global assets of their respective five largest banks are typically more than 300 per cent of their respective home country GDP. In the lead up to the European financial crisis in its various dimensions – unmanageable sovereign debt, bank failures, fiscal strains – credit and asset price bubbles had built up in several Member States, especially in the southern periphery, with sharp increases in leverage for households and, in many countries, a substantial increase in house prices. While risks were mounting, the overall resilience of banks improved little. From 2000 to 2007, solvency ratios increased by only 0.2 per cent. Leverage of many large financial institutions rose, reflecting a dangerous below-the-radar shift to short-term wholesale funding. Reinhart and Rogoff, *supra* note 2; Luc Laeven and Fabian Valencia, 'Systemic Banking Crises: A New Database' (2008) WP/08/224 *IMF Working Paper.*

Despite the urgent need for a banking union, the EU seems to be fighting an uphill battle for this reform.

The EU banking union would sever the link between national banks and national budgets. If banks are subject to common supervision and funds are earmarked at the EU level in support of troubled banks, this should relieve some of the financial pressure on Member States while exposing heretofore close involvement of national banks in national fiscal affairs. More prudent and transparent supervision and regulatory oversight would help troubled EU Member States to restore financial balance and lower borrowing costs, thereby further easing debt levels. Confidence should also improve with the knowledge that all banks in the economic area play by the same rules. In an EU banking union the European Central Bank (ECB) would be responsible for supervising all banks in the Eurozone. This politically contentious point, which involves a compromise of sovereignty, is hindering progress towards an EU banking union. In contrast to the current differentiated and country-specific financial supervisory system, under an EU banking union all Eurozone banks would be subject to the supervision of the ECB. The ECB would license credit institutions and ensure compliance with key banking requirements. The ECB would have the power to close down banks if necessary.

The historical non-arm's-length relation between the banks of EU Member States and their governments is a root problem addressed by EU unitary banking. In retrospect, the Maastricht convergence criteria were not up to the task, nor was the Growth and Stability Pact. Banking sectors that act as regional financial hubs require vigilant supervision. Euro currency integrity demands it. This applies especially to cases where potentially 'hot' capital flows on the liabilities side finance a growing pool of domestic assets. High level regulatory and supervisory oversight is required to ensure that undue investment risks are not taken on the basis of fickle capital. Such was the sorry plight of Greece and Portugal. EU banking union would break the vicious feedback between weak banks and weak sovereigns.

EU banking union would also help establish a proper transmission mechanism for European monetary policy. This, too, is crucial to the economic integration of Europe. Notwithstanding the question of whether Europe is a *bona fide* optimal currency area, monetary policy within the common currency area currently suffers for the inefficiencies that stem from the fact that Euro-monetary policy does not flow smoothly throughout the Eurozone, again because central monetary policy is filtered through diverse regional banks with local supervisory and regulatory controls.

Finally, EU banking union would improve the incentives for proper supervision and limit the susceptibility to any prospective regulatory capture. In essence, European banking union is a means to fully reap the benefits from European financial market integration, while at the same time containing the risks of financial contagion.

2. Obstacles to Banking Union

Resistance to European-wide banking regulation has its roots in conflicting views of the European project. For some early enthusiasts, the European project was a functional attempt to reduce trade barriers and keep Germany tied to a democratic Europe and committed to peaceful pursuits with its neighbours. For others, however, the European Community was the first step in a much closer economic and political union, with each new treaty and directive designed to trigger even further integration, a long and intricate process towards a goal. It is enticing to think that today we may be players in, or observers of, the long-life project that political philosophers refer to as 'functionalism' – extending Jean Monnet's vision of institution building to foster peace, stability and, in the process, prosperity within Europe. Some 55 years ago the Treaty Establishing the European Economic Community, known as the Treaty of Rome, was signed by Germany, Italy and the Benelux nations, launching the economic – and relentlessly political – integration of Europe. It is reminiscent of a delightful Chinese expression for large-scale policy incrementalism, 'Crossing the river by feeling for the stones', which has a strain of functionalism to it. The overarching objectives – which are mainly political and integrative in the case of Europe – are understood by those who design policy. The route to those objectives anticipates step-by-step advances as well as inevitable back-tracking and reassessment much like we have seen in Europe in recent days, weeks, months and years.

All of this suggests that modern Europe is learning by doing. It is engaged in a politically driven work-in-progress that is economically constrained and institutionally challenged.

Support for or rejection of the call for a banking union turns on the longstanding European concerns for sovereignty at the level of the EU Member States. Leaving that political issue aside, the merits of the case for risk mitigation and the institutional efficiency of the European financial system are overwhelming. But, of course, politics cannot be left aside. Integrating institutions include a European financial system that supports a commercial and factor-flow system that generates commercial gains that enrich Europe – although not necessarily evenly. The supporting European institutions do not emerge willy nilly. They must be designed, promoted, accepted and cooperatively nurtured. As Jean Monnet might have said, if we get the intra-European institutions right, we can limit brutal conflict to the football pitch.

Institutions that draw Europeans closer to complete economic integration necessarily demand common governance and relinquished sovereignty … and therein, of course, lies the rub. On today's Euro matters – in particular, currencies and debt – many of us, as technicians, tend to focus on initiatives to ensure the economic gains of more efficient markets, stronger institutions and more sustainable balance between the public and the private sectors. The impatient general public and the press are seemingly oblivious to the ultimate aims of the functionalist process.

The governing political and administrative principle of 'subsidiarity' underlies the political tension in Europe that is hindering the institutional development of pan-European banking and finance – *per force* a more centralized system in terms of both monetary policy and regulatory oversight. Those who push for tighter political union and union-wide regulation hang their arguments on this basic European concept. Subsidiarity is enshrined as a general principle of European Union law, *viz.* the EU may only act where action of individual countries is insufficient. The present formulation is contained in Article 5(3) of the Treaty on European Union (consolidated version following the Treaty of Lisbon, which entered into force on 1 December 2009):

> Under the principle of subsidiarity, in areas that do not fall within its exclusive competence, the Union shall act only if and in so far as the objectives of the proposed action cannot be sufficiently achieved by the Member States, either at a central level or at regional and local level, but can rather, by reason of the scale or effects of the proposed action, be better achieved at Union level.

The principle of subsidiarity seeks to determine the level of intervention that is most relevant in areas of competences shared between the EU and the Member States. This may concern action at European, national or local levels. In all cases, the EU may only intervene if it is able to act more effectively than Member States. The Protocol on the application of the principles of subsidiarity lays down three criteria aimed at establishing the desirability of intervention at European level:

1. Does the action have transnational aspects that cannot be resolved by Member States?

2. Would national action or an absence of action be contrary to the requirements of the Treaty?
3. Does action at the European level have clear advantages?

3. Banking Union as an Extension of Previous Treaties

In our concern for the role of banking for the integrity of the common currency and the successful integration of Europe – in the process defining the level of government that has the proper perspective and ought to have the authority and power to exercise pan-European monetary policy and effective supervision and regulation – the answer to each of the three questions above is unequivocally 'yes', with a concomitant call for more centralization, not less.

Banking is economic infrastructure. Banking is also a public good in the sense that its value to the 'system' exceeds the private value to bank owners. A look back at the evolution of modern Europe puts the overarching role and responsibility of pan-European banking in perspective.

The Treaty of Paris (1951) created the European Coal and Steel Community. That treaty was designed to help reconstruct the industrial structure of the European continent, to prevent war between neighbouring nations and to ensure a lasting peace. The aim was to pool Franco-German coal and steel production, as these two raw materials were the basis of the industry (including war industry) and power of the two countries. The vision was to put Franco-German coal and steel production under a common High Authority within the framework of an organization that would be open for participation of other European countries. The underlying political objective was to strengthen Franco-German industrial cooperation and banish the possibility of war. A few years later, the Treaty of Rome (1956) strengthened the ties that bind.

Such foundational treaties and the increasingly complex variants that followed, including Brussels (1965), Maastricht (1986), Amsterdam (1999), Nice (2003) and Lisbon (2009), established formal pan-European arrangements for trade, cross-border investment, labour mobility, EU expansion and the basis of an EU constitution (as per the Treaty of Lisbon), including the assignment of responsibilities and powers to specific levels of government – those that demand the perspective and power of the centre and those more effectively dealt with by the Member States. Subsidiarity became defined.

Through this process, banking and finance got short shrift. Attention was directed to overall fiscal and macroeconomic policy rather than to integrative institutional development. While the common currency agenda of the 1990s prompted the ineffectual convergence criteria for debt, deficits and inflation, the subsequent Growth and Stability Pact proved to be flawed fiscal rules that targeted neither growth nor stability. Meanwhile, banking and European financial market integration appeared to be mere afterthought. Europe needed another integrating force. Only when the G20 got involved in the wake of the financial crisis did Europe turn its attention to this crucial sector.

The G20 burst on to the world stage of financial reforms with the economic woes associated with the 2007 collapse. Washington, London, Pittsburgh, Toronto, Seoul – meetings in these sites rallied popular support for broad-based stimulus of unprecedented proportions followed by focused but more contentious programmes of enhanced financial sector regulation – Basel III and all that. By 2009 it had become clear that some degree of fiscal consolidation was called for. But fiscal contraction – or slowing expansion – is much tougher to achieve than outright expansion. Countries (like Canada) that weathered the storms quite nicely smugly preached fiscal consolidation to the rest of the world.

4. European Banking Union and the G20

By the time the G20 torch was passed to France, banking and financial regulatory issues had fully migrated to the Financial Stability Forum and all that was left, it seemed, was implementation. Rules for strengthening capital adequacy, liquidity and leverage were set on course with generous allowances of time. In some sense, the G20 passed the torch to international bodies, such as the BIS, and national bodies such as central banks. As international organizations have little enforcement authority, there was little else that could be done.

These developments parallel the G20's role in sovereign debt issues. A few points deserve to be made explicit. The early crisis began as a banking and financial sector collapse in the United States that went global. This led to a credit and liquidity crisis that called for collective fiscal intervention. In 2007–2008, a bank-centric crisis quickly evolved into a real sector collapse via a global credit crunch that created real economic contraction and rising unemployment. The solutions to the previous problems are not the solutions to today's problems. Failure to have resolved the 2007–2008 problems would have left us in a different situation than if the G20 fails to constructively address today's pressing European sovereign debt problems. Europe as we know it is on the verge of collapse. The broader and timely agenda for the meetings in Cannes, for example, was commandeered by an even greater urgency triggered in Athens. If one did not see this as breathless, then they were not paying attention. Pushed by events, the G20 and European regulators seem forced to react to quickly changing sovereign debt issues, rather than to devise a long-term financial institutional strategy.

Summit history will likely show Cannes 2011 to have been an alternative venue for European leaders to deal with their sovereign debt issues. The other noble G20 agenda issues – including reform of the international monetary system, global imbalances, the G20 social agenda, food security and agricultural price volatility, infrastructure and innovative financing – were eclipsed by the morass of sovereign debt. To paraphrase that great American epistemologist, Donald Rumsfeld, when moving forward there are known knowns, known unknowns and – most ominously – unknown unknowns. European leaders simply do not know what they do not know about a modern Europe without a strong centrally managed common currency and a sound pan-European banking system. Policy seems forged by fears of the consequences of failure rather than by a positive vision of integration. While agreement about what kind of financial union should exist eludes political leaders, they all seem to share a terror of the consequences of disintegration and a return to strident nationalism.

5. Progress to Date

Europe's largest problem – the route to sustainable solutions – is institutional, political if you will. In European fashion, perhaps more French than German, the economic institutions of Europe were born out of passion. Maastricht and the Treaty of Lisbon do not provide the complete basis for a properly functioning, flexible economic union. The span of monetary policy has no counterpart in the span of fiscal policy. Europe's monetary union – the 17-nation Euroland with its fixed exchange rates and common monetary policy – with no corresponding fiscal commonness or meaningful transfer mechanisms, is a stage set for continuing fiscal crisis – as in the present day sovereign debt debacle.

Breaking the circle between local banks and sovereigns requires both the bail-in of creditors and some centrally directed mutualization of banking risk. Apart from a credible fiscal backstop, a sound European banking system also needs a common deposit-guarantee scheme. Alas, ever-powerful Germany has resisted banking union in these dimensions and others ever since the idea was first mooted. Above all, the Germans worry about taking on new liabilities. The ECB eased the pressure with its promise to do whatever it takes to prevent the break-up of the Euro.

Meanwhile, the turmoil in Cyprus demonstrates why a credible banking union is so urgently needed. With a central supervisor and bank-resolution authority, Cyprus' banking problems might have been mitigated, or addressed sooner and at lower cost. The capital controls imposed on the island might then have been unnecessary or less onerous, particularly if the ECB had stepped in smartly to provide liquidity to smaller solvent Cypriot banks. The Cypriot chaos is telling. It revealed the ominous signs of common currency disintegration such as the widening gap in credit spreads between Cyprus bank debt versus those in the less-indebted north. Meanwhile, ironically, to the (great) extent that northern banks are creditors to the southern European periphery – again, writ large in Cyprus – northern banks are less solvent than some of their small southern counterparts. The Euro cannot survive such fragmentation. Only a proper banking union can repair it.

Despite the weakness of many European-level political institutions and resistance from national authorities, a good deal of power for financial supervision has been transferred to European regulatory organizations, but the process is neither complete nor completely clear. As a major step in harmonizing banking regulation, the EU gave prudential supervision of credit institutions to the ECB, laying the foundation for a Single Supervisory Mechanism. The ECB has been given some investigatory powers, but the supervisory tools are discretionary and the transfer of authority has not, as of writing, been approved by the European Court of Justice. The ECB's powers extend to Eurozone countries and those who have agreed to work closely with the Eurozone, but fall short of extending to all major banking relationships within Europe. Moreover, how the ECB will work with the European Banking Authority (EBA) is also rather unclear. But although the measure was strongly supported by the Germans, including many German financial institutions, under the EBA's purview the change of governance has met with heavy resistance. As one commentator put it, for the time being, the term Single Supervisory Mechanism 'promises more than it can deliver'.[36]

[36] For a useful discussion of the progress and limits of European bank supervision, see G. Schuster, 'The Banking Supervisory Competences and Powers of the ECB' (2014) 3–9; E. Gurlit, 'The ECB's Relationship to the EBA' (2014) 14–18 and S.H. Schneider, 'Sanctioning by the ECB and National Authorities within the Single Supervisory Mechanism' (2014) 18–23 in 1 *Europäische Zeitschrift für Wirtschaftsrecht*.

IV. CONCLUSION

Despite the recent dramatic challenges to global finance on both sides of the Atlantic, regulation still seems to remain largely a national undertaking. For some well-informed observers, G20 reforms of international financial regulation have progressed at a disappointing pace, failing to fulfil their initially promising reaction to the crisis and reform rhetoric. Neither individually – nor, more importantly, collectively – have major countries put a stop to the perverse financial incentives that led to reckless bank behaviour. National priorities, especially in countries in which the financial sector plays a very large economic role, have curtailed cross-border coordination.

A formal or informal consensus among major economies about the appropriate rules of the game for national and international financial organizations is still elusive. Even the most ardent optimists among reformers have to acknowledge the cross-border compliance (enforcement) mechanisms are a distant dream. Despite a world recession and the necessity of state intervention in banking, governments have been unable to agree on what needs fixing and who should do the fixing. While the governments and central banks have run up huge deficits, facilitated by historically low real interest rates, to ward off the effects of the crisis, they have shown little inclination to face up to their own role in enabling, indeed encouraging, private financial organizations to raise funds for public and quasi-public programmes.

1. Crises and Regulatory Reform

In many respects, this absence of political will should be no surprise. Some severe financial crises stimulate little reform, others some inappropriate reforms, while still others, such as the 1907 crisis in America, though short in duration, produce important institutional innovations, in that case the Federal Reserve Board. Making sensible changes often takes time and is sometimes not best achieved in a crisis mode. Nevertheless, in North America and Europe, many well-informed observers fear that we have missed the opportunity first engendered by the crisis and then the calm fostered by deficit spending and liberal central bank lending. The recent financial crisis is not the first that has stimulated worldwide financial soul searching.[37] The financial crises of 1907 and 1929–1931,

---

[37] Youssef Cassis, *Crises and Opportunities: The Shaping of Modern Finance* (Oxford University Press 2011).

for example, created within a few years vast changes in financial regulation, some of which had cross-border spillover, some not. Consider that by 1934, the United States had passed Glass–Steagall, created the Securities Exchange Commission and provided federal deposit insurance; and Germany had nationalized nearly all its large banks and instituted rigid currency controls. But in both those periods, various forms of friction between financial markets allowed governments more leeway in selecting their particular form of reform. Technology, the geographic spread of sophisticated financial activity and increased foreign direct investment of financial organizations make containing the activities of financial players in one place with one set of rules much harder without international political intervention.[38]

2. The *Défi Européenne*

The European Union presents special problems. Building a political or banking union takes time. Making the leap to a genuine banking union requires a dramatic shift of sovereignty. Even with a massive political pact, putting in place the logistics of a union could take years. Countries that have already formed a political union, such as the United States and Canada, took decades to create many of the institutions and organizations necessary for a unified financial system.[39] Institutions must be designed, complex new rules must be agreed. The most difficult challenge of creating a European banking union lies with the short-term steps towards its eventual implementation. Many banks in the Euro area, and especially in the crisis countries, are currently under stress and the move towards banking union almost certainly has significant distributional implications. Yet it is precisely because banks are under such stress that early and concrete action is needed. The first step should be to create a European supervisor that will anchor the development of the future banking union. In parallel, a capability to quickly assess the true capital position of the system's most important banks should be created, for which we suggest establishing a temporary European Banking Sector Task Force working together with the European supervisor and other authorities. Ideally, problems identified by this process should be resolved by national authorities; in the case that fiscal capacities would prove insufficient, the European level would take over in the country concerned with some

[38] Kobrak, *supra* note 13.

[39] Christopher Kobrak, Joe Martin and Donald S. Brean, 'Canada, the United States, and the European Union: Neglected Lessons in Building a Currency Zone out of Separate States' (2013)39:2 *Bankhistorisches Archiv* 139–152.

national financial participation, or in an even less likely adverse scenario, in all participating countries at once. This approach would require the passing of emergency legislation in the concerned countries that would give the Task Force the required access to information and, if necessary, further intervention rights. Thus, the principle of fiscal responsibility of respective Member States for legacy costs would be preserved to the maximum extent possible, and, at the same time, market participants and the public would be reassured that adequate tools are in place to address any eventuality. What is clear from Europe's experience is that a purely national approach to many aspects of financial regulation is no longer feasible. Success of the European project requires financial integration, which itself is part of a wider network of interdependencies.

Europe must take into account and accommodate the unequal strengths of factions for the success of institutional development. Not to put too sharp a point on it, with respect to the realignments of today, one might ask whether we are engaged in the Germanification of Europe or the Europe-ification of Germany? If functionalism does indeed succeed in integrating Europe, then the acrimony, alignments and angst that seem to threaten the progress to date will be viewed in history as just another trying episode. If not, and if it all unravels because of currencies and debt, then… who knows? If the remarkable construction of the Euro is lost, it will be a dark point in the economic history of the era. But Europe's problems may just be a special regional case of a much broader international phenomenon.

3. Financial Reform and Political Credibility

The most serious aspect of the recent crisis is perhaps the lost confidence in the political system on both sides of the Atlantic.[40] The ability of political and financial leaders to articulate sustainable expectations for that system and a reasonable balance between innovation and stability is not only crucial to our financial well-being but also to their own credibility. The financial crisis and its aftermath tarnished the reputations of financial actors and their regulators, adding costs and risks to doing business as well as to the very fabric of liberal democratic society. A

---

[40] Marc Flandreau, 'The Vanishing Banker' (2012) 19:1 *Financial History Review* 1–19; Ephraim Clark and Octave Jokung, 'The Role of Regulatory Credibility in Effective Bank Regulation' (2014) 01/2014 *Journal of Banking and Finance*; Legrain, *supra* note 15.

society that is continually asked to give up local control without understanding why and which has lost faith in elites to guide them is susceptible to the worst kinds of demagogy.

Index